Journeys with the Divine Feminine

Edited by Sue Fitzmaurice

Foreword by Patricia Iris Kerins

REBEL
MAGIC

JOURNEYS WITH THE DIVINE FEMININE

To contact any of the authors, visit: www.rebelmagicbooks.com or the websites provided in their bios.

ISBN: 9781693212222

**REBEL
MAGIC**

Cover art words: *Speak your truth. Tell your Story. You matter. You are a child of the universe and you are so deeply loved. You are a feminine child of god and are divine. Let it all go. All birds share the same wing and fly together. You have found your tribe. We are all just walking each other home. You must open your heart and let love unfold.*

People heal by being able to tell the story – the whole story.
Clarissa Pinkola Estes

·

My story isn't sweet and harmonious, like invented stories. It tastes of folly and bewilderment, of madness and dreams, like the lives of all people who no longer want to lie to themselves.
Hermann Hesse

Note to the Reader

The authors herein write in American English, Canadian English, New Zealand English, Australian English, Indian English, *English* English, and may have English as a second or even third language. Some *learnt* (rather than learned) to put a *u* in *neighbour*, that there is a verb *to practise* with an *s*, and that *minimise* isn't spelt with a *z*. Some have *traveled* with a single *l* and some have *travelled* with two. In editing, I've allowed the writer's own nationality of English to stand. We value your tolerance of our differences.

Contents

Foreword

It is a joy to lift a book that expands your consciousness and enriches your soul. You are in for a treat!

In this day and age with so much chaos kicking off around the world, here we have a haven of shared evolution and in particular that of the Divine Feminine within each of us, man or woman.

Not some abstract thought form as some may say, but an integral wisdom within all of humanity, waiting quietly in the wings ready to step out and take centre stage as the Divine Masculine recognises that it truly needs a worthy, valuable partner to dance with, to help humanity reach the ultimate goal of actualising its true potential.

They need look no further. She is here!

The re-emergence of the Divine Feminine from oppression, suppression, repression and ultimately depression is vital to restoring the balance of this world and all who live on this planet. Too long, we have been living a lopsided life as the forgiveness, love and compassion so sorely needed have been lost and are now being resurrected.

Going, if not completely gone, are the days when the opinions of women didn't matter. The transformation that is happening now is that we believe we do matter; we do count and what we have to say and contribute is valuable and important. We are also good enough in every way, in every circumstance.

This collection of words from diverse, unique women, outlining their journeys, are all very different and yet within them there is a common theme of self-discovery, self-remembrance, and a recognition of how they were as they started out on their journeys and how much they have changed and evolved as they stand more in their power of being a woman.

They have taken time to look back at the past and then stand in the power of the present ready to open and create the next chapter of their ongoing soul journey.

The road to this point can often be a bumpy one. What they have learned will undoubtedly help you to be all you can be. As they share their loves, laughs, trials and tribulations, you will remember similar circumstances in your life.

In sharing and collaborating, we help others to grow and thrive. For there will be triggers of resonance and remembrance from this and past lives – the memory of which are held in your DNA – that will awaken as you read.

You are not alone, you are one with all the women sharing here, their story is your story.

The question is are you ready to be the author of your own new story, and if so, what would that be and say?

An exciting opportunity to co-create your life with the Universe awaits; think big, be bold and take strength from the words your sisters have shared here for they have survived and they have thrived.

Honouring your beautiful Divine Feminine, I am

Patricia Iris Kerins DHP
Channel, Author, Modern Day Shaman, Sound Master Healer & Coach

Introduction

In December 2018, I was in the south of France visiting sites of significance to the tradition of Mary Magdalene. I had just begun my editing and publishing venture *Rebel Magic Books,* and whilst in meditation one day, I asked Louise Hay for advice. Her answer: *Gather women's stories and share them.* I began with the Divine Feminine.

I had been in serious pursuit of the Divine Feminine through the whole of 2018, from January when a stranger arrived and became my best friend, opened my eyes to new worlds, and then by the end of the year had become a stranger again. People don't always come into our lives for the reasons we think. Experiences don't always happen for the reasons we think. Every one of us here might say *If you'd told me twenty years ago… I never would have believed you.* And indeed, some do say exactly that.

When I asked thirty women to write their spiritual stories, I hadn't fully anticipated what that would mean. For everyone involved, writing their story was a journey in itself. Almost everyone, at some point, felt stuck or inadequate to the task. *Nevertheless, they persisted.*

From March through August, I received their words, tentative at first, then as they loosened up, it was full-blown *Eat, Pray, Love,* all of them. I have wept often on reading their stories – and laughed as well. Every woman involved has been utterly generous of spirit, from beginning to end.

For all of them, their experience of the Divine Feminine is necessarily spiritual – not any one type of spiritual, but a myriad of different meanings of that term. Spiritual doesn't *have* to be about God or Heaven – it's fundamentally about what gives us meaning and purpose, and the Sacred and Divine are as rooted in the soil as they are in the heavens. It would be fair to say, that for most, if not all, the women here, their stories do not encapsulate the whole of their spiritual life. Our paths are nuanced with a myriad of moments, thoughts, experiences, understandings and insights. It's impossible to portray it all.

Many of their stories begin with either an absence of the Divine Feminine, or a suppression of it. In this respect their stories mirror the development of feminism and equality generally, from the 1950s until the present, even as some hard-won equalities are horrifically reversing in some corners of the world. The freedoms brought by feminism have assisted in enabling the unfolding of the Feminine Divine (and vice versa) through more women's lives, where it was either absent or hidden in previous generations. And it is this *Sacred* Feminine that is the real gift – to women, men, society, the planet, and the future. The expansion of the Feminine will heal our world.

It's not easy to precisely define *Divine Feminine*, nor would everyone agree on any particular definition. You'll be immersed in it soon enough, which is always the best way to understand anything. Putting aside that this has to do with men and women per se (it doesn't), the Divine Feminine can be said to be inward looking, right brained, emotional, creative, intuitive, feeling, sensing, wise, protecting, and allowing. Correspondingly, the Divine Masculine is outward looking, left-brained, logical, pragmatic, courageous, strong, and action-oriented.

It is not the dominance of the Divine Masculine that has resulted in centuries of harm in the world, but an out of balance Masculine – an *Undivine* Masculine – that in its denial of its own true nature, as well as of the Feminine, has tipped away from pragmatism, courage and strength, into authoritarianism, control, fear and war.

The coming into alignment again of both the Feminine and the Masculine is the task of each of us as individuals, and of our species as a whole. That has been the journey of the women whose stories you'll read here.

You may reasonably ask then: *where are men's stories of the Divine Feminine?* For now, simply, this is not their turn.

You may also wonder: *where is the indigenous woman's voice?* Fair question. Whilst there is a little of that here, and whilst it would be an unfortunate generalisation to note that indigenous women's spirituality is more secure than that of many of us from the West, these stories nonetheless represent the myriad of Western women's journeys, either away from their own tradition, and/or much more deeply into it to relocate the suppressed and forgotten Feminine.

The twenty-five women here are aged between twenty-something and seventy-something, representing all of the phases of womanhood. Each one of them has wisdom to share. Most have faced grief, hardship and their own demons – both inner and outer – and most continue to do so, to greater or lesser extents. Many now categorise those demons as necessary contrasts – they are their shadows, their lessons, their inner critics, their shame – and rather than eliminate them, they have dived into them, integrated them, and even embraced them. They all know there is more to come, of both light and dark. Life is contrast and it is to be embraced, in all its facets.

The aim is that you will see yourself reflected here, that you will understand and feel understood, that you might see paths you didn't know existed, or that you'll feel freer to walk ones you've known but were perhaps afraid to venture down.

Finally, symbols have been part of the expression of the sacred since before recorded history. The Christian Cross is the most well-known – others include stars, circles and patterns of many kinds, animals, figurines, stones and jewellery, plants, mandalas and birds. Each author has selected a symbol meaningful to her that may or may not have obvious relevance within her story. My own is a triple korū design representing my homeland, New Zealand, and the triple spiral design of Celtic Ireland, the home of my ancestors. The korū itself represents new life and the unfolding of life.

Others choices may surprise you – it's not either of the Hindu women here that has the Om symbol, and indeed one has chosen something more Christian. They are reflections of complex, open and evolving spirituality.

Gracing the headings of other pages is a version of the Triple Goddess symbol of Maiden, Mother and Crone, each of which symbolises both a separate stage in a woman's life and a phase of the Moon.

My deepest thanks to these souls, these hearts, these voices.

Sue Fitzmaurice
Brittany, France
16 September 2019

Lynne Meyer

Sorting Femininity, Feminism, and the Divine Feminine

We know who we are when we come here. We know it and we do our best to express it. This world, though, is designed to make us forget ourselves. It sedates us, brainwashes us, and without an enormous effort of will, we become locked into spiritual stasis.

Who I was in the beginning, flits through my mind in mental images from early childhood. They click through my brain in a staccato, stop-motion film series of vignettes. I am three years old, lying on my back under my sister's crib, tracing the network of metal springs and rods that support the mattress with my fingers. Another scene: I am at the kitchen table, struggling to write my name. I proudly show the result to my dad. He scolds me for making the *n* backwards and says if I don't do it right, I'll never be allowed to use a pen. I am crushed by the thought of no pens.

I am at my great aunt's house where there is a wild floral and vine pattern on the black background of her living room rug. I drink lemonade and eat stale potato chips while following the pattern of the vines with my eyes. It moves along the baseboard, winds under the couch, twists between the legs of the coffee table, gets broken by the newspaper on the floor next to the armchair, and is illumined by twin beams of light piercing the lace curtains over the windows in the room. The dust motes in the light beams distract me from the rug. They look like slowly falling snow.

At four years old, dressed in lavender dotted Swiss, feeling grown up and beautiful, I am carrying a birthday present directly across the street to my friend's party. I love being with my friends. We have a great time. Later, I have to cross the gravel road and climb the shallow incline of grass that leads to my front door. I live at the end of a street that butts into a farmer's field – the end of a street with little traffic. I was watched as I crossed. Still excited from the fun, I enter the house wearing my beautiful lavender dress and get spanked for not looking both ways before crossing the street.

I am in kindergarten – the best place for fun – wearing an old shirt of my father's that serves as a painting smock. My heart is set on painting a picture of a lion when my teacher tells me I have to paint a seal with a ball on its snout. I argue with her, insisting on painting a lion. She sends me away from the easel, denying me any painting at all. I cry, furious at the unfairness. She punishes me by making me lay on my nap mat while the others paint.

Another day of being five involves the most hallowed of all good places – the public library – where my arms are weighted by a stack of books piled from navel to chin.

I am a curious child, frequently wandering away from the dead end of my street toward the main road, stopping to talk to every neighbor outside along the way. I hear about people's days. I learn of someone's aunt's surgery. I help someone else break green beans for dinner. I watch a man mix cement. I pull weeds with an old lady as she natters on about her garden. I make a new friend, one my age, who lives way down the block, well past the boundary of how far I was allowed to roam. She introduces me to others who live all the way down on that part of the street. I am thrilled with the increase in my social wealth. I am everyone's friend.

Through the years of early childhood, I was aware of things. For example, my mother had a cousin, whom we didn't see often, who had bought a new home. When we went to visit the cousin at her new place, I recognized the house immediately as we pulled into the driveway. I told my mother I had seen the house before. She said that was impossible, but I knew where every room was before going inside and I told her what I knew. When it proved out, my mother said perhaps I had dreamed it. I knew differently. I could also predict outcomes to unknown situations. I could *feel* what was coming. This served me when deciding to stay or go, and to speak or not. It made me able to exploit the political climate of groups: stay friendly with both sides, take any advantages that come.

I also knew when people were lying to me, and I would call them out on it. To tell another the truth about someone's unfair words or actions didn't make me popular at school; not tattling was a virtue back then. It didn't take long for me to learn that keeping quiet was the easiest way to avoid trouble. I watched. I knew.

There were ideas expressed in my home environment that I didn't like. People weren't people; they were categorized. Based upon last name, a person could be a spic, a wop, a kraut, a limey, a shit kicker, a dago, a bohemian, a pollock. The harshest word applied to black people. The words used also applied to my friends, which angered me. During my young days, there was an experiment in Chicago where students were bused from the inner city to suburban schools, and vice versa, in an attempt to balance out educational disparities. It was short lived and futile. Its very attempt, though, was excuse for loud raging. I liked the idea and said so. I said it wasn't the kids' fault that they were born where they were, and it wasn't fair that they couldn't get a good education there. Dismissal in the form of *you don't know anything* was the best outcome of situations when my ideas ran contrary to the ruling forces.

Home was a crowded place. Three adults and three kids lived in less than a thousand square feet of space. I liked quiet places to read, to color, to do puzzles, to draw. Mom's closet was a good place to be alone, as was under the back porch. As those sanctuaries were discovered, I was banished from them. Putting a book in my tucked-in shirt, I climbed and found happy solitude high in trees. I learned it's even easier to spot a child in a tree than under a porch. I got grounded literally and figuratively.

The inner me cared about what was pretty and fair and fun. I liked laughter and poetry and making up songs. I wanted to be like my beautiful first grade teacher, Sister Coralita, who embodied sweetness and smiles. I believed it was possible to be holy like her someday.

I was raised Catholic and went to Catholic school in the 1960s, which meant living within well-defined gender expectations. My innate nature, though, was curious and vocal, which didn't fit with the social program. I had the innocent nerve to ask questions like: *Why does the priest wear a dress? Do nuns go to the bathroom? Why do the boys get to help at the altar but the girls aren't allowed to? Why do girls have to wear beanies in church but the boys don't?* Somehow the answers all came down to a difference of what was holy for one was not holy for another.

The indoctrination of holy behavior at school did not mesh with home experiences. I recall family parties attended by priests and nuns who drank, smoked, and played cards as deftly as any of my relatives. Let's call the veil 'ripped but not rent' as my focus shifted from humans toward saints. Saint Theresa lived on top of a dresser in my childhood bedroom. Saint Anthony got my mom out of trouble regularly by finding things through her eyes and hands. Saint Christopher got us to school safely when the roads were icy. For years, Beings I could not see were relied upon and credited for actions occurring through the agency of the humans around me.

By the time I was in sixth grade (age eleven), I stood in front of my mother, metaphorically holding a tattered veil, and declared, *I don't believe any of this. I don't want to be Catholic*. What was unspoken was my doubt that anything anywhere was holy. My mother encouraged me with the advice to *stay at St Norbert's and graduate with your friends*. That seemed reasonable. I could play along until graduation.

Losing my religion could have been a moral dilemma, but the wider world brought ideas and changes as feminism entered my life.

Two weeks after June graduation from St Norbert's, President Richard Nixon signed into law *Title IX* of the *Education Amendments Act of 1972*, which prohibited discrimination on the basis of sex in any federally funded education program or activity. I entered high school at the end of that summer. Suddenly, sports – something I'd never had to think about seriously before – were thrust into my academic reality as one of two elective paths. I was caught between two worlds that polarized feminine and masculine structures. The old world argued for home economics electives; the new world presented its case for basketball, volleyball, softball, and field hockey. I had been baking and embroidering since I was five. I had hands-on experience with ovens and washing machines and with sewing on buttons. I knew for sure that those 'home ec' activities never came close to the fun I had catching tadpoles, climbing trees, exploring construction sites, jumping off tall dirt mounds, and riding bikes. Despite great efforts by my mother and aunts, all early admonitions to act like a lady resulted in Oscar-worthy performances of *acting* feminine. The heart and soul of me preferred loose clothes, loud laughter, and plenty of motion.

Because I was a student, and because *Title IX* really was the biggest buzz in the school environment, I had only peripheral awareness of other current US legislation. In 1972, Congress passed the *Equal Rights Amendment* to the States for ratification. Ratification by thirty-eight States was required for that Bill to become a law. I had no clue at the time how that was destined to impact my life for far longer than the time I'd spend in high school. On March 22, 2017, forty-five years to the day after Congress passed the ERA, Nevada became the thirty-sixth state to ratify it. On May 30, 2018, Illinois became the thirty-seventh state. It is forty-seven years since that amendment was passed and still we wait for that last, unknown, brave state to take a stand.

Meanwhile, American females of my generation had choices no generation before us had. As a result, we all had one foot in each of two worlds. We were awakening to the *idea* of choices—having them, making them, avoiding them, risking everything for them – on a collective level. Past individuals often made choices that ran against the cultural norm, which is how their names became known and how some achieved fame. My generation was experiencing social pressure to choose. Today it sounds ridiculous, but we faced choices as simple as ordering food from a menu for yourself and conveying that choice personally to a waiter. We faced choices as complicated as saying *not yet* or even *nope* to marriage. We had choices about higher education, choices about having careers, and choices about military service that, before 1973, had been confined mainly to nursing and other non-combat roles. The availability of choices led to new freedoms, but it also led to new anxieties and to forms of competition women could not expect or be prepared for. This was the backdrop of my learning to navigate the world.

One of my first jobs was at an auto body shop – a singularly masculine domain at the time – where I answered the phone and handled the payroll. My boss opined out loud that to be a real part of the office equipment the secretary had to be screwed on the desk. Imagine my incredulity. I was speechless with disbelief. I was sixteen.

All the women in my family worked outside the home. Being employed did not equate to any true sense of personal power though. An older cousin of mine was earning the lion's share of income for her family. Both she and her husband were realtors. She proudly said that every time she sold a house, she filled out the paperwork with his name, not hers, because *it's important to let your man be the provider*. In her case, getting screwed on the desk was a metaphor very close to home. Compared to other women in the family she earned more money, but she wasn't different from other female influences in my life. My plumber uncle's wife had a safely feminine job working in a sandwich shop. She worked there for years before I knew her job was as manager of the shop, responsible for the books as well as for creating seasonal menus. Her leadership role wasn't all she was quiet about. She invested her earnings and accumulated significant wealth. Another family member had a few secret savings accounts she kept from her husband's knowledge. He didn't know about the US Savings Bonds she bought with every pay check either. She told me that if I ever became engaged to be married that I should *insist on the biggest rock he can afford. You may need to sell it someday to survive.* My family's message about being a woman came down to: play your role, be wily, feather your own nest and keep quiet about it, and pay attention to what everyone else is doing. There, on the threshold of adulthood, I learned that to be feminine required strategy.

As I entered adulthood, women in the wider world competed with men for jobs. Women competed with women for status. In taking on new roles formerly held by men, women betrayed women by calling out false comparisons on each other. Working women were told they could have it all – career and family – but were punished financially and socially for trying, in ways men never were. Women outside the workforce who chose to be housewives and at-home mothers were told they didn't work. Each side looked down on the other with smug superiority, not recognizing that by not supporting other women's choices weakened both sides. By polarizing themselves, women inevitably betrayed themselves.

Politicians, clergy, and media fed the fury, further pitting moms against careerists, reinforcing glass ceilings, amplifying impossible standards of female desirability, condemning reproductive rights as wantonness, licentiousness, and sin; publishing lies, damned lies, and statistics… yes, my generation of American women deserved every valium swallowed to cope with it all.

In the lives of my generation of women, there were many wins, many losses, many triumphs, many bridges burned, and an inexorable march into a future that nonetheless remained tethered to mores of the past.

I lived through the social and familial sorting of a few decades without a lot of grace. I got married; it was what was done if one was a good girl. I dressed up when I had to, worked an odd assortment of jobs, and always preferred the days when I was 'home'. Being home meant not being at work; it did not mean being in my house. Home was on the back of a motorcycle, winding down forest roads and along the shore of Lake Michigan. Home was sleeping on the dirt of a campsite. Home was riding an elephant, or a rollercoaster, or the El into downtown

Chicago. Home was neck deep in the Kankakee River, or in Lake Zurich, or in a friend's hot tub. Home was on farms in Michigan and Southern Illinois. It was in the car on the way to Montana, Wisconsin, Missouri, South Carolina, Florida. Home was canning peaches at a friend's house or transporting live chickens in my tiny station wagon because that was logical in the moment. All my 'home' sites were places where I was my best as a woman.

Home also was a place where I was weak as a woman. It was easy to get sucked into family dramas, gossip, manufactured problems, real problems, illness, boredom, bitchiness, and a sense of powerlessness to change anything along those lines. Naturally, it seemed to me the circumstances – the outside – needed changing. I spent too much time giving advice. I heard too much about things I should not have known anything about. The normal family business of being in other people's business, wore me down and depressed me. I was stressed and nervous. I was frequently sick. My marriage was boring. After fifteen years of *go to work, watch TV, go to bed, get up and do it again*, I had enough. I saw that the pattern I was in was the same for the other women in my husband's family.

Things I wanted badly were not going to happen unless I made changes. I was determined to complete my education, to travel, to make a mark on the world. I wanted a life that made me feel alive. The writing was on the wall: staying in that family meant taking care of a boy who was never going to grow up. My marriage ended.

I had married at eighteen and plugged into an existing system of normal American life, complete with owning a television and subscribing to a daily newspaper. Newly single and in my early 30s, the reality of getting by on my income forced some external changes that led to internal changes. A day came when I decided to cancel the newspaper. Soon after, cable television had to go. The savings generated by these choices turned out to be more than monetary. I became aware that I could hear myself think. In due course, I stopped listening to the radio – even in the car. I was done being told what to eat, what to buy, what to wear, what to watch, what to think, who to listen to, and how to conform.

At first the silence was a little weird. It seemed as if a strangely loud, constant buzzing was in my ears. In time, though, I became aware that the thoughts I was having were genuinely mine. I moved through my days asking questions to no one specific – internal questions – and as I continued through my days, answers struggled to emerge. The quiet let me hear that my inner life was chaotic. I started university, which focused my thoughts on studies and squelched thoughts about the inner chaos. Two years into college, I met a man one July and married that stranger the following month. It really is no surprise that before long I was done being told what to eat, what to buy, what to wear, what to watch, what to think, who to listen to, and how to conform. I was too saturated with his voice to hear my own. I lost the ability to detect bullshit. I went into a defensive, survival mode.

By year five of the second marriage, I knew I was in a bad place. I made a promise to raise my child to adulthood no matter what it took, and if it took staying married to someone who really wasn't there for me, so be it. Rough roads all the way. I applied a lot of my early conditioning to stay stuck. The Universe stepped in though, and there was respite. My husband was hired at jobs in remote cities from where we lived, which required him to live hundreds of miles away. The peacefulness that set in when he wasn't around was welcome. The remote placements occurred such that we only lived under the same roof for half of the years we were married. My daughter entered her teens, so I re-entered college and completed my degree. My daughter was busy and well occupied, and I began to have alone time for myself.

I didn't know at the time that a convergence was happening. In my outer world, I was navigating finding a job and raising a teenager on my own. That world was very much masculine in its doing-ness. Yet because the job search was going slowly, I had a lot of free hours. I took up painting. Art unlocked the deeply buried feminine side. I had moments of flow and wonder and awe in the studio. There were long hours of in-the-moment presence. Without knowing what it was, I had encountered the Divine Feminine in the studio. Crafty one! She soon found another way to get through to me. Enter Meagan.

I had been a paper and red pen editor for more than twenty-five years when I got a new job as a technical editor in a paperless office. Meagan's job was to train me on computer software I had never dreamed existed. I was way out of my depth and suffering acute internal gender confusion. My usual work self was autonomous, made decisions, took risks, and *produced results* ahead of time if not right on deadline. In the new milieu, I was confused by new technology, overwhelmed by the learning curve, and as dependent as a child on Meagan's reminders and re-teaching. I was a veteran editor who felt as incompetent as a four-year-old first learning to use a pencil to write. Meagan was the first ever woman in my life whose nature was even-keeled. She would respond cheerfully when I asked questions. She was unflappable no matter what mistakes I made or how many times she had to explain the same things over again. She was encouraging all the time. But there was even more. I got to know her. I got to see how she acted with others. She didn't criticize. She didn't gossip. She patiently listened. Whenever she disagreed, she spoke her piece without a trace of meanness or superiority. She broke my heart open. From her, I learned I could trust. She personified femininity, and she was eminently capable in navigating masculine waters. I was shocked to learn that one of her hobbies was knife throwing.

Until encountering Meagan, my experiences of the feminine and of feminism were mainly internal processes pitted against the external voices of people around me, and media exposure that urged aggressive action, expanding consumption, fitting in with the right crowd, and getting more! more! more! from life, from jobs, from others. I believed in the equality of the sexes. I believed a woman's contribution was as valuable as a man's. What I had no clue about was how to balance the over-developed masculine characteristics I had acquired with my underdeveloped feminine qualities. The time had arrived to stop being a human doing and to start being a human being.

Association with Meagan on a daily basis forced me to see what was in front of me. Meagan didn't make predictions. She didn't position herself to take advantage of situations. She didn't orchestrate outcomes. She moved steadily with realistic expectations and high cheer. She knew how to accept that results will be known at the end. She had the ability to wait. Unlike me, she didn't start any process with the idea that it had to happen *now*, happen fast, happen in a way that beat the competition or happen anyone else's way. Meagan naturally did something I had never seen anyone do before: **she allowed**. I didn't understand any of it.

Our innate differences made Meagan fascinating, and I questioned her often about why she felt the way she did. She was all about feeling; I was a thinker. From her end, she was baffled about why I put so much effort into planning and doing. Over the course of the first year of our friendship, she let me be who I was without judging, while remaining curious and asking questions. Her ability to be present, to allow what is, started a deep healing process inside me.

Allowing circumstances to be what they are and flow where they will, is the primal reality of true feminine energy. Pregnancy is the process that illustrates it best. From the moment of conception, all growth that creates a fully formed, functioning, complex entity, occurs inside, out of sight, little by little. The mother's body allows it to unfold. While the mother's outer world may be filled with hundreds of ways in which she controls, manages, organizes, and influences people, places, and things, her inner world is the epicenter of creation. Within her, without her interference, a new world is coalescing, expanding, becoming ready to be revealed. Association with Meagan triggered an awakening. Everything I had taken for granted as being normal, became areas of focus. My ego started undergoing a gestation process. A type of spiritual morning sickness overtook me.

At the time I met Meagan, I had been married for twenty years. It was a legal bond; there was no real relationship. By then I had pushed down sadness and loneliness for twelve years. Relying on God, as I understood the concept, held me in place, but underneath that reliance was a lot of fear and guilt. A day came when the pressure inside built to a point of desperation. I left work early – I had to get out of there – but instead of driving home, I went to a cemetery where an elderly friend had been buried a few months earlier. I sat on a bench near her grave and poured my heart out to her.

I told my friend that I didn't know if what I wanted was right or wrong. I didn't know what I really wanted except to stop feeling so much pain. I confessed my inability to follow a path of religious rules anymore. I told her that right or wrong I could not live sort-of married, sort-of spiritual, sort-of socially normal. I wanted to live a true life. In the midst of feeling all that emotion, Mark Twain's character,

Huckleberry Finn, came to mind. Huck had to decide between two paths, one that society thought was right and one that he thought was right. Making his decision, he declared, *All right, then, I'll go to hell.* That was exactly the place I was at. That was exactly the decision I made.

A visit to a dead friend and the words of a fictional boy opened my heart to let in the Divine Feminine. I was scared, but I gave up pretending. Life was in constant motion with work and with the increasing demands of a teenager whose life was incredibly busy. I started meditating to reduce stress. Soon I discovered some beautiful chants and mantras on *YouTube.* At work I put my ear buds on and listened to the *Gāyatrī*[1] mantra, or to monks chanting on an endless loop, as I did my job. During the long drives to and from work, I put on chants and chanted with them all the way. These early steps led to realizing the truth of the adage *When the student is ready, the teacher appears.*

The first teachers were Kyle Cease and Matt Kahn. The multitude of their videos I listened to over the course of months helped center me, but the really great thing was that from listening to them so often, *YouTube* would put up suggested videos based on similar content. New teachers came in; Marissa Peer, Brené Brown, Marianne Williamson, and other women who talked about living authentically. They talked about healing shame and trauma, processing grief, and growing into healthy self-love. It's possible that I may have pushed too hard – old habits don't die easily – but every day I listened to talks and sought out more knowledge. Every night I listened to self-hypnosis videos by Michael Sealey or Jason Stephenson. Although I didn't know it at the time, what was occurring was **a shift from being a religious person to becoming a spiritual one.** I learned that developing a spiritual self was a messy business, requiring a lot of deep thought, a lot of emotional upheaval, a lot of forgiveness, and a lot of Kleenex. My 'knowing' returned. I re-learned how to breathe, how to calm myself, how to let things happen without force.

The entry of the Divine Feminine in my life appeared with both female and male voices. Its arrival steadily dissolved my old story. For a while, I stopped telling any sort of story about my life to others, mainly because a review of it caused me to question my perceptions of what had actually occurred. I reviewed everything. With those reviews came new perceptions, new recognitions, and compassion for myself and others.

I had prayed to be able to take responsibility for every aspect of my life. The answer to that prayer turned out to be, *Live and act with honesty.* Many people consider themselves honest. They'll turn in a dropped wallet or correct a cashier who gave them too much change. That's low-level honesty. To live in accordance with the answer to my prayer, I had to be rigorously honest with myself at all times

---

[1] The Gāyatrī Mantra is a powerful mantra from the Rig Veda, an ancient Indian collection of Sanskrit hymns.

in all circumstances. When I was, life worked well no matter how hard it was. When I backslid and believed my own bullshit, the ensuing course corrections were swift and sometimes brutal.

The honesty I was called to meant learning to say no. It meant learning to check in with what I really felt or wanted, rather than defaulting to people pleasing. It meant questioning my motives. It meant allowing things to take however long they took to unfold without me driving toward a set outcome. It also meant telling my real, messy, painful story out loud to the right people when I was in an emotionally fragile state. I admitted to myself and others that I was sad and lonely in my marriage because I was emotionally abused, neglected, belittled, demeaned, and traumatized. It's one thing to say that to a professional counselor. It's something else when you have to tell your boss that you are frightened your husband will turn up at the office and cause trouble. I admitted to others how at times things had become so lean that there wasn't enough food, and how neighbors shared their groceries for a couple of years until I finally found a job. Most importantly, **it meant taking responsibility for everything in my life without dishing out blame.** It meant feeling rage at times and then refocusing that hot energy into my role, my choices, and my actions.

The gestational mid-term occurred when I admitted I wanted a divorce. I was afraid of disturbing the hornet's nest, but it was the next phase of acting with honesty and allowing life to unfold. It wasn't pleasant. It brought out every bit of the drama I knew would ensue. The habits of meditating, chanting, self-hypnosis, and listening to *YouTube* remained in place. As I did conscious work on healing childhood trauma, the ability to manage emerging dramas related to the divorce process grew apace. Every internal act of honesty, every honest truth spoken, every step forward taken regardless of the sense of trepidation, increased self-worth and healthy self-love. It did everything I needed except speed up time.

I found in doing the work of reflection, admitting my shortcomings to myself, developing a spiritual practice, and staying true to advancing toward wholeness, **the Universe found ways to educate me.** The first thing I noticed were signs of encouragement – small comforts that came in all kinds of ways. Shiny coins, pens, and feathers were frequently in my path. There were frequent visits from butterflies and dragonflies. Unexpected social invitations let me practice new skills, especially in setting boundaries. I was pleased that saying *no* was both easy and could be done kindly. New, higher-vibrating friends came in. I loved all of that. The second thing it did was to test my sincerity about a stated willingness to go with the flow.

I needed to move house and thought to accomplish the move after I had time to collect funds. On a whim one day, well before starting to save any money for a move, I checked out an apartment in a desirable area. It was available immediately. I said yes, not knowing how I would pay for a security deposit or for the move.

The money I needed came in from an unexpected source at exactly the time I needed it. Almost as if to punctuate the sentence *Trust Me*, on the day before the move, my whole plan consisted of *I have to rent a truck tomorrow*. I didn't know how the truck would get loaded. The morning of the move, seven of my daughter's strong guy friends showed up, packed the truck, drove it to the new place, and unpacked it. Allowing everything to fall into place without trying to control the 'how' required a new level of trust, one that until then I didn't know I possessed. **The Universe really likes when you trust it.**

A different form of allowing occurred directly related to the divorce. When I hired a lawyer, the fee shock was tempered with an assurance that after a two-month, state-mandated, waiting period, the divorce would go through easily. My part was signed and ready to go. All that was needed was one signature from one person on one piece of paper. With that signature in place, I would have to appear in court to finalize. Two months turned into three, then four, then five. Every time I felt anxious or aggravated at the heel-dragging going on, I reminded myself to trust; to allow. These reminders went from hourly in the beginning, to daily, to weekly. One day, I felt an urge to call my lawyer to check on progress. I was told she was in court and someone would get back to me. No one called back. Instead I got a text that said, *Opposing counsel walked it through and it's done. You are divorced! I'll be toasting you tonight with a martini!* Days later, when I got the official papers, they were dated the day before I received that text. I had been divorced for twenty-four hours before I asked about it.
I didn't celebrate my divorce as I would have when I was much younger. Instead I celebrated by taking a new last name of my choosing, a name that honors my lineage.

The presence of the Divine Feminine within my life has grown. Women have entered life as friends who are farther along on the path. Younger women friends have entered whom I have been able to help. My reality as a loving, nurturing, courageous, creative female has re-emerged strongly. I am a good mother to my daughter and to myself. I am a good sister to my friends. I am growing at a natural pace. I am blessed. I am grateful.

Andrea Pollard

Seeking the Sibyls in Italy

I was dead inside. I felt nothing. I couldn't even say I was unhappy as that milestone had been reached and passed long ago. I prayed to *I-didn't-know-who* since I had no religion. And I wrote in my journal; it was always the same appeal.

Help me. Show me the way. Guide me to an interest, a passion, some enthusiasm. I promise I will run with whatever you send me. Just give me a clue, a direction.

Then I walked out to the kitchen and carried on with the dishes, next to my husband who was finishing the salad, while our two young sons played, building huts with the lounge furniture.

I worked full time and earned plenty. I drove a company car, carried several cell phones and wore black patent leather boots. I got drunk at work functions and laughed too much when the warehouse manager put his hand on my knee. I had a rock of a husband that treated me like a princess and my children were privately schooled. From the outside we had it all but I was suffering from the malaise associated with living a disconnected life.

Ten years on and I was just finishing up my latest, long, solo trip to Italy and I was at peace in my heart. I had thirteen hundred photos of the sites and reference points for the *Sibyls*. These were the women with the powers of prophecy that influenced the Kings, imperial rulers, and later the Emperors of Rome. I had travelled by train to see the frescoes at the *Villa d'Este* in Tivoli which feature images of the *Tibertine Sibyl*. I had romped through the ancient and deserted Greek settlement of *Cuma* near Naples to see the home of the *Cumaen Sibyl*. I had explored the Greek temples of *Paestum*.

Now I watched the moon rise over the Coliseum from the Capitoline Hill in Rome. My face was freckled and my pink travel scarf was faded from service. My wrists were adorned with the various religious leather thongs and cords I had bought along the way. My thighs were tanned and toned from hours of walking.

Thank you, Mary, I whispered in the warm evening air of Rome, *Thank you for bringing me home again*. Not only had Mary brought me back to my centre again but I felt vaguely as though I had lived here before, in some other lifetime.

This was my sixth solo trip to Europe over the past six years and my life was unrecognisable. I was happy, fulfilled and on a passionate journey of the soul. Mary had taken me by the hand, to show me the way.

Men.

My father didn't have much time for a little girl; his work required him to travel and put in long hours and then the weekends were tied up with keeping the section tidy. When he did turn his attention to the children, it was often to growl. He tested my knowledge with pop quizzes and his Virgo eye was always seeking fault. Although my mother told me he loved me, he couldn't really demonstrate it in a way a child could perceive. Unwillingly, it set me on a path where I would spend the next fifty years seeking the approval of men. Later I realised he had been living his own version of a disconnected life; he had given up dreams of travel and learning to fulfil the societal norms of marrying and having a family. What he did give me though was a vast curiosity for life.

I was born in New Zealand in the late 1960s and christened in the Anglican Church.

Why am I christened, we don't even go to church?

Everyone is christened, said Mum.

Well, why do I have to go to Sunday school? Not everyone goes there.

Eat your breakfast.

I suspected I was sent so that my parents could have a bit of time to themselves on a Sunday morning.

Mum was raised by her lapsed Irish Catholic mother who had married outside of her faith. Her father didn't go to church anymore, and much later he told us why. His father, my great grandfather, had become disillusioned when the minister had taken to publicly declaring how much every family tithed. They had never gone back. Within two generations, two church going people had turned away and raised my mother free from religion.

What religion are you, Mum?

I live by the ten commandments.

That's not an option on the form, what will I put?

Put Anglican.

Mum enjoyed an occasional tarot reading or attending a numerology night class. She dabbled lightly in the esoteric, and if backed into a corner became an Anglican.

Are you off to the ooky spooks again, love? My father was just as interested in it all as my mother but he made a joke of it. He had his own ideas. His bedside table contained books with covers about UFOs and the messages hidden in ancient Egyptian hieroglyphs.

His own mother professed to belong to the Church of England, and prayers were said before meals, but that seemed to be the end of it. His father did not mention any sort of faith.

I grew up with a broad scope to believe in what I wanted.

I chose boys.

They were the centre, the alpha and the omega. I would stand on a girlfriend, leave her somewhere, ignore her, even take her boyfriend, if it meant I could have a boy want me. I started sticking my fingers down my throat, and jogging from the age of eleven, in my quest to look good enough to get one.

After a series of boyfriends, I married young and divorced young.

When he walked out the door, my skin and flesh attached itself to his right shoe and went with him. I was left standing in the two bedroomed ex-state house, a skeleton. The following day when I went to work it seemed odd that no-one commented about my bones showing. He had fallen in love with someone else but he never said that. What he said was that he wasn't in love with me anymore. What I learnt from this was never to rely on another person again, that marriage vows can mean nothing, and that I better find another man as quickly as I could.

I married again. I wanted the babies, the house, the rug, and the matching plastic storage containers. The first sign that all was not well was when I found I didn't enjoy staying at home with those babies or attending the mothers groups. I did my very best to force myself to be everything a mother should be: baking for the school fair, knitting crayon holders, and stitching thirty felted wool hats for gnomes (the children went to the Rudolf Steiner School), but I was living in denial. After six years of raising my first son, then a year of raising the second, I flew away.

I've been offered a job.

Congratulations, what do the hours look like?

Well, the first Monday, I fly to Dunedin and don't come back till the Friday night. The second week, I have to go back to Dunedin again, and that time I need to stay for a fortnight.

What?!

I employed a nanny and at the end of each week handed her my entire pay. In the end my husband left his job and became a semi-solo parent.

He turned out to be the rock in this family. He introduced me to spirituality through his meditation and yoga practices. He committed himself to raising his sons, and was there for us all, day and night. His capacity for rocking crying children and listening to my grievances was incomparable. He balanced re-piling the house with collecting the raw milk for the co-op. He had his own journey navigating, then withdrawing from, a strict Presbyterian upbringing. The implications had left him in the wilderness before he found his own path.

The gift he gave me was to spend the next twenty years endlessly setting me free. Like a bird, I flitted off for work and pleasure, and yet found I always wanted to return. He accepted my need to exit and he opened his arms to my equally deep need to return, to his warm bed in the nest we had made for our sons.

On the outside, my life looked glamorous. Travel, hotels, restaurants, beautiful clothes and shoes, and a house-husband raising my children. On the inside, my gut wrenched with the sense of failure I had from having walked away from mothering and wife-ing. *Isn't having a husband and children what I had wanted?* My husband was having his own struggles, a sink full of dishes, the laundry full of dirty clothes, and no food in the house. We had our worst arguments through those years, about household chores, parenting, and competing over who was the most exhausted.

Why should I have to do all this after working all day?

I've been working all day too.

Couldn't you have done them as you went?

I didn't.

As the years passed, the rewards seemed less impressive, then shallow. And then the toll from doing a job that was so misaligned with my true nature, began to eat at my soul. I had sold out for appearances and money and opted out of bringing up the children I had craved.

Then there was the fourth man that smashed down the door to my heart uninvited, and stormed into my life. He led me to Mary and the Sibyls.

I wasn't looking for love, and when he presented himself, I didn't think much of him. It was a fleeting, throw-caution-to-the-wind kind of a thing, which morphed into something out of a cheap romance paperback. In one evening, he went from being ordinary to irresistible, when something like a bolt of lightning struck rendering me instantly in love. Fun, right? Except, it wasn't fun at all, not for me or for my husband.

I learnt that love is not a choice. It is an experience that happens to you much like being hit in the back of the head by a miss-thrown ball. I would never again judge anyone with their experiences involving love, as I had my first husband. We are at the mercy of the gods playing some celestial game, not, as I had once thought, victim to cruel decisions by uncaring people.

I came to learn that some kinds of love never go away, even after years of separation, and stuffing the feelings down, and refusing to acknowledge them; not ever.

I also learnt that there is no support from anyone in such a circumstance. Where I felt akin to having been diagnosed with an illness and that it was the kind of situation where visitors might come with hot meals and flowers, the reality is that society views people poorly under these circumstances, almost as a villain, and that they are seen to deserve every bad thing for having deliberately hurt their loved ones. It is a very private kind of suffering.

The effects were devastating. The end result of having spent my life without a clear sense of self, and focused on men, was that I suffered a crippling depression.

Creative Healing.

An idea emerged from the darkness that began my journey back. The thought was that **perhaps the hole in the landscape of my life was not from something destructive like a bomb going off, but from something designed.** Maybe hidden diggers had been at work changing the map of my life.

There was a new development underway, where the original meandering path had been pulled up and replaced by steep inclines, mountain views and precarious muddy ditches. Perhaps I was to make profound change much like *The Tower* indicates in the Tarot. Maybe the energy I was spending on this pain could be turned to a positive use.

I flailed around looking for where to start. I got on the library website and starting ordering travel DVDs and books. Italy resonated. I had been before but hadn't thought much of it at the time. I knew nothing about it except that my father had loved it. Systematically I took out every item the library had that in any way related to Italy. Films, cookbooks, books on architecture, gardens, cars, anything at all.

I investigated taking Italian language lessons. Strangely I found the idea embarrassing and internally sabotaged myself with shaming thoughts about my age and how stupid I would look. It took all the courage I could muster to enrol and start attending. I'm so glad I pushed through because I found my tribe there. There were other people that watched Italian films and read travel books about Italy; people that were planning their trips of a lifetime, and people suffering from the effects of love gained or lost. Even people older than me.

I started to write. I filled pages of my journal with my testimony to depression, as well as quotes and poetry, and then snippets that excited me about Italian history, culture and travel.

The real life-changer was the night I booked a flight to go to Italy. Solo. My husband had no desire to go, and yet again, in his deep generosity, freely offered his blessing. After I had hit the submit button on the airline booking site – a flight into Palermo in Sicily and out of Rome a month later – I was in turmoil. I sat in a chair in the lounge in the dark, wide eyed with terror. *What am I thinking? I really am mad.* My husband found me there and placed his arms around me, laying his head on my chest. Together we rocked till the anxiety subsided.

In 2015, I boarded a plane to Italy alone. It was a scary prospect as I had never gone to a foreign country alone and I spoke limited Italian. I had packed lightly, having planned for months in advance what my capsule wardrobe would consist of, leaving room for my hair straighteners and makeup. My flight was badly delayed in Hong Kong and I arrived in Frankfurt too late to make my direct connection to Sicily. Where my original booking would have arrived in the morning, I finally got to Sicily via Milan, late at night. My bag had not kept up and didn't appear on the carousel. The taxi dropped me off in a street that was not my destination, pointed at a door that was not my accommodation, and charged me an exorbitant sum. Only after he had driven away did I realise my predicament. I had left my mobile charger in my checked luggage and had a miniscule amount of battery life left. And I was lost.

Mary.

Mary was a young Italian woman, and, with her husband and small child, passed by on their way home from their evening meal and *passeggiata.*[2] She was young, petite and had long dark hair. I wiped away my tears and showed her my address and Mary and her family walked me to the right road.

In the morning, *Mary* was outside my room in the courtyard standing on a plinth in the centre of a water feature. I was staying in a convent and so *Mary* was also depicted in an image on the wall. At this stage, I didn't yet see Mary for looking, despite her tentative introductions. The first time I really noticed Mary was at the *Chiesa*[3] *Madonna della Rocca* in Taormina. I thought she looked serene. It was by now a few days later and my bag had been found and delivered. I hugged the nun that had carted it up the stairs to my room. Mary was gracious in accepting my profound gratitude. Over the coming days Mary started to become not only discernible amongst the crosses and statues, the vases of flowers and religious paraphernalia, but she was the star attraction. She appeared in a Sorrento cemetery, a niche in Naples, and a Caserta crossroads, as well as hole-in-the-wall places of worship in Rome. To me, it was as though she had just arrived, like a new and treasured gift. She was beautiful with her halo, head coverings and gown, and was often carrying her baby. In St Peter's Basilica in Rome, she held her crucified, adult son across her lap, and I felt such an empathy having two big sons of my own. Michelangelo captured Mary's qualities in his *Pieta*[4] as much as he did the star attraction. The scene of the *Pieta* was intensely moving. After a few moments I gathered myself and looked around to make sure no one had noticed my chin wobble and my ragged gasp.

In Santa Maria, in Trastevere, the presence of my Catholic grandmother blew through me like a cool, gentle breeze and it seemed Mary took a role in that experience.

Thank you, I said, addressing her directly for the first time.

We were slow to make friends but once we did it was solid. For the first time, I made tentative requests.

---

[2] walk

[3] Church

[4] A picture or sculpture of the Virgin Mary holding the dead body of Jesus Christ on her lap or in her arms.

Could you possibly keep an eye on me today so that I make my train connection at Piramide?

No answer.

I hate to ask something so trivial when there are so many more important demands on your time.

No answer.

And would you mind terribly watching over me until I find my accommodation tonight because I'm going to be arriving late?

As it turned out, she never replied but always obliged. I came to trust her. Our friendship developed into daily visits even if it was just a pop-in. There were churches everywhere, where I could step past the Roma woman with her paper cup, drape my pink scarf around my shoulders, remove my sunhat, and enter the cool sanctuary where Mary was always up the front and to the side. I would slip onto a wooden pew, bow my head, and for want of a better word, pray. No other such connection developed for me with any other characters present on the walls or among the statues and sculptures in the churches. It was just with Mary.

Near the end of that profound trip, my interactions with Mary went from being requests for help to expressions of gratitude. It was with a joyous heart that I returned to New Zealand.

The first days back I was brimming with my experience. I immersed myself in my photos and wrote posts for my new Italian travel blog. I returned to work. Slowly, fatigue and normal family life, and all the reasons it had happened in the first place, saw me slide back into my dark place. The depression returned.

Even after having had such a nourishing relationship with Mary throughout Italy, it never occurred to me to go seeking her once I was back home. It seemed the relationship only existed in Italy.

I joined a new organisation in my efforts to once again channel the energy of the gloom into something positive, and it happened to hold its biennial conference in Turin, Italy. There were plenty of other members further up the list that could have opted to attend than the newbie, but no one else seemed able to. It was a surprising turn of events that led to a whirlwind year of fundraising and hard work, culminating in a second trip to Italy.

Once back in Italy, I sought Mary out within hours. Reunited, my heart swelled and peace descended. Although it was a shorter trip, it filled the hole in my soul, but again on return the hole opened up. Seeking this temporary happiness drove me to annual trips over the next several years.

Connecting with the Feminine.

In 2018, after a long illness, my father died. It was as though his enormous masculine energy dissolved like the morning mist. My mother emerged as though coming out from under a duvet, unscathed but disoriented. All of the family were thrust into having far more interaction with each other than we'd had in years. I asked them if they wanted to come to Italy.

I had been writing a story based in Italy. It was set in pre-Christian times and a character had formed in my mind – a young woman, who is metaphorically lost, and decides to leave her rural home and journey to Rome. Once there she is faced with numerous harrowing obstacles which she overcomes to return home triumphant. Of course, it was my own story, except I had hidden myself so cleverly in ancient history I didn't recognise myself.

As long as I was immersed in my heroine's journey, the darkness didn't descend. The process was a pleasure and fed my introverted need for alone time, as well as my curiosity. I had to research every detail. The internal drive to write the story was overwhelming. Love is a powerful source of creative energy. If it is a big enough love and you can't find a way to channel its angst-ridden, obsessive energy, it can kill you, and so I wrote.

As I put the words onto paper and furnished the story with detail, I found I had a helper. I don't know if Mary had made her way to New Zealand or whether *the Genius*[5] had come to sit on my shoulder, but the story started to develop rich detail and exciting turns of events I did not feel emanated just from me. The protagonist turned out to be visionary and to be able to make predictions of the future, which catapulted me into a discovery of the Sibyls.

The Sibyls were oracles from ancient Greece, and a handful were also acknowledged from other countries, including Italy. The common thread is that they were all women able to make divinely inspired prophecies that came to them via underworld deities. The ancient Romans gave much weight to the powers of the Sibyls and consulted their books of prophecies in times of turmoil. Virgil wrote about them. Michelangelo painted them in the frescos of the Sistine Chapel, and Raphael did the same on the wall of the *Chiesa Santa Maria della Pace* in Rome. Shakespeare referred to them in multiple plays, and the Siena Cathedral

---

[5] In **Roman religion**, the Genius is the divine nature present in every person, place, or thing, not dissimilar to a guardian angel.

shows them on its pavement. I studied the fragments of what is known of these fascinating women so that I could incorporate them into my story. They were strong, independent women – outsiders, forced or content to be different.

My mother and sister nervously paid deposits for their flights to Rome.

What's the other place you want to go to again, the one near Naples?

Cuma.

What's in Cuma again?

The first Greek settlement on Italian soil where the Cumaean Sibyl lived, Mum. Oh yes dear. And what is that?

We flew into Rome and I took them to meet Mary. We travelled to Molise and visited the Temple and Sanctuary at Pietrabbondante where the Samnites worshiped female deities such as the Sabine[6] goddess Ops Consiva.[7] We drank beers and talked about the man my dad had been. Mum cried. My sister, who I had not spent much time with since we were teenagers and who I thought I had nothing in common with, turned out to be very like me. We even had the same obscure music on our phones. After two weeks of close proximity, with our beds lined up in our hotel room marae[8] style, listening to each other's gentle snores and private calls and ducking each other's rinsed out undies in the bathroom, we found our sameness. Then we went our separate ways. Mum and my sister went north to Florence before flying out, and I went to the deep south of Calabria. I had the archaeological finds of the *Oenotrians*[9] and their worship of Athena to visit. And after that, there was one last thing I had to do. I needed to return to Rome. I had discovered Mary had a predecessor.

The Great Mother.

In 204 BC, the Romans were under duress from Hannibal at Carthage, and they were desperate. Meteor showers, failed harvests, and famine, seemed to be portents of Rome's impending defeat. The Sibylline books were consulted. They were stored in the vault under Capitoline Hill in Rome and had been sold to the King of Rome, Tarquinius Superbus, three hundred years before by a Sibyl, the

---

[6] An ancient Italian people living in the Apennine mountains.

[7] A goddess of agriculture and wealth.

[8] Maori communal meeting, and often sleeping, place.

[9] An ancient Greek people.

Hellespontine Sibyl. Her recommendations, if they were interpreting the words correctly, were that they needed to import a new Goddess. The name of this Goddess was *Cybele* in Greek; in Latin she was *Magna Mater*, or to us, the Great Mother. A second Sibyl at Delphi confirmed that their interpretation was correct. Magna Mater was transported to Rome and placed in a new temple on the Palatine Hill. Rome was indeed victorious in Carthage. The Magna Mater cult became one of the most important in the Roman world. She set the scene nicely for the coming shift from Pagan to Christian Rome. When the Emperor Constantine converted to Christianity in 312 AD, Mary seamlessly filled this maternal feminine role and the Magna Mater faded from memory.

Perhaps Mary and the Great Mother are one and the same. Perhaps my beloved Mary is every Goddess and Sibyl. **She is the Feminine Divine in all her various guises and we can connect to her restorative, healing and creative powers in whichever way we choose.** She has been my friend, carer, nurturer and silent witness. For me, she is most strongly felt in Rome.

My trips to Italy over the past six years have taken me on a journey within. I developed faith in myself and my abilities, and I am guided and supported by these powerful feminine allies. I came to see myself as their instrument in making use of my life. Their guidance with my writing has brought me peace. Rome became as familiar to me as my home suburb. I came to trust that everything in my life is happening as it should. I developed hope for my future. **I became unafraid, either to die or to live.** I felt my connection to something more than myself. I came to inhabit a space in the world independent of the male influences in my life although I did need to keep practicing this as I was prone to fall into the trap of babying my giant, grown sons. **I had always been brave and resourceful but I had now become beautiful**, which I never was when I needed a man to tell me. I stopped travelling with hair straighteners and makeup.

The moon was full on the 16th of June 2019 and it rose above the Coliseum about 8:30pm. I was walking down from the Capitoline Hill, where once the Temple of Jupiter Optimus Maximus had stood, and in a vault beneath my feet, the Sibylline books had once been stored. My feet were sunburnt from five hours on the Palatine Hill learning about the Magna Mater and exploring the House and Temple of the Vestal Virgins in the Forum. I was walking towards the Coliseum metro to make my way back to my convent bed by Santa Maria Maggiore, the largest Catholic Church in Rome dedicated to Mary. The next day I would start the arduous twenty-four hours of flights to New Zealand. I was going home to spend the rest of the year writing.

Maggie Pinsent

Living with the Feminine Divine

Growing up in South America, I was unknowingly – organically I guess, in the way that children absorb life's gifts so easily and with open minds – introduced to the idea that females, women, girls, Goddesses, played a significant part in the creation of everything around me. Of life. For both women and men.

Yemanjá, goddess of the seas. Ayaó, goddess of the air. Oxún, goddess of pleasure, beauty and love. And others. Their rites and rituals, ceremony and festivals, are such a rich part of life, and a very visual experience, in Brazil especially. I lived alongside Afro-Brazilian Orishas, the pantheon of Goddesses and Gods, warriors, both male and female, lusty lovers, magical beings that control the elements, our surroundings, the things I could palpably recognise in my life and which made them divine. Without realising or understanding, the seed was planted.

I was christened a Roman Catholic where the females are either pure-in-spirit mothers and aunties, or prostitutes. A lot of good versus bad. My heart battled with the teachings of my parents, my schooling, and society, but I conformed nonetheless. It was confusing to say the least.

Then, in the USA in the 70s, I discovered there was a similar group of Native American tribes that honoured comparable divine beings with powers to transform, heal, and understand the Universe, as well as an elemental father and mother. I was hooked. I'd always known as a child that my reality was only accessible through understanding the Universe, the female, the luscious green yumminess of Mother Earth. The female became the Feminine Divine for me, and I started my journey of discovery, learning, and development.

The woman of Willendorf was discovered in Austria in 1908. This little clay figure, just over four inches tall is thirty thousand years old. I discovered her in 1999. Once again, I fell in love. And a whole new world of Celtic and Indo-European female divinities came into my life, and transformed me, my thinking, and my way of living. I could see how the ancient and the more modern beliefs, and their divine representatives, can walk together.

Coming back to England, with my ten-year old son Dylan, after thirty years away travelling, and living mostly in South America, I started reading the myths and legends of the Celtic, Saxon, Roman, and Indo-European people, and was stunned to find a whole host of women divinities that I had never heard of. I had to take it further and I did.

So, my childhood was immersed in the world of Afro-South American divinities, my youth in North American Indian tribal teachings, and it was as a young mother that my journey with the Divine Feminine led me to the roots of my own lineage, and to embracing Her across time and belief systems, through myth and mythology, ancient stories, archaeological findings, and my own research. The main thread through all I had learned thus far, and was learning now in my reading, was that the female would always be my natural place for inspiration.

My family had always said I was strong. All my life people have said how strong I am, and yet, I know now that any outward strength I showed was acquired because **I had learned to believe that being a woman was enough.** I didn't feel strong, but I dealt with those hard events we all have thrown at us throughout life, in unemotional, straightforward ways. Asking myself what a goddess might do in the circumstances, and sitting with the hurt and pain, I would invariably feel touched and inspired by a divine guide. My prayers were more of a chat and answers came to me in the same way. I love ceremony, so it always helped me to set the scene with a ritual that involved one or more of the Feminine Divines I had come to love. It's possible that each time I needed to go through this process, I became stronger, more able, maybe even wiser. Little did I realise how much stronger I would one day need to be.

Living in South America was very different to anything resembling the lifestyle of Europe, the United Kingdom or North America in the 1950s to the present day. My family moved from southern England when I was seven years old. We lived in Venezuela, Brazil, and Colombia, and I spent the next thirty years flitting from one country to the other, with England in between for short periods; then boarding school, finishing school in Switzerland, and the United States for a few years. As an adult I returned to Brazil and worked as a translator. Brazil is an amazing paradise of colour and music, but it is also a place of deep poverty and discrimination, corruption, and little respect for the sanctity of life. The 50s and 60s had seen a resurgence of the 14th century African religions of Umbanda and Candomblé, with trance dancing, animal sacrifice, ritual and ceremony in open spaces. Today Brazil is riven with new-age, money-making, so-called Christian religions such as the *Universal Church of the Kingdom of God,* which has recently built a massive temple in Sao Paulo costing over US$300m, in an area where people clearly live in terrible poverty.

Candomblé was created in Brazil when the 16th century religion of the slaves from West Africa, Umbanda, prohibited by law, and the official religion, Catholicism, were merged to make it acceptable to all. Today, and in my own experience, Candomblé has grown steadily away from Catholicism, and closer to its original African Umbanda roots.

When I was eleven years old in 1962 in Brazil, it was a time when I could be left to find my own fun outside; a carefree, happy time of my life. We lived outside the city, and we were often in contact with native people. They were noticeable because they wore very colourful non-western clothing, and because they would gather in the evenings in different places close to the house. I was entranced by the rituals and strange ceremonies that these tall, dark-skinned, loud and laughing people enacted in public places. Crossroads. Corners. Underneath special trees, on the sea, at the beach. Unlike the Catholic ceremonies I was taken to by my parents, inside a stuffy, uncomfortable church, where a man droned on as we bobbed up and down, these amazing people danced and drank, sang and played drums. The women were the centre of attention in their beautiful white dresses that flowed out in circles as they twirled. I loved it. The sight would fill me with delight and a longing to be part of it. At the end of a rite, an offering to the gods and goddesses, a *macumba*, was created in the form of a small pile of wood and sawdust, dead birds and chickens, rice and flowers, all manner of organic things, and topped off with sprays of alcohol that they were drinking as they danced. Last of all, different coloured ribbons were placed on the top, each colour with its own special significance, representing one of the Orishas,[10] or sometimes a prediction. During these rituals, I'd watch from afar, fascinated by the magic of it all, until one day one of the women invited me in to sit on the edge of the circle with other children and watch. Much later, in the dead of night, one of them would set fire to the pile. Next morning I'd go out and find smouldering embers, burned bones, empty bottles. And coins, lots of coins. I knew not to touch it or take anything away from there. I was entranced by the mystery of it, and respectful of the ceremony.

There was story-time too, when we were told about the trials and achievements of the many Orishas; stories that transported me to magical and wondrous places. I fell in love with Yemanjá and Iansã, two female deities. Yemanjá is very powerful and the goddess that rules the seas, but she is also a protector of children, a guide for women of all ages, and a symbol of motherhood. Sometimes mermaid, sometimes beautiful young woman with dark flowing hair, she wears a light blue gown or cape. At the turn of a new year, a statue of Yemanjá is placed in a small wooden boat, painted white and pale blue, and decorated with flowers and garlands. The boat is carried by men dressed in white, as the women in their white dresses and pale blue sash, dance and chant in procession to the beach. The men carry Yemanjá out beyond the waves so that she floats away. It is a sight to behold, exciting and emotionally stirring at the same time. It has never ceased to ignite my inner goddess. On the beach itself, candles are lit, forming altars with flowers and food and drink, in sand pits all along the beach. The chanting and dancing continue throughout the night until dawn.

Iansã, another compelling goddess, owner of all the directions, rules the weather and has the power to cause sudden storms and terrible winds, ferocious rain and

---

[10] Gods and Goddesses.

fiery lightning. She is also sought out by women for guidance in tough situations and difficult times. Iansã, goddess of death and rebirth, resists male authority and is a role model for passionate women. She is one of very few Orishas concerned with death, taking souls over the bridge to the other world. She is Yemanjá's daughter, and she carries a machete or the sword of a warrior and is always depicted wearing a red gown.

These two women formed my early idea of what it is to be a woman; they were my goddesses and I kept them close. As I got older, I read more about their qualities and took them to heart. There is much to study about the female divine in Candomblé and Umbanda.

At the age of twelve, I went to boarding school in England at my own instigation. It was a Catholic convent, rather like living in a womb of women of all ages, with a clear idea that there is only one God, and he is a man. *Ha!*

God might be a man but the Divine Feminine was very present at *Poles Convent FCJ*[11] for me. The nuns were dedicated to loving their God but I never felt religion was pushed down my throat. In fact, I was allowed to pursue my own enquiry and I was given a lot of encouragement especially when I became fascinated with the similarities in Mary and Yemanjá, Mary Magdalen[12] and Iansã. The colours they wear have symbolic significance in both belief systems. Their life stories guided me to look at my own role models and the qualities I wanted to learn and take on myself. In my usual way, I took on life at school full-hilt, and became the Priest's assistant. To me, it was like being close to the source. I spent many hours at the foot of Our Lady in the chapel, just talking, and I always felt a sense of being guided and protected by Mary. Many a tear was shed here, but comfort was also there for me.

In an earlier Church of England school in Brazil, Mary Magdalen was mentioned in passing or not at all, but at *Poles* she was very much a part of the community's life. The nuns never referred to Mary Magdalen as a prostitute, but rather as a helper, a companion, and a disciple that stood by the prophet. I remember being astonished later in my life, reading and hearing her referred to as a prostitute, and wanting to correct that. The nuns encouraged us to talk about Mary and Mary Magdalen, their lives and teachings and, during our silent retreats, to read and learn more about the life of other women of the times.

Going through boxes of books after my recent house move, I came across a tryptic flier given to girls interested in joining the FCJs. In it, the Founding Mother, The Venerable Marie Madeleine Victoire, Viscountess de Bonnault d'Hoet, says: *My name is Magdalen: I wish to follow in the footsteps of my patron saint. She and*

---

[11] Faithful Companions of Jesus

[12] I was taught this spelling of Mary Magdalen and I believe it is the Roman Catholic spelling used in English

*Holy Women did not leave Christ in the hour of His need, but throughout His life they proved themselves His **Faithful Companions**. Such is the name we shall bear – I and those who will associate themselves with me… The foot of the Cross will be our rallying point.*

While I was at *Poles*, I had several moments when I felt touched and guided by a divine presence. It filled my heart with exultation and often gave me the comfort I needed. I would feel infused with light, and I knew it to be a feminine essence. It was never Jesus or any other male; it was always a motherly touch, or a woman's wisdom, that would come through to me. Several times when I was worried about my exams I would go to chapel, and sit in meditation and, in minutes, I would feel the glow of love surround me. I was thirteen when I learned my parents were getting a divorce. I was devastated. Not only were they divorcing each other, it felt like they were divorcing our family as each found a new family with children. I felt utterly alone, as though I had to fend for myself. Again, I went to chapel and kneeling down, hands clasped, I cried. Within minutes I felt a gentle hand on my shoulder, comforting me. I thought it was a nun, but there was nobody there. I knew then that I was being comforted by my divine mother. Reverend Mother did all she could to console me, but it was only when I remembered to sit in chapel or to find a place in nature, to speak to my goddesses, that I could see the reality of their lives, and my own. I wept and found solace in the chapel and walled gardens of Poles Convent.

Once again, it was women who had a hand in moulding my mind and guiding my heart. There was a definite focus on the female, and that is probably why, before I left school, I professed a wish to become a nun in the Order of the Faithful Companions of Jesus. However, Reverend Mother Mary Christina was a wise woman, and suggested I go to finishing school, where my cousins had been before me, and hone my language skills first. Then I could take a teachers' certificate at the FCJ teacher training college in Preston, in Lancashire.

I went to finishing school in Switzerland, which could not have been a more different environment, although again I was living within a community of women my age and older. I studied and had fun, and that was it. I did learn French and Italian, but I didn't enter the Order.

Many years passed in which I drifted, allowing life to take me along rather than leading a life I wanted by planning it or seeking guidance. It was as if once I was loose on the world, I lost the paddles of my boat, and my navigation.

I roamed between my parents, living in different countries, working and partying, until I fetched up in Massachusetts and discovered the native people of North America. It was 1974 and I was horrified to find how badly the Native American was treated. Disdain and disrespect were commonplace for them. It was heart-breaking.

I read all of Carlos Castaneda. I smoked dope. I learned to journey in meditation, seeking the realms outside of my earthly reality. I learned about the ways of the Native American, and was pleased to find similar beliefs to those of the Indians of South America, especially with regard to the way women are treated within the tribe. While I am sure there are exceptions, it seemed to me women were (hopefully are still) treated with protection, love and respect by their own men, be they father, husband, brother or son. They are the creators, and their guidance is sought even by the tribal leaders. Women become elders, whose experience and wisdom are meaningful and important to all the generations of men and women in the community.

I was in my 20s, and still cushioned by the knowledge I'd acquired up to that time. Discovering a new aspect of the sacred feminine way of living was a revelation that remained with me, and became a part of who I was. I immersed myself in learning all I could about the ways of the 'Red Indian', as they were known in the 1970s still. There wasn't much contemporary literature on the lives of the different tribes so I depended on the old stories, mostly about battles and written by men, the victors. History has a way of doing that, doesn't it?

It was at this time that I came across *The Suppression of Women's Rights* (aka *When God was a Woman*), by Merlin Stone. This book became a treasured item in my luggage as I travelled around, before getting married and settling in Boston, USA. Stone's writing made so much sense to me; I could relate to her writings, as if she spoke for me. By 1977, my world was changing rapidly again. It was a whirlwind, especially on a personal level. My marriage lasted but two years, ending when my gentle, handsome husband was diagnosed with paranoid schizophrenia and institutionalised. Paul had made several attempts at taking his own life, and I seemed unable to help in any way, much as I tried. I felt blamed by his family who, in their words, had thought that *I would be good for him*. I obviously wasn't good enough. They forced me to agree to electric shock therapy, which I was completely against, but I gave in. Paul went from bad to worse, a shell of the man I loved. I fell apart, left the United States, and went back to South America where my father was living in Venezuela.

It was when I started working and earning my own living that I understood that this is a man's world, where the feminine is cunningly and violently stamped out. I entered a time of enabling men, and of allowing the machinations of a materialistic world to divert me on a path that was bereft of the influence of women, divine or earthly. I call it my dark time, when my heart and spirit, my flame, had to be suppressed to enable me to survive in a world driven by a different force: an aggressive, worldly, ambitious world led mostly by a domineering male energy. I didn't have the skills to understand a world run by men. I thought women were enough. And yet I felt continually let down, disconnected from my higher self, used and abused, and helpless to fight back. I had failed at marriage, like my parents. Christianity had failed me. I had ignored my goddesses so they had gone too. I lost my balance and I teetered badly.

In 1981 soon after my divorce was finalised, I married again; on the rebound, I guess. He was a brutal misogynist. Having wooed me up the aisle he now felt able to control me through violence. He beat me, and I felt deserving. I rapidly fell into a quagmire of self-loathing, hatred for him, grief for the life I had expected, and pure unadulterated self-neglect. And then I found I was pregnant. That's when I began to come back to me. Somehow, being able to carry a child, to grow a new being, made me aware of how indestructible I could be. My feminine strength reawakened, I listened to my goddesses again. It took some time but when my son was just over three years old, I finally broke away to save his life and mine from destruction. My child was my life and he was the flame that sparked my inner goddess into life. I was fierce, a warrior, and reborn to protect my child. I was thirty-six by this time, fully self-supporting, and back in control.

When Dylan was ten, I left the Americas and brought him home to England. Being Dylan's mother brought me utter joy, as well as a realisation that I had full responsibility for this beautiful being, to show him the ways of women and the Feminine Divine. He would learn about a man's world just by living in it! It took some time to adapt to Anglo-Saxon ways again, but I was lucky enough to find work in a place that was less *macho*, less aggressively money-making, more interested in facilitating my personal desires for further learning and study. As a staff member of the University of Oxford, I had access to the best libraries in the world, including the *Bodleian*.[13] I could not have found a better time and place to delve into a subject that I had always loved, and I was fascinated to know more. A more formal study of the Feminine Divine began.

I read copious amounts on the Indo-European goddesses. I travelled to India, and became completely enthralled with the many female divines, their stories, ceremonies, rituals, and their wantonly colourful representations. Ribbons and beads, flowers, garlands, incense, singing and dancing. I was back in my childhood in Brazil. I came away determined to discover a way of incorporating these lives and stories into my own, and Dylan's.

Ruskin College[14] in Oxford offered me the opportunity to throw myself into research. I needed direction and help, as I had never done any form of formal research or academic writing. My original title was *The Study of Indo-European goddesses and their place in our lives*. I was overwhelmed with the amount of information I uncovered.

---

[13] The main research library of the University of Oxford, and one of the oldest libraries in Europe.

[14] Ruskin College is totally independent of the University but they have a long-standing relationship, whereby its students have access to the University's libraries among other things.

I had started visiting sites of Celtic significance in Britain. As a child I'd often enjoyed a picnic with my family at the foot of Stonehenge, and I'd been to holy wells in the past, so I knew there was plenty to discover. I found more stone circles, more sites of divine reverence at wells, rocks, hills. I became a Celtic tourist; holidays and weekends, where possible, were taken up with finding out more about this bountiful heritage of my ancestors. I found that, although the Celts left no written history, their stories were told and retold. Stories have a habit of changing with the telling, and being embellished along the way of course, but there is nothing like being physically at a site of significance, where the people prayed, lived and died. The Romans absorbed and recreated a lot of the Celtic divinities, giving them new names and a story. Such as Sulis, worshipped at Bath, later Romanised into Sulis Minerva, seen as a nourishing, life-giving mother who could also be called on to vanquish an enemy. The Celts honoured goddesses of nature and natural forces, much like Yemanjá, Iansã, and Oxún. They had skills as healers and warriors. They were beautiful and hideous, young and hag-like. They transformed their appearance into associated creatures such as crows and wolves. The study of the ancient Celts and the pantheon of deities is a massive task. And I was fully immersed once again, in a mystical, magical journey that engulfed my senses. Wells are not just where water springs, they are where a Goddess lives and shares Mother Earth's life-blood. Rolling hills become a goddess lying across the land, her belly large, her breasts engorged, caves her dark cunt. Saying that, reminds me of a *Sheela-na-gig*.[15] In my research I kept coming up against her being either a representation of fertility or a warning against lust. That, of course, is a man's interpretation, and don't they love to put women into those categories of makers of babies or seductresses. It's also a way of demonising pre-Christian deities, especially the female. My own theory is that she is the Creatrix, Mother of all, the One who birthed the earth. She is the beginning. The look on her face isn't frightening (apparently to warn the viewer); it's the look of agony and anguish as she holds her labia apart, to allow the world to come into being.

This was when I came across the *Woman of Willendorf*, also known as the *Venus of Willendorf*, a very old lady indeed. Her head has no face, it is the world. She is voluptuous, with a fat belly and large breasts. I engrossed myself in making her in clay, and working with clay became a much-loved hobby. I created madonnas and many other figures that represent the figure of the Feminine Divine. This photo is my version of the woman of Willendorf. There is something about moulding and hand-forming a lump of clay into the figure of a woman, a goddess, that is highly satisfying. It puts me into a meditative state, where I feel Her presence and guiding hand. Each piece is unique, and each one is infused with a divine energy, channelled through me. Hours go by and I come out renewed and refreshed.

---

[15] Figurative carvings of naked women displaying an exaggerated vulva; found all over Europe – particularly in Ireland and Great Britain – on churches, castles and other buildings.

left: the 30,000 year old limestone figurine, now in the *Naturhistorisches Museum* in Vienna; *and right:* my clay figure.

My research project at Ruskin College was ultimately titled *Celtic Mythology with a Focus on the Feminine Divine.*

Reading in the Bodleian and writing up was one of the most intellectually stimulating and personally enriching experiences of my life. I confirmed to myself that what I had experienced as a child in Brazil, and what I was discovering in my home country, and the teachings I came across in between, were in fact all connected. In the same way, I believe we are also all related, all connected. *Mitakuye Oyasin,*[16] as the first people of North America say. Every time I delve into the stories of ancient people in different parts of the world, I am astounded how correlative our deities are, and especially by how many of those deities are feminine. The Divine Feminine connects us.

That feeling of connection to a universe of women gave me strength I was forced to call on in 2017. My world crumbled, and I found myself, not in a whirlwind as before, but thrust into a soundless numbness. I don't know how I survived Dylan's death. My Sonshine. He was a boy who became a man, but I could see in him a divine presence, and it was feminine. He taught me true love – unconditional and all-embracing love – among many things, and now the fragility of life. My life shattered. My heart broke in a million pieces, and I am a different woman.

Nobody but a bereaved mother can know how a life can be changed so dramatically. And nobody, other than a bereaved mother, can understand the longing and profound agony a mother feels at the death of her child. I don't need anyone else's attempts at understanding though. What I've needed, and still need,

---

[16] All Are Related. From the Lakota language, it reflects their world view of interconnectedness.

is genuine friendship and compassion, and it hasn't been easy to find. My grief has been so engulfing and so life-changing, and to some extent so destructive, that I lost my identity, my sense of self. With Dylan gone, I drowned with him; and yes, I blamed all higher powers for not keeping him safe. Yemanjá, goddess of waters; Iansã, my muse as a mother. Where were they now?

My gentle and passionate, beautiful, brave son – this free spirit adventurer I birthed and nurtured – should not have died so young. Dylan was born on a Monday, and died on a Monday. He was 33, the age I was when he was born. I struggle with life and a reason to continue living without my son, and that, I suspect, will never change. The grief is bottomless. I live the unanswerable questions: Why? Why him? Why me? Looking for blame where there is none and yet blaming myself for not protecting my son from death. And knowing in my heart, there was nothing I could have done. I miss him so! I am alive though, and on my best days another new me is emerging: a wiser, more compassionate woman. I'm discovering a new way to live, closer to mother Earth.

A year or so after Dylan's death, I was in my own biblical wilderness when I met two wonderful women who have become genuine friends: Sue and Detta. Sue opened my mind again to new possibilities and a new purpose, and Detta opened my heart to find the love inside me that can walk alongside my sorrow. Through these two living goddesses, I am slowly finding a new path, a purpose for living. It is genuinely a turning point for me. I will unearth my little thesis and publish it. I will make new and wonderful goddesses in clay, and offer classes in clay and mosaics to like-minded women. It is through Sue that I have rediscovered the Marys too; and now I can fully identify with Mary the Mother, who also lost her beloved son. It meant little to me before – now it has opened a door for me to engage with her again. Yemanjá and Iansá are waiting to be invited in.

The Divine Feminine has been a part of my life always, and whereas for a while I laid that part of me aside, I am convinced that my world, or the world that nourishes me, comes from the feminine.

In the end, **are we not all goddesses?** The embodiment of the Feminine Divine? Aren't we women the Feminine Divine ourselves?

Some of us are Kali, Pele, Rhiannon, Oxún, Diana – warriors and huntresses, protectors and protesters. Others are loving mothers, nurturers, and spiritual guides like Mary and Mary Magdalen, Yemanjá and Sulis. We are wisdom keepers, frivolous dancing queens, mothers, daughters, sisters, grandmothers. We are all women with an inner goddess of our own. And we are all connected.

Rema Kumar

Threading my Path to the Divine Feminine

The first years of my life were in Kerala, in the south-west of India. Every second Indian and every tourist advertisement calls Kerala *God's own country*, for its verdant beauty, the backwaters, the beaches and the temples. It also ranks the highest for female literacy rate in India, with a history of matriarchy, which was often a part of discussions during my childhood. So, growing up in Kerala, I never felt inferior as a girl, as a female. I was blessed with a carefree childhood. My sister and I went to a convent school nearby, wading through the paddy fields and the banana trees, running and hopping with our friends, absorbing the sights and smells of the changing seasons, be it summer or monsoon, during sowing or harvest.

It was at convent school that I was introduced to Jesus and Mary. While some of the sisters who taught us were kind, some were strict disciplinarians. I distinctly remember the screening of a film on Jesus but do not recall any Christian friends. The majority of the children were Hindus and we were a happy bunch. Christmas brought us as much joy as our special festival of Onam.

My earliest and strongest religious and spiritual influence was my paternal grandmother, my Ammumma, who spent her childhood in Neyyoor, near the border between Kerala and Tamil Nadu. A very spiritual lady, she had suggested my name *Rema* after her spiritual guru, Sree Rama Devi Amma, who she revered. It was also one of the names in the list drawn up by my maternal grandfather, a Sanskrit scholar. And so I was named *Rema* – one of the thousand names for the Goddess Lakshmi.

Ammumma was extremely disciplined about her morning prayers. Her day would begin at dawn, with a shower, then lighting the lamp in the puja room,[17] singing *shlokas*[18] and *bhajans,*[19] followed by yoga, before entering the kitchen to settle into her daily chores. Our mornings began with listening to her soft chants. She

---

[17] Place of worship.

[18] Sanskrit poetry.

[19] Religious songs.

initiated my sister and me into this world: the shlokas or verses for different Goddesses and Gods; the bhajans – light classical songs sung in their praise; and the chanting of mantras.[20] We absorbed them all like sponges. My mother taught us the *gayatri mantra* – her favourite, especially in times of stress. It's so much a part of my DNA that I chant it subconsciously whenever I am in need of inner strength. We learnt the *Goddess Lalitha Ashtothram* – 108 verses in praise of Goddess Lalitha Devi, considered to be a manifestation of Shakti/Durga. We recited it every evening when the oil lamp was lit, and we would sing and pray for everyone's well-being. A visit to the nearby temple during auspicious days and festivals was and still is a tradition. Having lost her father even before she was born, Ammumma was extremely close to her aunts and cousin sisters with whom she grew up, and every time we would visit the family Bhagavathi[21] temple in Neyyoor – her ancestral home – I would try to imagine her childhood when the matrilineal society had been in full glory.

Growing up in India amongst the Gods and the Goddesses, devotion, religion, and spirituality are almost taken for granted, especially in the southern part of the country. Every Goddess and God has an exclusivity and one's devotion depends on one's own experiences, one's own journey. You could be a Hindu, yet reach out to a Muslim Saint or a local Church, or even a wayside deity in times of trouble depending on your belief or your spiritual vibrations. When you begin something new, you might take the blessings of the elephant God Ganesha who is believed to be the remover of all obstacles. When you are appearing for an examination or interview you might seek the blessings of Goddess Saraswathi. Unmarried young women might pray to Lord Shiva for a good husband. When you want to do well in business, you might pray to Goddess Lakshmi, and so on. To each his own.

My belief in the supreme power of the Goddesses is very deep-rooted as a practising Hindu. According to Hindu mythology, Adi Parashakti – the Goddess or Devi[22] – is the supreme being and therefore the source of all other Goddesses. Her name is appended to many place names to indicate the local deity of that place. In every nook and cranny of a town or a village in Kerala, there are temples for Bhagavathi. Even the men worship the Goddesses. Every Hindu home has a special place for puja[23] and Goddesses reign supreme. I grew up with all of them – they were and are a part of me. Kali[24] and Durga,[25] are the fierce forms – sometimes they are separate and sometimes they are one and the same, being

---

[20] Sacred utterance, not necessarily with any meaning.

[21] Another term for goddess.

[22] Goddess.

[23] Worship.

[24] Known also as Kali the Destroyer, she is the Goddess of Time, Creation, Destruction and Power.

[25] Warrior goddess, protective mother goddess.

incarnations of Parvathi.[26] She embodies the divine shakti – feminine energy – that is used against the negative forces of evil and wickedness. She protects her devotees from evil powers and safeguards them. I pray to her for strength to face my demons of all kinds: physical, material and imaginary! Lakshmi, being the goddess of wealth, always looks beautiful and grand, and is most often depicted with a never-ending shower of gold coins from one of her palms, symbolising abundance and prosperity. I believe that without her blessings it is impossible to progress in my business. And Saraswathi is very important as the Goddess of education, wisdom, music and art, all of which are very important in Kerala. I did well on the academic front throughout my school and college, and having chosen to follow the creative profession of being a textile designer, every single day of mine is dedicated to her.

When I was twelve, we moved to Chennai, Tamil Nadu. It was a turning point for my family. Achan, (Father in Malayalam) being a film-maker, was based here. We hardly ever saw him. I remember writing many letters to him asking when he was coming home, though I do not recall any reply from his end. In those days also, we did not have a telephone at home, so communication was sporadic. Amma, (my mother) a doctor, began to worry about her daughters moving into their teens in his absence and found it quite a daunting challenge. I, for one, had already begun to exhibit strong signs of rebellion. Being the mother of a teenager now, I can totally understand her dilemma. She had to make a firm decision – whether to continue single-parenting in Trivandrum or to make the big move and live together as a family, even if we had to struggle it out. She finally took a stand and we moved. Ammumma, widowed by now, came with us. Thank God for that. In her own quiet and passive way, she gave us a sense of stability. But I don't think my sister and I were well-prepared. It felt like we were transplanted from our cosy cocoon of innocence into harsh reality.

However, a lot of credit for who I am goes to this beautiful city and its people who played a major role in my formative years. A city that has a rich cultural history, Chennai perfectly balances its heritage with its thriving modern lifestyle. The mornings would begin with *shlokas*, and then playing in the neighbourhood. We would pass temples on our way to school, with Fridays being extra special. This is where I learnt about the significance of Friday as an auspicious day for the Hindus because it is dedicated to Shakti and her multitude of incarnations including Durga and Kali. During any of the city's frenetic festivals, one could see Chennai's spirituality on proud display as temple idols are paraded through the streets, and pavements are painted in mesmerising geometric patterns known as *kolam* or *rangoli*, which bring good luck for the coming year.

---

[26] Goddess of fertility, love, beauty, marriage, children, and devotion; as well as of divine strength and power.

Ever so gently and slowly we began settling into our new life as a complete family. Now Achan was overshadowed by four women at home. The fact that he was not an authoritarian and had a great sense of humour helped. An eternal optimist, with deep-rooted faith in the power of the Gods, his film banner was also named *Almighty Films* with a logo that incorporated all the various religious symbols on a six-pointed star. He would try his experiments in the kitchen and regale us with tales from showbiz. We were initiated into using public transport as our school was a few kilometres away, and we learnt to speak Tamil and began to converse more in English. (Earlier in Kerala, though we studied in an English school, we only communicated with our friends in Malayalam).

Growing up in Saligramam, near Kodambakkam, the heart of the moviemaking world of erstwhile Madras in the early eighties, was a different world altogether. We had to pass through film studios and cinema halls on our way to school and it was a common sight to see actors – both small-time and big-time – whizzing past us to reach their shoots every other day. Huge billboards, shoots, and cinema gossip were all part of our daily diet.

And whenever a movie required a school as a backdrop, hey presto, ours was one of the most sought-after venues. Excitement would build up once we reached school during such mornings, with unit hands setting up their equipment for the upcoming shoot. Then we would keep our fingers crossed to see if our class would be included in the mock assembly scheduled in the middle of the day so that we would fill in as glorified extras required for the scene. Anything to break the routine of classes. And of course, during the intervals, there would be a mad rush to get the stars' autographs in our school diaries. A few years later when some of these movies showed up on television, we would try to spot our classrooms and excitedly check if we or any of our schoolmates were lucky enough to get our one millisecond share of silver screen presence. It was a big deal then for us innocent kids.

Back where we lived, bus stops would spring up overnight out of nowhere and vanish just the same way, and then we would realize that they were part of movie sets. There was an artist's studio around the corner that painted hoardings, and my sister and I would be fascinated by the drama that unfolded before us on huge canvases. We would know about upcoming new releases before our friends, from the hoardings that were commissioned to this local artist. South Indian cinema in those days often had movies on popular Goddesses and Gods from the Indian mythology; the epics: *Ramayana* and the *Mahabharata*, as well as spiritual gurus, saints, and a few that had storylines about how unquestionable faith in one's God ultimately helps the heroine or hero to triumph in the end, beating all odds. These were lapped up by the masses. The songs, the costumes, the jewellery, the colour, the grandeur, the magnificent sets with popular actors playing the major roles, ensured that these films ended up as super-hits. We grew up in this milieu.

It was also in Chennai that I was introduced to Amman, who symbolises sacrifice, motherhood, abundant wealth and good health. Mariamman,[27] being of rural popularity is represented by natural features of Mother Earth, just as any folk deity is worshipped for the fertility of the earth, animals and humans, prosperity in the form of rain, good crops, protection from natural calamities, even ghosts and demons. Mariamman worship is not just through Sanskrit hymns – you can hear songs blaring out of loudspeakers in praise of her, based on popular movie tunes. It is believed by devotees that Amman does not fail anyone, provided you go to Her with a sense of complete surrender. She already knows the devotee's pleadings and the devotee does not need a middle-man in the form of a temple priest.

We frequented another temple, *Melmaruvathur Adi Parashakti*, where the devotees thronged in red robes or clothes. The red colour symbolises the pigment of blood, which is common to all human beings on this Mother Earth, irrespective of caste, creed, gender, religion or any other discrimination. One of the unique features of this temple was that it did not have appointed priests to perform or conduct daily prayers, unlike others. The devotees, including women, were allowed to perform puja. Women were even allowed during their menstrual periods to perform regular prayers at the Sanctum Sanctorum (which is prohibited in other Hindu temples all over the world). The explanation given was that according to the Goddess, it is only a natural phenomenon which should not prohibit women from worshipping God. For the adolescent in me, it was quite a liberating fact to learn amidst the prevalent taboo about menstruation.

In October, we welcome *Navratri*, a nine day festival dedicated to the worship of Goddesses, in particular Lakshmi, Saraswathi and Durga. There are different worships every day and every evening there is a puja and the women sing devotional songs in praise of the Goddesses. The first term exams are timed to finish before Navratri, followed by a long holiday of almost ten days, so we doubly looked forward to it. Navaratri means *nine nights* in Sanskrit – *nava* meaning *nine*, and *ratri* meaning *nights*. It's at the end of the monsoon and is one of the most important festivals, celebrated all over India in honour of the Devi, the Goddess, the Divine Feminine.

In Kerala, because Saraswathi is especially important, the last part of the festival is a celebration of books and learning. We would place our school books before Saraswathi for her blessings. All studies and most work requiring skill are suspended, so we looked forward to this day when we only played all day. On the day of *Vijayadashami*, the books are ceremoniously taken out for reading and writing after worshipping Saraswathi. This day is considered auspicious for initiating children into writing and reading, leading them on their first step into the world of knowledge. It was also on this day that the Goddess Durga killed the

---

[27] Goddess of rain. She is the main mother goddess in the rural areas of Tamil Nadu.

demon Mahishasur, so *Vijayadashami* also celebrates the victory of good over evil.

In Chennai, I was fascinated by the tradition of *Bommai Golu*. Women set up their own creative themes in their homes, and friends and families invite each other to visit their homes to view *Golu* displays: steps adorned with dolls, toys and figurines. We would dress up in our finest silks, and in the evening we would be *Golu*-hopping from one home to another, where we would sing devotional songs praising the goddesses, and were treated to delicious snacks and sweets, eventually going home with gifts. More than anything else, the festive atmosphere was a joyous celebration of womanhood, with little girls in their innocence likened to Devis.

Interestingly, my first brush with Islam happened in Chennai too when I joined a Muslim College for my graduation and post-graduation in Textiles and Clothing. The fact that I did not get to go to medical school following Amma's footsteps (which everyone had expected) seemed to have worked in my favour, because it was here that I made some lovely friends for life. Every assembly began in the name of Allah, the beneficent, the merciful. And slowly the Urdu words, their pronunciation, the religious focus of my friends fascinated me. And from then on, every time I hear those prayers anywhere, I recite them along silently in my mind. It was also here that it slowly dawned on me the fact that I enjoyed a lot of freedom in comparison to many of my classmates who came from orthodox Hindu and Muslim families, equally patriarchal in their approach to life.

Then there was the mother of all moves. We shifted base to Delhi when Amma got an offer to work in the Indian Council of Medical Research. This was something we had never contemplated at all. Not even in our wildest dreams. It turned out to be an absolute game-changer for me, because it was here that I met my husband, Puneet. And it was here that I was able to give wings to my dreams of making a name in the world of textiles. It took me a while to get over the culture shock, the sea of difference between the north and the south of India, and to get used to Delhi and its ways. The toughest part was making new friends. Being an introvert who takes time to venture out of her shell, and not holding a regular office job where you had colleagues to interact with, did not make it easy.

A tremendous amount of self-motivation, strong unconditional support from family, and unwavering faith in my creative abilities, helped me through those years and gradually I found my way. Meeting Puneet was the icing on the cake. He is a restless soul and an exceptionally brilliant artist – one of the finest in India. He can work wonders with art and craft – textiles, jewellery, paper, beads, ceramic, metal, wire, resin, leather, yarns, wood, mirrors, scrap. Give this man anything, and sheer magic is what follows! He inspires me to better my craft every day and he loves textiles with a passion. To the outside world, our marriage might seem to be a match made in heaven. But ask us about the hard work that goes behind the scenes to keep it going, and we can write reams of our story, as two strongly opinionated creative people sharing a workspace and going through our share of explosions, frustrations and fireworks!

I always knew I would marry someone who respects women. The first time I meet any man, I look for this. In India, men reveal themselves very quickly as being one or the other. If that respect isn't there, I keep my distance. I only connect with the men who have respect for women. Marrying Puneet was a coming together of the North and the South, embracing all the customs and festivals from both sides. Living in a joint family was something I had never pictured myself in. It took some time to warm up to the idea of being the first daughter-in-law of the family. And Puneet being so passionate about the grandness of every festival, from dressing up to getting the temple ready for puja – initially it was all so overwhelming for my simple, quiet ways of worship.

A couple of years along the way, our daughter Yashasvini came into this world. I had quite a smooth pregnancy which made me believe that it must be a girl. Both of us only wanted a girl and fortunately for us, we were blessed so. We would have been so lost if it was a boy, it was not even an acceptable thought. What would we do with all our love for textiles, crafts and art then? We were not into any sport and didn't know how we would keep up with a boy's energy in that direction? Of course, these were the stereotypical thoughts of gender bias, but we were quite anxious, hoping for a girl all through. Now, sixteen years bringing up Yashasvini (another name for Goddess Lakshmi) has been a beautiful journey. She has travelled with us right from her infancy on our various trips to the villages of India where we work with the craftsmen and weavers. Musically inclined and naturally endowed with a great voice, her spiritual self comes alive through her music. Though I would like to believe that she might have imbibed at least a part of my religious beliefs, she has not shown any devotion towards a special Goddess or God so far. I do not insist on her accompanying me to temples on auspicious days. Many a time, I feel that she has taken after Puneet. His upbringing was very different. He is not religious, but he's very spiritual. He's not interested in worship and rituals, at least not for himself; from a cultural point of view, he's always fascinated with it, but as an observer, as an artist. In my house, growing up, we had all the different Goddesses and Gods around. For Puneet, worship is just lighting one lamp at home. You need to light the lamp every day – you don't have to have all the forms displayed for that. Yasho is also like that.

I am not very religious, but believing in God is a part of me. This is my spirituality as opposed to my religion. It's not about being Hindu – I would feel the same in a church, a gurudwara or a monastery. It's about the calmness around, the positive energies. **I have always been very calm and have complete faith that there is something divine and that there is a grander cause, and that whatever happens is fine,** even if something goes wrong. I have always felt that 'the one up there' has something planned for me. I have always been spiritual in this sense. **The one up there isn't male or female – it is Light up there.**

Sometimes I also refer to it as The Universe. **For me, being spiritual is being comfortable in my own skin, feeling calm, believing that everything will be okay.** Being at peace with myself. I like to be in nature and let it soak in and not think of the mundane life. It's not about God. Mostly for me, there is this one big milieu of religion and spirituality with blurred lines in between.

My work in the field of textiles takes me travelling all over India. Working with weavers and craftsmen sitting far, far away from the hustle and bustle of the city and its noise and the stressful urban world, touches my soul. It's like oxygen when I am choked by the toxicity of aggression that is Delhi. It rejuvenates me to be a part of these simple creative lives even for a brief period. This is also the time I come closest to the Divine Feminine. The womenfolk in the rural world are so devoted to their job at hand, be it helping their husbands in weaving, doing their household chores, taking care of their kids, looking after the elderly, or running errands.

The settings are different in every weavers' village but the essence remains the same. Sharing a few excerpts from some of my travel notes:

> A typical day in my weaver's household in Chhattisgarh begins like this. The school or college-going daughter pitches in by filling the bobbins before and after going to college. Her friends, all covered with scarves, with just their eyes showing (to prevent dust from hitting their faces while cycling), patiently wait for her to join them. After getting back home, she quickly finishes her notes and studies before it gets dark. The weaver's wife finishes her chores in the kitchen early, so that she is able to help with the spinning, disentangling the yarns and filling the bobbins with the requisite colours. A weaver simply cannot function without support from as many hands as possible from his family. When new designs are being tried out, her work doubles, as we always run out of colours and we do not want to waste much time. Morning turns into long, balmy afternoons and then it's suddenly dark. Just watching the designs come alive is so therapeutic that one loses track of time.

> An evening walk around Raghurajpur village in Odisha and you feel like you are walking through art. Every humble home has men, women, girls and boys painting, engraving and engaged in all kinds of handcraft activities. When I peered into one, the women seemed so delighted in each other's company, sharing conversations while painting the coconuts, with clothes hanging and strewn all around. The one nursing her baby in the background was the most jovial and kept smiling all through. She was the one who called out to me when I was hesitant about stepping into the scene. The sight of all the colours fills up my senses.

When I met the weavers of Shakuripara village, Mulberry, Assam, I was taken in by their quiet strength. Particularly Pranita, one of the group leaders who mobilises and continuously inspires and motivates the group. She was happy to present to us a song, written by her, set in a popular local tune, which broadly meant this –

We, from the village, are backward and need to go forward and link up with people who are educated, without forgetting our own culture, ethnicity and language. We should take pride in our weaving skills, weaving the clothes we wear, our identity.

When the women sang together, it made such a strong impact on me. Here was a woman from a village in the north east, appealing to her own sisters to not forget their heritage, while many of us in the cities have long forgotten their value. We too have to find every way possible to make everyone aware of our textile heritage and the beauty of handmade crafts. The crepes, the georgettes, the satins and the chiffons maybe beautiful and sensuous, but these mill-made fabrics do not have stories to tell – the real narratives are created by hands and hearts, not machines.

When I question myself as to where my life is going, my life's purpose, I get temporary answers, and then you go on for some time and then come back to the questions again. At the end of those questions, I always send this request to the Universe: *Please show me the way*. Something always happens. I do get my answers. And I continue my journey.

I know my purpose is to work with weavers and promoting our Indian culture and traditional weaving and textiles – but **the way forward I haven't always got figured out. I go through this all the time. It's not going round in a circle – each time it's moving on, and it gives me faith that there is a purpose.** You don't have to plan. Whatever happens, happens for the best.

I meditate off and on, but my morning walk is my real meditation. This is my communing with Mother Nature and the Universe and where I get my insights, my inspiration, my happiness, and I feel alive. Displaying my creations before any exhibition is also a kind of therapy and meditation for me. I go into a state of deep contemplation about the individual textile journey of each creation of mine, from where it was woven, to the surface detailing, finishing, and finally all set to go into another home, literally spinning a different yarn, a new tale yet to begin – much like all our lives.

I consider myself fortunate to have been allowed to grow and blossom in a conducive atmosphere at home. This is not the reality through much of India though. I fail to understand how on the one hand there is this divine equality and on the other hand there are such extreme gender issues here. Even among people

I know from Kerala, there are still so many women who have to seek the permission of the men before going ahead with whatever they wish to do – they don't have a say in their lives. It's ironic. Because of the high levels of literacy and other cases of equal opportunities in Kerala, people tend to assume that there are no issues. This prejudice exists all over India, but it's much more prevalent in the villages where not much has changed in all these years of so-called development. It's baffling to see that men can worship the Goddesses but at the same time not respect their women at home. When they come to the cities, they see the difference in the sense of equality, where women work shoulder to shoulder with men, sometimes even as superiors.

Every morning our house help walks in and shares new episodes from her previous evening at her own home – some happy, some sad, some bitter, and some angry tales that go with bringing up four daughters aged eight to twenty-two, almost single-handedly since her husband is partially paralysed. After years of practice as a Hindu priest, one day he converted to Christianity. She and a couple of her daughters, however, refused to convert and still follow the various Hindu rituals of fasting during festivals, puja, and so on, while the youngest accompanies her father to Church and sings in the choir. She has both *kirtans* and *jagrans* – all night worship – for Hindu deities, and Bible reading sessions at home. She exclaims that her life has not changed at all – the husband who used to spend the day reading the Bhagavad Gita, now reads the Bible – while she does all the hard work to put food on the table. All laced with humour and a toothy smile, I am sometimes blown away by her spunk and inner strength. In many ways, it reflects the intensity of the Divine Feminine all around me.

I see the Divine Feminine in different forms every day. I see it in the hearts of the women in my family, in the eyes of my dear friends, in the hands of the artisans I work with, facing the innumerable challenges thrown at them with unshakeable faith and immense belief in their own self. And I sense it in me. Every single day.

C. Ara Campbell

Rosaries & Rebels: Reclaiming the Goddess

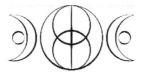

When I was growing up, you went to church. Not because you wanted to, but because it would appease overzealous grandparents eternally hounding your parents to save your young soul. I felt the influence of other people's faith through all aspects of my young life.

You said Grace at Grandma's table before you ate. You listened to the choir when you sat on the pews with Baba, even if you didn't understand the language. You never questioned the tales told by the preacher or the words in the holy book.

With roots in both Ukrainian Catholic and Baptist faiths, I learned early on that there's more than one path for people to believe in. Which can be both a blessing and a curse.

When I listened to Bible stories in Sunday school, I was confused. I kept wondering, where were the women in these tales? I was surrounded by women in my own world; where were they in these pages? I'd always had a strong sense of justice, equality and curiosity, and it seemed strange that this book of wisdom comprised only men's opinions.

There was a God and a Son, and a Holy Ghost who I was also told was male. There were disciples and martyrs. There were Johns, Pauls and Peters. Where were the female names? Didn't they have some wise words to contribute to this book? I had three sisters, multiple aunts, female cousins, grandmothers and a mother. If I had that much feminine influence in my life, surely this wise God could find a thought or two from some women?

Sure, Mother Mary was painted on the walls of the chapel – virginal perfection in her shroud of celestial blue. Eve was the bringer of original sin for her actions in the Garden of Eden. And of course Lilith, the fallen one, was cast out for her disobedience to her husband. Mother, sinner and whore – the faces of the feminine, written by the patriarchy that I didn't understand then. Women were generally missing and those few that were there had no voice. I felt this deeply. And I had a feeling it affected us all.

Later I realised that these tales of submission were a training manual for our mothers and grandmothers, the absence of strong women creating a void within them. I knew there had to be something else: a kinder, more understanding path, that wasn't rooted in sadness or oppression.

My heart was soft but strong, filled with compassion towards other living creatures, especially animals. I brought strays home with me, wanting them to be safe and loved, not wanting anyone to be alone. I collected flowers and rocks for my mother, feeling an unspoken magic in them I wanted to gift to her. I felt a power coming from the Earth, a wild wisdom that I didn't understand.

My mother's nickname for me was *Spitfire*. In kindergarten, I was playing on a giant snow hill with my little friends when the older kids began tormenting them and pushing them off the hill. With my inflated sense of justice, I found this intolerable, and little Wonder Woman that I was, I retaliated. I was small, but that didn't stop me kicking the 6th graders off the hill.

I earned a trip to the principal's office and was admonished for my misbehavior. In my eyes I hadn't done anything wrong. If not me, then who would stand up to those bullies?

My antics continued into high school. My dedication to standing up for what I believed in was deeply rooted; I didn't stand down for anything. I stood up to the principal quite often, for which I earned more than one suspension. I expected a woman in her position to empower other women, but instead I saw the familiar conditioning silencing us, as it had for generations. I often clashed with the authorities when I made my way into academia.

As a teenager, I was connected to the Earth. I spent long hours in the company of the forest, marveling at the medicine of the natural world surrounding me. Growing up alongside a lake surrounded by the wild wood, I found solace and healing in the Earth and her mysteries. My imagination flourished, as did my love of all things wild.

For a few years in elementary school, my aunt was my teacher. From her great wisdom, and love of reading, I developed a thirst for the written word and first discovered the Goddess myths. She taught us the tales of the Greeks, Romans and Celts, and I learned the stories of Athena, Diana and Brigid. I was elated to discover them, and to see the face of the feminine and hear her voice. I was empowered by her, finding a new avenue of belief. I began to see that the more paths to spirit that existed, the less likely it was that there was only one road to follow.

Still they were tainted by the patriarchy. There was something wrong with many of the myths. There were dire punishments for spurning the advances of Zeus. It was unthinkable to say *no* to a God, after all. Vengeance at the hands of jealous husbands like Hephaestus to Aphrodite, the man she was given to by Zeus and forced to marry. Retribution was handed out to women but not to men.

I was confused by the imbalance. I didn't understand the lopsided justice that was doled out to women. After searching for the Goddesses for so many years, I felt betrayed. Why did men make the rules and get away with everything? Why were women held to a different standard and more harshly punished? What the hell was this? Where were the Goddesses I was seeking? The *fierce* feminine? The *wild* women? Those who were not struck down for standing up and speaking out? Where was equality?!

Where were the faces that looked like mine – outspoken, loud, and standing up for what they believed? I was angry that there was a different line in the sand for women. The alternative was silence. The lesson was that you lived your truth at your own risk.

It was hard to take. I was an outspoken and fiery soul, so what did this mean for my dreams? Should I guard my desires for fear of reprisal? I began writing during this time, hoping I'd find something important to share with the world one day. Should I fear my voice and my words? If I brought them into the world, would I too be misunderstood and punished?

How often had we done this, we wild women with our roots deep in the earth? **How many times had we held our breath and our voices and kept silent.** Because what if the world didn't want to hear us? What if we made waves and no one loved us as a result? Our veins were woven with the fear of disobedience and we stayed small to survive. We were compact and undetectable. We stayed under the radar.

As we grow up, we are sold a picket fence existence. We are taught to find love, a partner, a little house, and to settle down; have kids, save for retirement, and live for a tomorrow that seldom comes the way we envisioned it. In my twenties, I bought into society's plan, and my dedication to my voice and my passion, to truth and justice, faded. I moved away from my connection with the natural world and from the Goddess. My writing ceased. I'd been taught that my passions didn't equate to a good living. I doubted my own gifts and never let my dreams be my focus, and so I moved along a safer path.

I aimed for what I was taught would make me happy and sustain me. I went to college for something I thought would open doors for me and focused on my business diploma. I graduated, got my name on my office door, had the right sort of social life, a partner and a home. I put my energy into a life that on the surface looked perfect. I held my tongue too many times to count, fearing the consequences of my voice.

I began to write again – but in secret – journalling the growing disillusions of my life. I was convinced more than ever that no one felt the way I did: alone and swallowed alive by a joyless system. I felt lost and I knew there was something missing. I realised I no longer stood up in outrage at the injustices of the world. I didn't have faith in my words.

When we disconnect from our truth, it's easy to become entangled in others' truth. I looked back at the businesses that I had been a part of over the years and realised I had been living someone else's dream instead of my own. I'd given all my energy to others' dreams while mine starved. I had left them behind in order to follow this sensible path.

I'd severed my connection with the Earth and her magic. My roots in the Goddess hadn't been nourished and I'd lost my voice. I hadn't honored my heart and I had no idea what my truth was.

In exchange for a life I'd been told would sustain me, I had starved myself. My path had become what was expected, not what I desired.

I left the work that starved my soul, leaving behind people that I had come to call friends. A desire was growing in me for great change, to strike out in the direction of my dreams of being a writer, though I didn't know how to find the path forward. I gave up the comfort of a steady paycheck, friendships, and a familiar routine, for the unknown. I wasn't sure what was coming and I felt very alone. But my truth could no longer be ignored and I felt it bubbling up, a foreign language I needed to decipher.

There is a dark night of the soul that calls to many of us in this life, fueled by disconnection from our truth. I was pulled into an abyss of uncertainty, questioning everything. Here at the crossroads of nothing and everything, I surrendered the chains I had been taught would be my salvation. I let go of the life that I had always been told to want.

When I was thirty-three, I was called to a three week immersion into the Goddess, with Chameli Ardagh. The Goddess Inanna[28] revealed herself to me, becoming my rebirth back into the Divine Feminine. Inanna was a Queen, a Goddess, who felt something missing in her life and had moved into the unknown to find it. She sat with me in the darkness, and I was inspired by her path of peeling away earthly trappings and moving into the underworld. There she became whole, merging with her shadow self and embracing all that she was.

Like Inanna reborn on her journey into the underworld, I rose up, tattered, but connected to my truth. Naked and raw as Inanna had been, I faced my fears and cut away the relationships and connections that no longer served my highest good. I began to trust in the voice within me, and the words that yearned to be born. I stepped towards my dream and the desire to share my voice with the world.

---

[28] Ancient Mesopotamian goddess of love, beauty, sex, desire, fertility, war, justice, and political power; associated with the planet Venus.

The Goddess doesn't desert you when you leave her behind. She waits patiently in the darkness, like a Mother, ever vigilant. When the time came for me to peel off the dusty layer that had built up over my soul, there she was, holding my medicine in her fingers as a reminder to all that I was.

My journey back to the arms of the Goddess had taken years, but once I stepped away from what no longer served me, the path opened wide. **That's the thing about honoring your truth – it creates doors where there used to be walls.** With each breath I consciously chose reverence instead of ignoring it. I honored my intuition. I focused devotion back on the Earth and her medicine. I created a life out of doing the things that called to me. I would no longer let myself be defined by someone else's rulebook.

I moved deeper into connection with the Earth and her cycles, feeling at home in my rediscovery of the Goddess path. As a Priestess of the Earth, my temple of worship was rooted within Gaia.[29] The wisdom of the stones spoke to me, offering ancient guidance when I worked with them. Within the wild world, the animals and birds showed me their medicine and their connection to the spirit of the Earth. Her wild wood was my temple, and the whisper through her trees my prayer. I celebrated the cycles of the seasons, tapping into the magic of the changing landscape surrounding me. I worked with the moon, with astrology, and with the messages of the eclipse cycles. Inspired by the depths of my journey with Inanna, I gravitated to the Goddess stories of Lilith,[30] Aradia,[31] Hecate,[32] and Cassandra,[33] the goddesses who walked in darkness, who knew what it meant to sit with their shadows and to dive deeper.

My path was understood by very few. I was considered a heathen, a witch. I was looked down on by much of my family. My mother was supportive though, as she too was rooted deep within the soul of nature. She grew herbs, and looked to the guidance of the moon for her planting, moving with the seasons and cycles. She healed with herblore and knew the medicine written within the leaves of the plants. She could grow things like no one else I knew, as if she spoke their language, comprehending their every need. She also read the tales of the Goddess, rediscovering the path to the feminine that had been tainted for her by a patriarchal and oppressive Catholic upbringing. Others were not so tolerant. I was admonished and reminded that non-believers were sinners that would be punished. I was reprimanded by my grandmother for gifting my sister a protective stone talisman, as it was a totem of evil. In my innocence, I didn't understand. I

---

[29] In Greek mythology, Gaia is the personification of the Earth. She is the ancestral mother of all life, the primal Mother Earth goddess.

[30] Represented in Jewish mythology as well as having several earlier origins, eg. Mesopotamian, she is often cast as a demon and as sexually wanton.

[31] A pagan figure of French and Italian origins.

[32] A Greek goddess associated with witchcraft, knowledge of herbs, ghosts, and sorcery.

[33] Given the gift of prophecy, but then cursed by Apollo for refusing to have sex with him, so that thereafter her prophecies would not be believed.

wanted to protect her. How could that be evil?

There came a point in my existence when I realized that the thing that always got me into trouble was my greatest gift; my words and my passion. I started to speak; I put my words out there. After my journey with Inanna into the darkness, I created *The Goddess Circle* in 2014 and I urged other women to embrace their truth and their medicine. I encouraged expression and free speech. I dedicated myself to serving the rising voice of women. I connected with women around the planet, learning so much from their stories and their trials. I devoured the teachings of wise women, from Clarissa Pinkola Estes and Maureen Murdock to Layne Redmond and Zsuzsanna Budapest; their words an inspiration. I was going to be a channel to aid the feminine however I could; to hell with the consequences. The fierce feminine voice had been silent for too long. I vowed to never be a grave for my voice.

By leaving behind the safe path, I embarked into the unknown, dedicating myself fully to my gifts. *The Goddess Circle* became the channel where I brought my offerings to the world. My rediscovered words became podcasts, blogs and online courses. My connection to the unseen energy of the Earth became astrology publications and tarot readings. I was able to reach women around the world. I combined my love of rocks and crystals into an *Etsy* shop, expanding the knowledge of the stones. What I created on a leap of faith became something that sustained me, financially and soulfully. My goal is to one day publish my words into books and reach even more women.

However, the path to revolution is not always paved with roses. To put oneself out into the open is to invite the retribution of those who are triggered by your words. I've been harassed and threatened, and propositioned in horrible, vulgar ways that no one should ever have to hear. This has been done in an attempt to silence me, as it has been done to women for thousands of years. But I will not swallow my voice. Being faced with this has only shown me the wounds that still need to be healed in the world. I had to try in my own way to bring the voice of the feminine into being. For every push against me, I would rise up, armed with my words, connected to my truth. Their hate did not silence me, but fueled my dedication to my path, inspiring me to speak out and reach women challenged in the same ways. In our continued celebration of our gifts, by bringing our voice into the world, we inspire others to do the same.

Maybe the majority of my family would never understand my path or my plight to bring respect back to the feminine face of faith, but that would never stop me.

With age comes greater wisdom, or at the very least, acceptance. As I grew into my path, I began to see the women in my world in a new light. I made my peace with their beliefs and with the paths they walked because that was all they knew. I forgave their rosaries for their treachery and accepted their prayers when offered. They were, after all, coming from the hearts of the women themselves, and not from the faith which I held in disdain.

I understood why it didn't matter if we believed the same thing. It wasn't my truth they needed to agree with. They were already rooted in their own sacred devotion. Their religions had created a legacy of hurt that was passed down to their daughters, my mother no stranger to the damage inflicted by a pious parent. My Baba was not an easy woman to deal with, and I wondered if the oppressive feminine role she was taught to play had any part in it. But now it fell to us to heal the wounds of our ancestors.

When my Baba passed into spirit, all I wanted as a memory of her was one of her rosaries. Not as a symbol of the religion that I never belonged to, but as an emblem of the devotion and belief that she held. As a touchstone for the love, faith and sisterhood that existed within something that I had always found so bleak and oppressive.

As I sat in the small country church for her funeral, staring at the brightly painted saints adorning the walls, I realized I had been wrong. **The Goddesses were never meant to be found in the pages of the holy books and stories written by the hands of man.** They had been there all along, caring for the sacred altar of the feminine. They had been guiding my life from the very beginning. They had crossed perilous oceans for me to be here on this soil. They had paved their own way even when their belief system would hold them down and keep them silent. The fierce face of the Divine Feminine was found all around me and within me.

She was me, fierce and passionate, Goddess of justice, brandishing my flaming sword of truth, refusing to back down from subjugation and silence, determined to heal the wounds that history had imprinted on the spirit of the feminine.

She was my mother, guardian of the Earth, growing herbs and moving with the cycles of the moon, connected to Gaia and paying homage to the ancient ways with her worship of the seasons and animals.

She was the caregiver of those holy church walls, my Baba, a sacred priestess, she and her fellow church sisters clearing the sacred temple, caring for its aging needs. Replacing candles and sweeping the hearth. There was no pay, no glory, and their hands were withered by the sands of time as they carried out these hallowed tasks. Still they came, these sisters of the sacred, entrusted with this holy devotion.

There they were before me; maiden, mother, crone. The triple aspect of the Goddess running through my blood. Even in death it could not be erased.

Women will always find a way to gather and grow, whether it be by sacred fire deep within the forest, or on hewn roughwood pews in a Catholic church nestled on the mountainside.

The flame of the feminine can never be extinguished; it only burns brighter with time. We thrive in darkness as well as light, bursting forth from the Earth like a seed stretching towards the heavens.

The Goddesses are among us, as they always have been and always will be. We are here, as is the ancient lineage that we hold within our blood. We don't need them to write our stories, as we will write them ourselves with our own hands.

Judi Hobbes

Everyday Goddesses

Divine Feminine wasn't a term I'd used until recently. In my adult life I developed a meaningful awareness of the Spiritual. I'd studied Goddesses: Greek, Roman and Hindu. I had a concept of the Divine, of Spirit, but it wasn't gendered.

It's been a challenge and a journey to reflect on and write about the Divine Feminine as a part of my development as a woman through the 'everyday' goddesses who have influenced me and helped me to realise my true self and my path in life. For me now, the Divine Feminine is embodied by women (and men) whose light shines brightly, who radiate love and light, and who offer new ways of seeing and being.

Most spiritual traditions commit to the path of love. To me, the Divine Feminine is an expression of that love. It can be gentle, nurturing and receptive, but also challenging and fiercely protective.

Recently I had an encounter with one such woman. My friend, Lore, runs a small organic bakery in the town of Orgiva, near Granada in Spain. We have a house outside the town, and I went into town for some shopping. I stopped by the bakery to say hello, and we moved immediately into deep conversation about how to stay centred and grounded in the midst of the heightened challenges we are facing at this time. Since the internet and social media, we both find it hard to stay focussed in our here and now life. In Orgiva we are fighting the placement of eighty metre high electricity pylons that would ruin this peaceful, clear and beautiful valley, so the challenges of our world are literally in our own back gardens.

Lore told me of her struggle to clear her mind, and her inner critic, and of fearful agitated feelings. We talked of when to surrender and when to act, and located the place for answers in our hearts and souls, looking for the divine guidance within us. Lore recently lost her beautiful dog, Estrella, to old age. Our dogs are so often our comforters and our teachers: they radiate the loving energy we need to stay connected within ourselves. So she was struggling more than usual with intense feelings and the intensity of the world today.

I felt my own light grow as we spoke of what is fundamental to withstand the storms of this world: our trust that if we can stay present and open and connect with what comes from within us and beyond the everyday world – spirit – we'll know what to do.

And then there's love – in this case the love of friends – which helps us connect, trust each other and ourselves, and trust that it will open us to any support and love from the beyond, however each of us experiences that.

I wasn't always a spiritual pantheist as I am today. I was brought up Jewish in a small New Jersey town. As a child, I liked being part of a community and the idea that our purpose was to create a better world on earth rather than hope for a perfect world when we died.

But my rational mind was always watching, and apart from moments of oneness being in a congregation praying together, I didn't *get* spirituality. I couldn't relate to this man-centred religion. A woman's place then was as homemaker and mother, and the cliché that food was love was only a cliché because it was true. I never learned to cook 'just enough' for any number of people – my mother taught me that only 'too much' is enough.

Jewish women could be formidable – my paternal grandmother a case in point. But as a kid it was all about stuffing in more of her food than you could possibly eat so as not to offend her. What I didn't learn until later was that she'd travelled from a *shtetl*[34] in Belarus to New York at sixteen, in charge of her fourteen-year-old sister. Her father had preceded her, and as he could afford to, was sending for family members, children first.

The two girls spoke only Yiddish and a local Russian dialect, and travelled overland to Liverpool. During this long journey they only knew one family in Germany, otherwise they were on their own.

I recently Google-mapped her journey, to get some visual perspective on where and how far she travelled before getting the boat to New York, landing at Ellis Island, her first glimpse of *Liberty*.

My great-grandfather eventually brought all of the family over, at a time when pogroms destroyed many Jews.

My grandmother grew up and married, and she and my grandfather, who died when my father was twelve, joined the socialist party and began the left-wing dynasty that is my American family.

---

[34] Yiddish for 'town'.

I didn't know any of this until after my grandmother died, so my memory of her was of a scary, formidable woman. No wonder! She's one of my goddesses now, and I only wish I had known her story when she was alive and I could have celebrated her amazing life with her. Jewish women could be powerful, robust, and have agency,[35] but I only saw that in a domestic context growing up.

The Jewish tribe, as I've come to see it, was invested in education for both boys and girls, so I was sent to university and got a good degree. But my early years had nonetheless implanted the idea of homemaker and mother as my fate, and I was supposed to leave my partly-honed mind outside the front door.

When I was at university, I went to a class entitled *Philosophy and Literature* – I was an English Lit major at the time. Thelma Levine, Professor of Philosophy, came sweeping down the aisle of the full lecture theatre, long black hair and red-lined black cape flowing – and proceeded to blow my mind. (I was a 60s baby boomer after all.) Here was a Jewish woman who showed her brilliance out loud, and by the end of the course I'd switched to a joint major in philosophy and psychology. I became passionate about how people used their minds and came to think what they thought. I wasn't yet conscious of how this Jewish goddess challenged the script I was supposed to follow.

I inevitably married, had two kids, and moved to England with my English husband, into a house that had been in his family for generations. When we left Washington DC, where we'd both been at university, we left family and friends, with our three-month-old daughter in tow, to begin what I hoped would be our big adventure.

I discovered that a common-*ish* language didn't guarantee a smooth landing into a recognisable way of life. We knew virtually no one in our new village. Using my practical mind and my American go-getter spirit, I joined many groups until I made new friendships. There was much that was different in the lives of the women I met, but also much that was the same, as my main friendship group were housewives and mothers. I focused on what we had in common, and determined not to become too British, as I saw it: buttoned up, not touching, and needing a long time, if ever, to share deep thoughts, feelings and experiences.

I began training as a psychotherapist – my interest in others' minds and feelings finding an outlet. It was when I wanted to go out to work part-time that I discovered my husband embodied my mother and my Jewish culture. He was obstructive in any way he could be.

While reading *The Women's Room* by Marilyn French, I came across an exchange that opened my mind to new possibility (as did most of that book). The protagonist, Mira, was in a similar predicament to mine, as she pursued a

---

[35] To make free choices and act independently.

university education and met a new group of women. As Mira was bemoaning her domestic situation to one of her new feminist friends and blaming herself for upsetting her husband with her newfound desire for a life outside the home, her friend said something like: *You don't have to change yourself; you can change your address.*

At the time, this was a revolutionary thought for me – a lightbulb moment – and I started to slowly make my way back out into the world of work, defending against the ongoing pushback from my husband. I tried for years to find the right way to communicate with him and make him understand, thinking if I could say it right, he'd get it. He went into counselling for a short time, but when he started doing scary things and eventually became violent, I couldn't allow that, and also feared for my children's safety. He never hurt them, but I couldn't take that chance. It was my cue to *change my address*, which I eventually did when I thought I could manage looking after a two-year-old and a six-year-old. I expected hard times ahead – the consequences of my choice – and manifested the practical and strong me, burying my vulnerable self. This was a habit I had learned in my family. Some years later, as often happens, I was hit by a freight train of feelings about breaking up my family and losing something I really wanted – a family that included a father, a mother and two kids living together and making that life work.

In the early 80s I met a powerhouse of energy, Linda, who invited me to help her organise a festival in Manchester. Its purpose was to showcase local talent in every way. There were taster workshops from therapists (I was practicing by then), reflexologists, massage therapists, musicians, jugglers, and every alternative approach to health and well-being embodied by a Manchester practitioner. The festival grew out of Linda's alternative magazine, which included articles and listings of local practitioners. She'd seen a need for this and just went ahead and did it. She was also Jewish and also from the greater New York area, and we hit it off right away. Linda's main profession at that time was as a teacher of *T'ai Chi*, and so I joined her Monday afternoon women's class. Although *T'ai Chi* is a martial art, being part of a women's class was definitely a soft experience, feminine rather than masculine.

I had experiences in the class, doing the slow, flowing movements, that awakened me to something new, something beyond the everyday. I felt myself being drawn upward in a way I couldn't explain, and experienced calm, soothing energies. I felt both opened and more grounded. This is when I first experienced something I could name as spirituality.

I didn't recognise it as spiritual to begin with. What I felt was an opening up energetically, which I noticed became stronger. It manifested as a calm and beautiful feeling as well as a longing for something more. That 'more' I started to see as beyond the everyday, beyond my everyday experience. It wasn't like falling in love, it wasn't like a close and satisfying exchange with a friend, it wasn't quite like being in nature and seeing the beauty there, but those were the closest similarities I could find to naming it. These days I would consider all those experiences as spiritual.

My physical experience was of being drawn upward and outward. I felt a new energy rising in me. It's hard to describe because it was subtly different. The more I did *T'ai Chi* and relaxed into the flowing movements of the practice, the more I felt my centre sink down and a connection with something above or beyond me drawing me upward. The feeling of longing developed over time too. Longing for something more, that wasn't stuff or people or everyday experiences. This is what led me to understand the experience as spiritual.

My view of the spiritual before this time was cognitive rather than experiential. When I went to synagogue as a child there was talk of God. I said prayers and sang. I enjoyed the social get-togethers with kids and teens my own age. My first love was a Jewish boy who went to our synagogue, but I don't equate any of that with spirituality. Especially the kissing!

I didn't believe or disbelieve. My parents weren't especially religious, but they wanted us to follow Judaism so they took us to synagogue when we were kids, celebrated the Jewish holidays, which I enjoyed, and insisted that we be *Bar* and *Bat Mitzvah'd*. It was something I had to do that I didn't particularly want to do, and it didn't have an effect of uncovering any spiritual aspect to myself. I don't remember having talks with the rabbi or my parents at that time about a spiritual meaning of my *Bat Mitzvah*, though the rabbi may have tried.

But doing *T'ai Chi* was an experience of something new and satisfying, and I wanted to experience more. Soon after this I began practising meditation, and in retrospect I see that I was searching without really knowing it.

Linda became one of my closest friends soon after the festival, and we shared the intimacies of our lives. She died eight years ago and I still miss her. She was a strong leader who people were happy to follow; she cried at the drop of a hat, and wasn't afraid to show her vulnerability – in conversation and in her poetry. She was also much better at moving on from things that she felt were finished for her than I was, so that she could get on with the next important thing she wanted to do. She taught me much, including the appeal of the combination of vulnerability and strength.

I started practicing as a psychotherapist in 1978, and I understood, theoretically, how vulnerability and strength made a powerful pairing, but I hadn't yet found a way to live both. Strength – that's how everyone saw me; vulnerability – not so much.

I got a part-time job on a deprived housing estate in North Manchester and worked with first and second-time young mothers who wanted to understand themselves and their relationships with partners and children, expand their options and find some agency in the midst of poverty and new parenthood. I also set up a part-time private practice in south Manchester and worked with women and men who were interested in solving personal and relationship problems, and to know and realise themselves.

I was drawn to this work after being part of a research project at the Department of Psychiatry at Manchester University, my first job in the United Kingdom. This was in 1975-1976. I worked alongside a psychiatrist, and together we looked at GPs' attitudes to their patients' emotional problems, not foreground for doctors at that time. While my colleague sat in and observed doctors' responsiveness, my job was to use a questionnaire to interview patients in the waiting room. I started with general questions about how they were feeling that day, and ended with questions about thoughts or attempts at suicide. I found my position as objective researcher at times very challenging when people would share with me difficult feelings and I could do nothing but ask the next question. I was empathetic, but my role was to collect information. We went to ninety GP practices in and around Manchester, and some way into this job I decided that I wanted to offer counselling for people who didn't have access to counselling through their GP as they do now. At the time I was working on this project, all that was on offer was hospitalisation if needed. Everyday emotional and relationship problems were, on the whole, ignored by the GPs we studied. I began training as a psychotherapist while I was completing the project. As part of my training, I went into therapy myself, working on shedding the skins that no longer fit me and finding the person underneath, finding some agency of my own and learning more about who I am and how I wanted to live.

Because of childhood experiences with a loving but emotionally unpredictable mother, and a physically abusive and bullying older brother, I had learned to highly attune to others to try to predict their moods, and to adapt to what was expected of me. I had stayed out of their way as best I could and learned to look after myself. This is when I decided I had to be strong and not show vulnerability. My father was loving and generous, but also passive, and so wasn't much help. In therapy I began to understand how these experiences resulted in me being a *lone ranger* – someone who could trust only herself and who didn't look to others for help. Somehow, I retained a sense of self, though I mostly kept it hidden. In therapy I was able to express feelings about all of this and to accept support. I stopped hiding my feelings with people I could trust, and I explored ways of doing things and being in the world that came more from what I wanted than from what others wanted me to want. I think part of what drew me to becoming a therapist was taking the role of helping others, where they revealed their inner worlds to me, but I didn't have to reciprocate. I didn't realise this when I was training but in therapy came to understand it. This is a life's work, and I was in a wonderful development group with colleagues and got individual help if I needed it.

In the forty-five years I've worked as a psychotherapist, I've found my work to be my vocation, my purpose. Though I'm mostly retired now, I still supervise therapists two half days a month and run personal development weeks several times a year.

Four years into this exploration, I met Robin, also a psychotherapist, who was more of a playmate and soulmate than the controlling 'parent' my ex-husband had been, and we've been married for thirty-six years. While no relationship is perfect, we've learned a lot from each other, and encourage each other to be and do what we want.

Not long after we met, and not long after my *T'ai Chi* practice opened up the desire for something more, I received information about a workshop in London entitled *Psychotherapy and Spirituality,* run by a well-known psychotherapist and trainer, and his wife who was a counsellor. They were from Australia, and Robin and I were both intrigued to see what they were offering.

Elizabeth was *yin* to Ken's *yang*, both open-hearted, knowledgeable and available, and they radiated a loving and soothing energy that attracted me. They had devised a way to understand and teach Eastern philosophy and meditation techniques from a Western perspective. Being psychologically minded, they provided a clear link to my understanding of mind, body, and now spirit. I came across a quote from Lau Tzu that I think summed up their approach at that time.

> *He who knows others is wise.*
> *He who knows himself is enlightened.*

I found that being with Ken and Elizabeth and experimenting with the meditations they offered opened me up emotionally, and I shed many tears and felt much anger. I also felt joy and bliss. We had the opportunity that weekend to be initiated into a mantra. I continue to meditate with it to this day.

Over many years we went to workshops when Ken and Elizabeth were in the United Kingdom, and also to Australia several times. Meditating connected me to an awareness and experience of the divine beyond me, in others, and within me; to feelings of love, security and joy, as well as to feelings of pain, sadness, fear and anger. I was opening to an energetic connection to life in a new way, to people who radiated light and love; and to nature, which gave me a sense of peace and harmony.

I was evolving a focus on love in all aspects of my life. My sense of the spiritual was energetic – feelings of bliss, expressions of emotion, shaking, stillness, seeing colours, feeling love for specific people, for everyone and for nature. I valued all of these experiences (though some were painful) and found them releasing and steadying. I continued to do personal therapy when I was stimulated by life experiences and encounters with people who triggered old and painful memories. My spiritual practice enhanced my therapy and vice versa. I learned to show vulnerability as well as strength, though my default position is still strength first, vulnerability maybe later.

I started to distinguish between *yin* and *yang* within myself and within relationships, noticing and accepting the light and the dark, masculine and feminine energies, and other opposing forces and feelings. My love of nature, and the divine within the natural world, I saw as feminine. The goddesses I encountered in my life represent the Divine Feminine to me as well.

My growing experience of spirit led me to think of ways I could include this personal and spiritual growth in my work as a therapist. I began asking clients if they'd like to experiment with guided meditations, and to envisage their higher self and mine present and available in the room with us and supporting the therapeutic work we were doing. Some wanted to, and I was thoughtful about who to ask.

Much of my work was focussed on love – opening the heart, accepting and loving yourself. I felt love sometimes towards my clients, which I know they could sense. I still think therapy is all about loving and accepting yourself to allow you to be who you truly are rather than changing yourself. I can't now separate a feeling of love as a human being with the spiritual love that is at the core of us all: divine love within us and beyond us. I know that people who are spiky, resistant, and 'difficult' are at their core lovable and loving beings. The focus of my work is relational and developmental: our difficulties evolve from our relationships as children and how our developmental needs were responded to. **If we can see and understand where our needs weren't met or how trauma and the cruelty of adults and siblings impacted on us, we can seek and have new experiences of relationship as adults that can be healing.** This is part of my role as a therapist: to offer a safe space for being with whatever arises in your experience, and to help people develop new ways towards filling developmental gaps as adults as best we can. We can't change the past or erase all wounds but I think we can heal old wounds effectively in positive experiences of relationship.

As a child and teenager at services in the synagogue, God was presented as a man whose name you could not speak. He resided in the Heavens. Now, if I think of anything as God, I think of the Divine in nature, and being in nature is one of my greatest pleasures and feeds my soul. The Divine in nature I see as Feminine. I see the Divine in people as Feminine and Masculine and believe we embody both. To me the Divine Feminine in people is a loving and receptive energy, it's an openness, a warm presence. It's also strong, protective, sensual and sexual. So what then is the Divine Masculine? It's so easy to stereotype this energy as the shadow side: arrogant, domineering, bloodthirsty, destructive. But the Divine Masculine is confidence, being analytical, setting strong boundaries, fathering. If this has any truth in it, I see this energy in men and women, and non-binary people, as I see the Divine Feminine in us all. I see it in myself. I'd say the combined Divine Feminine and Masculine are qualities of God within us. Sometimes I have the experience of looking deeply into someone's eyes and seeing God there.

I have been blessed to meet many women and some men who embody the Divine Feminine; my closest friend, Marcia, whose personal and spiritual journey I've shared as she has shared mine; and Evangelia, a Greek goddess I shared my waking and sleeping dreams with during the three months I spent on a Greek island coming back to the centre of my life the year I turned fifty. Both fully realise the Divine Feminine in their hearts, souls, lives and relationships. I've become more clearly aware that an energetic connection with others of love and light, being in nature and in sacred places, enlightens me and feeds my spirit. I'm grateful for all who've nudged me along this path and for those I've yet to meet.

I'm finding my purpose now in both personal and community spheres: producing art works and joining the climate support movement. I hope to bring the experiences of my life and my work to supporting life on this planet. I was on the streets protesting and worked for political change in my late teens and twenties, and I'll be doing that again in this third age of my life.

Marian Hamel-Smith

The Dragonfly

My Journey in the Divine Feminine has always been and will always be. I feel that this is the backbone of my life. Looking back and pondering over my life, it has always been there.

I was born and brought up in Trinidad & Tobago, in the West Indies, of French, Irish and Trinidadian lineage. I was the fifth child, and the first girl. We lived in the Cascade Valley, just north of Port-of-Spain, the capital. As was the custom in Catholic families at the time, often one of the girls (or maybe some of them when there were many) was consecrated to Mary, the Mother of Jesus. I didn't know that then but it is very obvious now, because I was always dressed in blue. Not dark blue, but Mary's blue: light blue, sky blue on a cloudless day, or lagoon blue. My younger sister was always dressed in pink. My mother made our clothes so it was a deliberate choice on her part.

Another thing that made it obvious was my name. I was named Marian. The Irish priest who baptized me remarked to my mother that it was not a noun but an adjective! I stayed an adjective. This point was obviously important because the story was passed down to me. I cannot tell you what time of day I was born but I know that I am an adjective.

So as an adjective, my life path was defined.

If anyone had told me how my story would unfold, I may have hidden in a cave, afraid to go on the adventure, but luckily, I didn't. It was in this way that I discovered every emotion that exists.

I was born with a very heightened awareness of God, and of good and evil. This was nurtured by my religious practices and as a very young child I went with my mother to early morning mass, before school, at a cloistered Dominican convent about three minutes' drive from our house in Cascade. There I saw many women who had devoted their lives to God and seemed fulfilled with this choice. I pondered on this lifestyle.

Movies, and going to the movie theatre, was and still is one of my delights. Musicals were definitely my thing. I loved singing, to the point that I irritated everyone at home especially my elder brothers. Julie Andrews was my heroine before I was ten years old. I can't say how many times I saw *The Sound of Music*. A woman who sang, and a religious, spiritual, romantic choice. I could see myself in her. She was a Maria; I was a Marian.

By the time I was twelve, I had the nickname of *Mother Marian*. I sang in an all-girls group called the Goretti Group; and at our church's Saturday evening mass. The Church was changing. Saturday evening youth mass with guitars and modern music! This was new for the Church, scandalous for some, but it allowed people to actually have a lie-in or a longer day at the beach or with family gatherings. The holy day of observation was being changed. And, *we*, the female youth, started to go to Church, in pants and trousers. My mother didn't like it *at all.* These changes in the Church were a result of *Vatican II*, the second French Revolution, *May '68*, and Woodstock. I didn't realize either that as a young teen, I would feel the consequences of all of this, that I would *live* history, all through my inner self-search.

Being a teenager is a challenge, and for a young girl at this time, it had its good moments and its bad ones. It seems so long ago now, but I feel that the teen years are the ones that form our characters the most. The bonds we made at that time, remain. The backbone of that time though was still my faith and spiritual quest. It is what made my choices. I plunged into the arrival of the Catholic charismatic movement born after *Vatican II*. I attended youth groups, masses and open-air gatherings with conferences. It was at one such conference that I heard that anything to do with astrology was a no-no. I was very disappointed but obeyed my Church and its teachings. On another occasion, in a conversation with other practicing Catholics, the topics of yoga and transcendental meditation came up and were very negatively perceived. From then on, *meditation* became a dirty word for me. Instead of being an opening after *Vatican II,* the Church seemed to become even more closed to practices that came from the east. Or at least that's how it seemed to me.

There was a terrible inner battle raging between living my teen Catholic life and adventuring into the forbidden places of 'boy meets girl'. Alcohol, finding Mr Right, and going through the teenage years with parents who weren't getting along, complicated things. But the Catholic Christian faith has these beliefs of perfection, and of heaven and hell, that keep you in line. So when you step out of line, you have the guilt trip and the priests to absolve you. Then you return to your quest of perfection and buying your way to heaven by your good deeds. And I was going to get there! I was taking that train, on that straight rail, getting me through the Pearly Gates! I was going to do everything it took. I was trained at an early age to be a giver, a people pleaser, a do-gooder, never saying *no*. I was a Marian. I was devoted to Mary. Who was She? She was the Handmaid of the Lord. And who was I? I was *her* handmaid. What better way was there to get to heaven than to become close to Her? I went to a Dominican primary school and then to the secondary school, so I learnt everything one needs to know about doing this. On graduating, we got a school ring with the Dominican crest and our school motto *Veritas*. I always took it to heart and it has always been my mission to seek the Truth.

When I was seventeen, it was decided that I would go to England to do my A Levels. After my O Levels I did a one-year secretarial course, and then ventured to Europe as the family had done for generations. I was to do a one-year course at the *Oxford College of Further Education,* doing A Levels. This was a joke of course, because at the time, I definitely wasn't an academic-minded student, and what was to come would reduce my chances even further. My mother's sister and her husband welcomed me to their home which was about half an hour away from Oxford by train and I would commute to school every day. This was at the end of August 1978. Come October, I was to learn that my parents were to separate definitely. My mother had left in May that year, a week before my 17th birthday, for about a month. Both these periods were difficult times for me. Especially on my spiritual journey. It had been drummed into my religious upbringing that marriage was for life. Divorce was not a thing at that time like it has become. I wanted to go back home and patch things up! But my aunt told me there was nothing to be done and to enjoy the year as best I could. Any studies I might have thought of doing, flew out the window. I met new people and enjoyed my year, though I struggled within. I continued on the road of my faith. My aunt, who I admired immensely and who shared my faith, helped me through this difficult period. In February of 1979, my father sold our family house, the only home that I'd known, and this was a *big* blow to me. I would have to go back to everything new. I held on to my religion like a buoy in the middle of a stormy sea.

Back to Europe.

In the midst of storms, there is hope. I was still so young and naïve. I had a list of things I wanted to do, so after two and a half years living with my father in Trinidad, my native island in the Caribbean, I headed to France to learn French, as an *au pair,* in Paris. It was the easiest way of learning the language and being able to have the money to do so. That was the summer of 1982.

France is the magical country of half of my ancestors (on my mother's side), and most of all, land of my faith. After Rome, France is one of the most revered spiritual countries in the world. So many Saints and Marian apparitions have come from here: Our Lady of Lourdes and Saint Bernadette, Saint Theresa of the Child Jesus in Lisieux (my second patron saint), Saint Michael the Archangel in Normandy (Mount Saint Michel), and the list goes on.

After a year in Paris, I went to Lille to pursue my search of knowledge about my earthly mission. I don't know when the notion of a mission per se would dawn on me but I kept looking for whatever I was being called to do. I felt like Barbara

Streisand in the film *Yentl*, yearning for knowledge that was kept only for men. I was still wondering if I should go into a religious order and be like the Dominican nuns who had inspired me in my youth. But like Maria in *The Sound of Music*, I was still very hesitant. I was encouraged by a boyfriend to go to the Catholic University in Lille to study at the *Institute for the Formation of Catechists by Audiovisual and Art* where we were taught theology, exegetics, and techniques for teaching catechism. Was this to be my mission? During this year I shared a house with five other students from the school and two other university students, and this is where I met Anne-Cécile. She came from the east of France, from the Voges region, to do her studies in Lille. We were to become best friends and remain so today. The year after this, I went on to study theology and continued studying French.

After three years in France, I returned home to Trinidad. No calling, no mission. The search was still on.

A month after returning, I got a job as a bilingual secretary in a construction company where I stayed for nine months before the itch to return to Europe came back. This time it would be Spain, as an *au pair* again. Anne-Cécile had called me in February to tell me that her eldest brother was getting married in July and asked if I would come. I was a part of their family by then. So back to France it was, where I would work as an *au pair* again during summer, while waiting to go to Spain and the wedding. This is where I was to meet my future husband, Pascal. Anne-Cécile played a big part in this adventure. Pascal is her second cousin, and a farmer, and that's how a suburban West Indian, small island girl became a French farmer's wife. It was the 26th of July, Feast of Saint Anne, who I found out was the Patroness of Brittany, where I would then live. Saint Anne is the Grandmother of Jesus. I had also chosen Ann as my confirmation name as I was baptized in the parish of St Ann's where I had grown up. Eureka! I was being led and guided and my life was going somewhere. On my bucket list of things that I wanted to do and learn was farming – *The Little House on the Prairie* kind, where there was always a happy ending. Things were never that easy and I would find out the reality of being a farmer's wife.

We got married in December, 1987.

When I was first married, I taught English in eight primary schools, for five years. I also did one year of evening classes for adults. This was never on any of my lists. It just happened. During this time our two eldest boys were born. I got involved with my parish church, leading the church and choir with the hymns. Now the lady with the English accent was extremely well known. But like all highs there are also lows. When our eldest son went into the second year of primary Catholic school, I contested one of his French reading books. Having studied theology, I was much too aware of underlying currents to corrupt young souls. As I had done the catechism the previous year in the director's class, I thought the director would understand why the book was unacceptable for the children. He didn't. At the end of September, we took our son out of the school and put him into the lay school two kilometers down the road from the farm. (To understand the weight of this act, one has to go back to the French Revolution!)

Next change to come was the Parish. I was still singing there but things in the *Little House on the Prairie* weren't always as easy as I would have liked. So I plunged down deeper into my faith, trying to find solutions to improve my marriage and surroundings. Trying to make everyone happy, I came upon a book called *How to change your husband* by changing yourself. (The second part was in smaller letters at the bottom of the cover.) Eureka again! Things would improve! I felt a call to become holier and search into the women of the Bible for models. I felt called to be more and more submissive, to follow the patriarchal upbringing that I was brought up in, to make my husband happy. I wanted to cover my head in the Sunday masses and felt called to wear skirts and dresses more often. I wanted to bring out the feminine in me. My childhood and youth were coming around again: dresses to church and a veil on my head; though at first, I started wearing a shawl. Feeling the pressure of the congregation and my intensifying faith, we decided to go to the Sunday mass at the old people's home where I didn't know anybody and wouldn't be laughed at for my appearance.

During a pilgrimage to the shrine of Saint Anne, we met a Dominican priest who was confessing, and then later met his whole convent. We learnt that it was a traditional Catholic community where women wore dresses and veils on their heads. The masses were in Latin. This became a whole new chapter in my life.

In 1999, I joined my husband on the dairy farm, now organic, replacing my mother-in-law. My religious ways extended even into the farm and I started to wear skirts to do my farm work, like the generations before me. I no longer owned trousers. With three children to look after, in my role of *Caroline Ingalls*, life revolved around the farm, the home, school and Sunday mass. I was learning every homesteading skill necessary to live there. I did the kitchen garden, which has always been one of my dearest pastimes, and like all the pioneers, I learnt how to cook, bake bread, preserve foods, and make all sorts of dairy produce: yogurts, butter, cottage cheese, desserts. We had our own meat, and I had hens for eggs. There were *always* things to do. I was still trying to be a perfect farmer's wife, mother, and Christian, and I was still aiming for heaven. I was doing what all the women saints in my Church had always done! Mothers, nuns, lay women, all sacrificing themselves for the better of the family, society, and Church. I was being faithful to the sacrament of marriage, however hard that was. I had three boys, and soon a little girl and another little boy in 2003 and 2006.

We no longer had contact with the local parish or the local schools. We went to a traditional Latin mass in Rennes and went to a school connected to the church. The mothers all wore skirts and there were uniforms (in France, children don't wear uniforms). It is in this community that I met an American lady who started to open my eyes. She, like me, came from elsewhere and had had different experiences before coming to France. She was ten years younger than me but we got along well. She opened my eyes to different beliefs even though she was in this community. She was a lot more opened minded than the rest. We talked for long moments about all sorts of things: religion, spirituality, world politics etc. She broadened my outlook and I felt enabled to venture out into spheres that I wasn't allowing myself to go, because I was afraid of disobeying and going outside my faith.

In 2013, things got tough(er). The year started off with a bang. Our second son returned home from his work with a medical problem; the week after that, one of our farmer friends killed himself because of financial pressure. This was an enormous shock to us all. In April, Pascal decided to stop the farm and sell the cows! As a consequence, lots of things happened. The two youngest came back to school in the village nearby. This was a good thing; I was so exhausted doing two hours driving a day just for that special school. Money of course, got really tight. It's six years ago now and I don't even remember how we got through that time. I was still gardening, so there were still vegetables, eggs, fruit, and meat. I sold some eggs and vegetables but it was a difficult time. Then the wake-up year followed.

The Spiritual Catalyst.

I guess when one is stubborn and doesn't want to listen, the wake-up call has to be a hard one. Today I would translate that into a different language: When things are completely off balance in every sense of one's *being*, something has to happen to recreate that balance. Up until now, my life was a projection of perfection. This was all I was taught. *Be perfect, as your Heavenly Father is perfect.* Also, *Love thy neighbour* and *Do unto others as you shall have them do unto you.*

Things got rough between Pascal and I; there were problems with banks and with our relationship. We had a huge verbal fight and the next day I woke up with vertigo. At first, I didn't see the connection between the emotional state and my physical state but then I did. This was in early March 2014.

Then the unthinkable happened. Peter, our second son who was nearly 22, who had just arrived at a new job and had just talked to me on the phone, went missing. I was informed the next day. But I would not accept any possibility yet that he was dead. They found his body two weeks later, and we buried him ten days after that. It was a very hard time. (I may be still in shock, I'm not sure.) Nobody knows for sure what happened, although some foul play is suspected. Maybe one day the truth will reveal itself.

The night before they found his body, a dragonfly visited me in my green house and stayed there until the next morning when I set it free. At that time in my life I had no connections with dragonflies. When it knocked on the light in my green house, I didn't even know what it was. I had never seen one on the farm or in my life (except maybe a tiny one or in a book but I had no memory or affiliation with this insect). This thing was huge! It had a yellow head, a green body and a blue turquoise tail. It stared at me and I got frightened; I didn't know if these creatures stung like wasps. I crept out of the green house, but it was still there the next morning. It should have flown out because the green house had openings all over. I believe it wanted to tell me something. It was that afternoon that the mayor and two policemen arrived at the house to give us the news that they had found Peter's body.

In the week that followed, dragonflies appeared everywhere! A lampshade, my sister-in-law's brooch, in a letter, on a shop front outside the church where the funeral was taking place! *Hey Mum, don't worry, I'm not far away.*

Since then, I know lots of things about dragonflies. One thing I learnt is that they can change direction in an instant but they don't go backwards. In French, they are feminine – a she: *une Libellule*. She has become a big messenger, teacher, guide, and presence.

Every possible emotion, as you might imagine, came out of this event. Only change was possible. And everything changed. Balance had to be found.

Here we return to the image I used before of the train of perfection that had to go straight on the tracks, the religious tracks, the patriarchal tracks to get to heaven. Peter became my spiritual catalyst and my train changed direction before more disaster could continue in the spiritual realm. He opened so many new doors. He allowed me to start thinking about myself.

> *A true Spiritual Catalyst does not change the eventual outcome of a person's journey into truth, they only accelerate it.*
>
> *A true Spiritual Catalyst will not impart their own truth onto others, rather they'll present an alternative possibility or challenge a key building block of someone's own reality causing illusions to fragment and fracture, thereby opening space for a more evolved version of their own truth to emerge and flourish. ~Open*

What was death now? Was it that place of fear? Where were heaven and hell? Where was Peter? Why did this all happen? Why him? Why to me, to us? How was I to go on? What meaning did life have now? Survival? And balance? If I had to continue forward on my bike, I had to pedal, keep balancing. If I stood still, I would fall off. I still had two little ones to take care of but in reality, they took care of me. They gave me a reason to get on that bike again no matter how badly I hurt; I had to ride and find that balance that I had always needed.

To get that balance I had to change all the vibrations. To do that **I could no longer *not* speak my truth.** Because I was hurting so much, there was no more room for anyone else. I had to start to take care of *myself*. Like the stewardesses tell you on the plane, *if there is a lack of oxygen, the mask will fall in front of you. You must put on your mask first before helping anyone else.* So that's what I had to do. **I put my oxygen mask on and took care of myself first.** I couldn't help my husband. I had to speak the truth about our marital situation. I could no longer hold him up. The wind of change was now blowing a hurricane. At the end of August 2014 things blew up between us. I was on a new path and I started to think differently. I could now think out of the box. I was awakening.

Peter had changed everything.

I had to learn deep forgiveness in all dimensions. I had to realize that looking for revenge was not possible. It was *so big*, where could I even start? He wasn't supposed to die before me. I hadn't protected him. The torment went on and on in my soul. I looked for answers. I listened to my sister who was far more advanced in her journey of the Divine Feminine. She had been less trapped and influenced by the Church. She was younger than I was and had had different experiences, different friends, a very different path. She is now a yoga teacher and a doula. She helped me go forward in my mourning.

I started a B&B and two guest houses. It was therapy; it kept me occupied, distracted, gave me some kind of purpose. I am a very sociable person so while doing my job and meeting people, I couldn't think of my pain. Little by little it eased. It didn't go away but it has changed.

The feeling of being in a huge fog has stayed with me, knowing that I could only go forward with baby steps. My motto since that time has been *Fake it till you make it*. I have also come to believe that the Creator of the Universe, or the Multiverses, must have a plan. **And our soul has a plan for each one of us.** Getting down into the silence of the soul must be the hardest thing one can do. Getting connected with self. This connection with self brings us to the divine in us. We are souls having a human experience. But we cannot *not* consider the vehicle that transports us. It is totally connected to the Source. We have to cherish it, nourish and consider it, because whatever happens to the mind affects the body and vice-versa.

This Goddess who had always been there and had been screaming to come out, was trapped inside by an age-old system so powerful that, in the past, it had deemed any female, connected to Source by nature and healing, a witch. For centuries, women in their Divine Feminine state, where they were naturally of service for good and healing, were done away with by a patriarchal setup. I love the divine masculine and I have come to learn, that in all of us, we have this essence too. But in my journey, I hadn't been taught balance.

The biggest element of change in my life has been the goal. It is no longer one of pure perfection, it is now about living an experience. Living in the moment. This is not easy because we are often either in the past or in the future, seldom in the now. Nature has taught me about balance, cycles, spirals and health. And about life and death.

I have looked back on my life and I've wondered, what can I do with all this now? I have knowledge to share – things I have learnt about food, health and people – and I wanted to learn more. I wanted to study. In 2018, I took a very beautiful course at the *Institute of the Psychology of Eating* and became a Certified Mind Body Eating Coach, a step in my journey that means so much to me at this young age of fifty-eight. It is my first significant diploma, being practically autodidact all my life. This course hit me deep down into the core of my *being*. It tied up all the loose ends and I learned that we only need to be one step in front of another person to be able to help them.

Now, in 2019, the fog is slowly lifting. Being in a fog can also be a gift and a protection because knowing too much about the next step can be scary. It can also take away spontaneous meetings with beautiful people, such as Sue, who fell through the fog, into my life, onto my Facebook page, and then onto my doorstep, like my dragonfly, as a messenger! She has included me in an adventure that I have dreamed of but never thought would ever come into being. I feel I'm going somewhere, forward, pedaling, and I feel empowered. The Divine Feminine that was always there, with absolutely no self-confidence, has awakened and has a voice. There are now many sisters to share with and it feels good to grow, learning from each other with respect for each other's paths and gifts. It's exciting and encouraging and it has given me hope.

My life today is no longer a purely religious one, living by rules of good and bad. I have turned a hundred and eighty degrees. I am proof of change. I would never have imagined me as I am today. It is an amazing metamorphosis. I am pleased to be where I am. Doors and windows keep opening, bringing in the new. Surprises that help me continue the journey. Sometimes I stop pedaling because I get tired or sad or I overthink the craziness of this world and my life. Then my soul shakes me up and seats me back on that bike and says *Pedal!* It's not the goal but the journey that makes it worth everything.

My life 'before' seems far away. The intense religious life that I led, with all the different people and the lives of Jesus the Christ, His mother Mary, to whom I was so devoted, Saint Anne and all the women and men saints, seems so distant now. It's strange but it's now as though in a dream. I have totally changed my inner life as though I went to live elsewhere, into another realm, another energy flow. I am no longer looking for answers in that direction. Maybe I'm just being carried. I explain this by the shock of losing a child. A gigantic stick hit the gong. It's possible that my head is still vibrating from it. A vibration that is healing me slowly and that has turned me into the direction where I can say that my life seems to have a purpose now, even a mission. I am discovering *me* for the first time and what I came here for, and am now open to this adventure that is present and that awaits me. There will be more ups and downs but that's part of the adventure that my soul has decided for me so that there will always be growth in this journey.

Stella St Clare

Mother Earth Mother Moon

As I walk out into the night, I feel the darkness descend over me. It is a slow, soft process, this entering of the sacred world and completing the task of the sacred dark of the moon ritual. To become accustomed to this place, that is and isn't my ordinary back yard, to enter the realm of sacred and Divine Feminine, I must allow the earth under my feet to pulse up through me. I must allow the wind to enter me. I must allow a child's imagination to conjure up, out of my old, warm puffer coat, a cape of brilliant red velvet, with garnets and opals stitched around the hood. I must invite the transition: from dinner and dishes and talk of the day and plans for tomorrow, to the magical stillness that becomes the sacred act of witnessing and honoring the unseen, the invisible. This is the dark of the moon, especially magical tonight because it is also the eve of *Imbolc*,[36] the first quarter holiday after Yule, the winter solstice. There will be signs of spring soon; sweet, fragile, snow drop flowers will soon break through the snow. The earth has been sleeping; the unseen moon will be seeded this night. She will begin her gestation and She will birth Her light as the full, glowing moon in two weeks' time. I feel the tenderness of Her in my breasts and my belly and I ask gently that She seed me as She is so seeded. I pray for a wish, a dream, a desire to come to fruition as She grows round and full. I picture myself enjoying the achievement of my desire, and when I re-enter the ordinary world, I will write my intention again and again and cast my intention, my spell, out into the universe. I commune with the dark Goddess Moon for as long as my feet can stay in imaginary warmth, and then I speak my prayers of gratitude for all that I have received, and I pour the wine that I saved for this moment back into the sleeping earth. I blow a kiss to the dark sky, to the unseen moon, to the beautiful Goddess, and I wander back inside the house, my red garnet and opal velvet cape sliding off my shoulders to wait for the next time.

As a child, the moon was my first royal invitation to the Divine Feminine. I would learn, years later, beyond my early instinctual awareness, to call her Goddess, Queen, La Reina Luna; but as a child I learned to attend her without even understanding that I was in attendance. After sixty-two years on earth, I still mark much of living and dreaming and sacred connection, by the cycles of light and darkness of the moon.

---

[36] A traditional Gaelic festival marking the beginning of spring, held on 1 February; widely observed in Ireland (where it's also called Brigid's Day), and Scotland.

She has always been female to me. On summer evenings, as She rose, adult relatives around me would point out the face of the man in the moon, but I didn't see it. I didn't see him, I saw Her. I saw Her round, full face as a watcher, a protector, something palpable, mysterious and magical, that could shine in the darkness. I believed we had a connection, the Moon and I, before I knew what connection meant. I believe She showed herself to me, as She shows herself to every child, and invited me to believe in Her magic. And I believed completely. Maybe because I needed Her light so much? Even within the safe circle of my sisters, I had learned early on, that summer nights could turn bleak and vicious without warning. My mother hit the Bourbon and her children, without discrimination. And on a long, beautiful summer night, my mother could drink a lot of Bourbon. If you happened to be within her sights and you seemed a little too boisterously happy, she would follow you and find you and make you pay. The unpredictable nature of the cruelty was the most frightening, and so the steady, dependable cycle of the moon, even on the darkest new moon nights, became my guiding spirit.

And there were sweet, fragrant nights when only the moon would follow me, no matter where I ran, wild and shrieking with laughter as my sisters and I pretended to fly, believing we were human by accident (so unbelievable to us was any connection to our mother), and that in the moonlight our true fairy forms could be remembered and brought back to life. Even inside, sent to bed while the adults would linger on the porch, their voices softly trailing up to our bedrooms, curtains and windows open to whatever bright breeze could whisper its way in, I watched the moon's magic patterns of shadow and light on the walls of my bedroom. Long after I was supposed to be sleeping, I played my own solitary game of bringing to form and life Her stories. I would fall asleep to Her blessing. Her light would continue to follow me into my dreams. She was eternal for me before I even wondered what eternal was.

By age eleven, I was sneaking out of the house at night – or more like escaping, as the craziness grew to terrifying levels in our home – to wander the neighborhood, no matter what the season. Winter was the best season because of the way the moonlight could make even the smallest snow-covered shape glitter magically. Snowy hillsides and ice-covered trees appeared dressed in diamonds and emeralds and pearls. If the houses around me happened to be decorated with Christmas lights, so much the better; it was like an unreal dream time to slowly wander through familiar yards and woods that were transformed by moon and snow. This magic would delight me for hours and *oh!* it was so much better than trying to sleep during the screaming fights. There was a particular blue spruce, in a neighbor's yard, that was always strung with lights during Christmas, and I remember standing for hours gazing at it as something so beautiful and strangely full of comfort. An hour would go by without my knowing time was even passing. After such encounters, I would slip back into the quiet house, past midnight by then, and slip into my chilly bed, my body and mind filled with warmth and calm, even in the middle of winter and within a family in chaos. Clearly, something otherworldly traveled with me through these wanderings and connections.

Age eleven was a pivotal time for me. I got my period. I put on more weight, particularly in the breast and hip areas. I was suddenly almost fully developed as *female,* and that, apparently, was not a good thing. I was still the accidental human girl, in search of my lost fairy form, but the world no longer seemed to see me that way. I alternately responded to and then rebelled against, the constrictive, demeaning misogyny that I woke up to when I turned eleven. I was angry most of the time. This anger was deemed highly unfeminine, despite the fact that my mother engaged in pretty regular displays of verbal and physical rage. It was explained to me that anger was not seemly in a girl of eleven and that I had hit an unacceptable level when I refused to join in making bullshit Christmas cookies (*bullshit* became my favorite word for a while). And that is why, during Christmas vacation of 1968, I was sent to my grandmother, to learn to cook our traditional Italian Christmas foods and to learn more tolerable ways of being female. I did learn much about cooking and learned to hold my temper, at least around my Nana, who with just a look, could silence me into a demure and smiling creature. I cleaned pounds of squid and shrimp and smelts without complaint. I learned to reconstitute dried cod in cool water that had to be drained and replaced every two hours, round the clock, for forty-eight hours (my Nana actually set an alarm for me). I peeled and chopped so much garlic that the tips of my fingers puckered and burned. I baked and boxed thousands of cookies. I rolled and cut and filled enough ravioli to feed the army of family who showed up at Nana's house on Christmas Eve, and as I passed around drinks and anchovy toasts, I was quiet and smiling and gracious. In truth, I was quite proud of the feast I had helped prepare. I also had a hidden agenda.

I had been promised by my Nana – if my parents would let me stay on till New Year – a trip into the city for the *After Christmas* sales. The possibility of taking the street car into downtown Pittsburgh was thrilling to me. There was a chance that I would not be permitted – my mother, ever unpredictable, was capable of saying no to just about anything. I held my breath as my Nana requested my continued company. My parents agreed, partly I suspect because they did love me and hoped I would blossom into a more suitable girl for my own sake, in a world that was dangerous for rebel girls.

And so I went shopping at *Hornes* department store with my very thrifty Nana, who had been married off at age fifteen, lived through the depression, divorced her abusive husband, and raised her children as a single, working mother (when that sort of motherhood was seen as sinful). *Hornes'* sales were legendary, and in 1968, shopping *in town* was a big deal. I could barely sleep the night before, and when the morning finally arrived, I thought I would never be able to wait till we were ready. We dressed up for this expedition. People did that back then. Nana wore a dress and stockings and her good coat, with shoes to match. I wore my new Christmas hat and scarf and carried my new purse, which held my life savings of $20 in Christmas money, and another $10 earned from babysitting. I was to look for sensible sale items. Nana made suggestions regarding socks and underwear, but I found my way to the perfume counter, where I must have sampled a hundred fragrances. One in particular, *Shalimar*, stopped me in my tracks. My Nana must have been with me, I don't think she would have let me go off shopping by myself in *Hornes* department store, but in my memory, it is just *Shalimar* and me. I fell under a spell of dark, spicy, secret female power. The sparkle and shine of *Hornes'* store decorations seemed to spotlight the beautiful *Shalimar* bottle, and my hand seemed to move of its own accord, removing the perfect, blue crystal stopper, to dab my wrist with a scent I can still only describe as divine. Divine and female, together, for me, for the first time ever. I spent all my money on that one bottle. And I do remember my Nana scolding me, telling me I was too young for such a thing and reminding me that I had spent all my money and would not be getting anything else so don't ask. I didn't care. And I didn't want anything else. I had the most wonderful thing ever in the world!

This experience in *Hornes* was also my first encounter with The Triple Goddess of Maiden, Mother and Crone, though I was not aware of it at the time. It's only been in the last twenty years or so that I have come to see the tableau at the perfume counter as something more than the purchase of a fragrance. I see myself, a Maiden just on the cusp of womanhood, with a defiant desperation to connect to positive and powerful female energy. I see the *Guerlain* sales clerk as a deliciously sexy Mother, with her full, red lips and red nails and lovely smiling approval of my awkward step forward into the realm of female power. And I see my Nana as Crone, elder female, matriarch, with strict lines of conformity and disapproval, yet with her own sort of power. The three of us are locked in my memory, surrounded by shining glass and crystal, velvet-lined shelves full of beautiful and mysterious bottles, scents and fragrances, the Christmas lights and the jingle-jangle, gold and silver ornaments decorating the artificial swags of evergreens and Christmas pine trees, those ancient vestiges of the The Goddess, The Old Ones, The Druids, that centuries of purveyors of Christianity could not completely obliterate.

This may seem an odd sort of meeting with The Divine Feminine (and possibly a far flung jump into the exploration of the shift from a female Goddess spiritual perspective to a male dominating God religion) but I think it was like many of my encounters with Her, uniquely mine, unique to my life, my time, my ancestors and my culture. But at the same time, **there is an archetypal, almost divinely planned map or path I have followed, that seems in retrospect marked with significant points, through maidenhood and motherhood, all directing me to where I stand now, in my own dwelling place of Crone.** When I ask myself how I survived, the only way I can see is with the help of Divine Feminine and Divine Spirit. I think of my sister, who did not survive, dead at thirty, by her own hand. I mourn my brothers, both lost to me for reasons I will never understand. I wear the crown of Crone because I earned it and allowed myself to be led by something beyond physical, intellectual and emotional. And, I was lucky. I was so lucky.

I had the natural world. I believe it claimed me early on. And that world is still my deepest connection to the Divine. Throughout my life I have known, and still carry in my heart, soul places, experiences of the Soul, where my spirit has been lifted out of the ordinary, out of the everyday, out of despair, out of struggle and into something, someplace, that I have limited language to describe. Maybe *In Perfect Love and Perfect Trust*, the same words I learned to speak when casting the sacred circle. As a practicing Wiccan, I have learned to use the language of the Goddess and the Divine Feminine in the traditional sense, but all the words and traditions come to me with tinges of my own life, my own memories.

The Big Swings. I think I was fourteen the last time I visited the big swings but it was a mainstay of my childhood and early adolescence. Someone, long ago, had fashioned a wide, heavy plank of wood into a swing, hung with thick coils of rope from a huge, ancient oak tree. All the children of my neighborhood would go there to swing and play and dream. I ran away many times to the big swings, more specifically to the steady, sturdy oak tree where I could stretch my arms out around the massive trunk, not even close to reaching fully around, but close enough to feel comforted when there was no human comfort to be found. I would go there by myself when there were no brothers or sisters or neighborhood kids to play with, and spend hours just being a spirit child in the human world. This is where I first learned to feel the earth and the trees and wind as caresses from the Goddess. Each season offered splendid gifts, but in fall, when the oak leaves fell and mixed with the fallen leaves of maple and birch, all the children would bring rakes to sweep colossal piles of leaves to jump in, sometimes jumping from mid-swing. In winter, whoever managed to race their sled through the snow, all the way to the big swings, was legendary. I hold this place forever in my heart.

Honeymeade Farms. Where I could walk for miles through the pastures and fields, pretending I was walking the moors. I wore a cape. It was impossibly romantic and ridiculous and beautiful. I would carry apples and carrots, and sometimes the old horses who wandered the outer pastures, free from work, would let me get close enough to feed them.

The Hawthorn Area Memorial Library. The beautiful library in the small town where I grew up. I could check out books, take them to my favorite maple tree, and in a perfect spot which overlooked a beautiful view of the Ohio river, I could read all afternoon. That tree and that view are more home to me than any part of Hawthorn, including my family home. It's the last spot I visited before I left forever. I stood there for a long time, watching the wind whip up white caps on the water. It was so cold that day. It was sunny, but the wind was so strong and so loud that I couldn't help but hear goodbye, goodbye, goodbye.

Under Wisteria. I am at the main entrance to *The Culinary Institute of America*, where I first knew I was in love with a man who called the moon La Luna and named me after the stars and the saints he loved so much. I can never smell wisteria without feeling flooded with love and excitement, and for a moment I remember that I believed in the effortless future of romantic love. And though that future did eventually arrive as illness and death, I still believe in the magic powers of wisteria.

The Hudson River Valley. The most beautiful place I have ever seen. The trails through the woods will always run in my veins, in my blood. The fields of purple loosestrife will always be the color I see, just for the briefest moment, before I fall asleep. And the wild wide Hudson River, flowing through every memory. The Hudson River, who sang me to sleep, every night, for twenty-five years, will always be my kin, my brother.

Omega Institute. Where I was lucky enough to work for three years and where I was allowed to be part of an accepting, nurturing community and where I first tried on the wings of Wicca and re-learned that witches were once revered as wise women. I say *re-learned* because I remembered one day, during a lunch conversation with a colleague, that I had written a grade school essay on how hundreds of thousands of innocent women, and men and children, had been tortured, burned, hung – murdered – for the crime of witchcraft. I also remembered that my teacher had not believed that my essay points were accurate. Even when I brought in the volume of the *Encyclopedia Britannica* and showed her, she insisted it had been a 'misprint'.

Omega Institute is where I was befriended with love and acceptance and where I learned to cultivate a whole garden of friends and colleagues. They were a wonderfully diverse bunch of spirits, living in the human world, who celebrated holidays called *Beltane*[37] and *Lughnasadh*[38] by dancing around bonfires, drinking mead, eating cakes, and wine-soaked honey bread. **I learned to call Halloween *Samhain*[39] and to understand it as a culmination of an entire year of seasons and life and death. I learned to welcome the ghosts of ancestors on Samhain Eve and to speak the names of the dead and to pray for peace for us all, the living and the dead.** I learned to love the grinning faces of carved pumpkins, lit up in the darkness, as heralds of the coming winter, when seeds would sleep, waiting to be reborn in the spring of *Ostara*.[40] **That there was actually a whole system of ritual and belief that honored the earth and the seasons with ancient holidays and that churches were not needed to be entered to walk this particular path, was astounding to me.** And yet, hadn't I been seeking it all along? And hadn't that path been seeking me? The Goddesses and Gods who had begun to show themselves to me, in dreams, during walks in the woods, in synchronistic signs and 'accidents' – hadn't they been there all along? I believe so.

I call myself Witch and Wiccan and Pagan now. Sometimes I call myself nothing and gently ask the Goddess to name me, to show me, to love me. I follow *The Wheel of the Year* and I celebrate each season's commemoration day: *Yule, Imbolc, Ostara, Beltane, Litha,*[41] *Lugnasadh, Mabon*[42] and *Samhain*. Sometimes I celebrate with friends and sometimes I follow my mostly solitary ways. These solstices and equinoxes and their quarter holidays feel profoundly significant to me. They are also **reminders to take stock, to ponder, grow, sow and reap, make magic – to find magic and miracle in the earth and the stars.** The moon has remained my constant reminder of light and dark, of birth and gestation and death, of remembrance and reverence. She still follows me and I follow her.

The Full Moon Blessing. As I walk into the center of my back yard, with the glowing, full moon suddenly hidden by drifting clouds, I take the momentary shadow as time to gather my thoughts and prayers. I ask to be opened and share that I am ready for what will come. I concentrate on my breathing, in and out, in and out. Slowing down. What comes to me is gratitude and peace, and oh I have

---

[37] Gaelic festival held on 1 May, marking the beginning of Spring in Ireland.

[38] Gaelic festival marking the beginning of harvest, traditionally held on 1 August.

[39] Gaelic festival marking the end of the year and beginning of winter, held on 31 October.

[40] Also Ēostre, a Germanic and Anglo-Saxon goddess, namesake of the festival of Easter.

[41] Midsummer.

[42] Autumnal equinox.

been longing for the feeling of peace in these past months. I locate my center of stillness, and my breath becomes slower as I let my prayer speak itself, as the clouds shift and the moon shows herself in glorious light:

Oh beautiful Goddess, Oh Beautiful Light
Giver of peace and long-time protector of the girl that I was
And the woman I strive to be
Thank you
Thank you

Sarah McCrum

Yin and Yang

You have a male soul, my new mentor told me. *That means that in most of your past lives you've incarnated as a man.* It was a new concept to me, but it made sense of many things.

I'd always found it hard to relate to femininity. From early on I couldn't understand why women wore makeup and I didn't feel comfortable in feminine clothing. I felt I never belonged in girly conversations. I didn't long to have children in the way I heard from so many women. It was a world that seemed slightly alien to me and I didn't know why.

At the same time, I didn't feel like a man either. It seems that being born with a female body, in a culture that has gender-specific expectations, makes a difference. The mentor who introduced me to my soul explained that the reason for me to be female this time round is so I can learn a softer, more feminine way of being powerful. In the entire thread of my twelve previous lives before this one, it emerged that I'd occupied one powerful, spiritual/religious male position after another.

You can probably imagine what that meant in terms of behaviour. It was a litany of abuse of power. From Druid priest to Tibetan monk leader to bishop during the Inquisition, it seemed I took every opportunity to put myself in the place of God and create an experience of fear, control, powerlessness and misery for those around me. The only female life that showed up was cold, hard, bitter and cynical, and very powerful again, but in that particular context female power had to be expressed in a manipulative, behind the scenes kind of way. It wasn't any more attractive than male power.

Whether those lives were real or not wasn't so important to me as discovering the patterns that helped me understand my relationship with power in this lifetime. As a child I was always the leader. It came naturally to organise large groups of teenagers in wide games that lasted for hours and extended over many acres of local English countryside.

I was in my element and played so wholeheartedly that I learned how to inject spirit into the entire game, manage the timing so it was satisfying for everyone involved and be an example of how to play for the sake of the game, rather than merely to win. It always surprised me when other people organised games that were purely competitive, because they lacked fun. It seemed so pointless.

I had a strange relationship with competition. If it was Monopoly, I was out to win. Looking back on it, what a terrible example that was. The game taught that to make money you have to crush everyone else, extort as much cash from them as you possibly can and rent properties at prices that ultimately no one can afford.

There was only one boy who could beat me. When he was around, my leadership was always threatened. He had a natural charisma that I lacked. I still remember with discomfort the time he persuaded me and another girl to play strip poker. I didn't know how to play poker and very quickly the two of us were stark naked while he hadn't removed a single item of clothing. It wasn't a particularly sinister event. He didn't try to take advantage of us in any way. It was simply the humiliation of losing without any chance of an alternative outcome.

As a boarding school girl from the age of eleven, my main exposure to spirituality came through twice daily chapel services and church on Sundays. The local Canon, who led our Anglican church services and often visited our school, was one of those old, dry men who had no clue about making religion appealing for the young.

Every Sunday morning, we lined up to be inspected by the school Matron, who was extremely masculine, hard, and verged on cruelty. We wore special Sunday suits (skirts with matching jackets) with white gloves, and hats in the summer. Everything had to look perfect to prevent her from raising her terrible voice, that echoed along the corridors, and getting into her bad books – a fate worth avoiding. We walked, two by two, in a long line through the town to the parish church, sat in cold, dusty pews and endured forty-five minute sermons by playing word games and trying not to giggle too loud and get in trouble. I don't remember feeling touched, emotionally or spiritually, by any experience in that church.

My best times came after a few years when I put myself in charge of the music for our school services. We had a beautiful modern chapel, full of light, and our headmistress sometimes told good stories. But my greatest joy was setting the mood as the girls entered the chapel, waiting for the service to begin. I learned how to create a magical atmosphere, playing Mozart, Mahler and Vaughan Williams. I loved the feeling of this special space being filled with the most gorgeous music. It was my way of influencing the experience for the whole school and it made my heart sing. This was my first inkling of a living spirituality which was inclusive and expansive and powerfully uplifting.

Those moments of beauty as a teenager were followed by many years of inner wilderness. In my twenties I prided myself on saying, *I'd rather go to hell than heaven because it's more interesting.* I was clever and my mind dominated everything. I had an inner sense that I was supposed to do something significant in my life, like a trace of the power from previous lives, but my daily reality felt powerless and strangely weak. I no longer had the natural leadership of my childhood. I felt blocked and unexpressed.

It took the death of my younger sister, when I was thirty, to wake me up. Three weeks after her idyllic wedding on the small Maltese island of Gozo, we were visiting her in London's top neurological hospital. She had a brain tumour. When my mother called to give me the news, I couldn't believe something like this could happen to our family. It seemed so unreal.

They operated on her hypothalamus, which is deep inside the brain, so it was never expected to save her. She lived for another twenty-one months and we got used to a very new life. When she came home from the hospital, she'd lost her short-term memory. She thought her husband was an old boyfriend and kept calling him by the wrong name. She'd go into the kitchen and not be able to find her way out because she couldn't remember where the door was, and she'd try to find her way out through cupboards. She forgot when she'd last eaten, where she was, where she was going or what she was doing.

As a child she'd been extremely difficult. She had tantrums every day for years, and looking back, it seems as if the whole family was constantly treading carefully around her, trying not to trigger her. The last year of her life was my first introduction to healing, although very unconsciously. I spent far more time with her than ever before. We drove together across Europe, from England to Gozo. Over and over again she would ask me where we were going, because she couldn't remember anything. I had to watch her all the time so she wouldn't get lost. It softened me and I learned to become very patient.

In her final few months we played many games of gin rummy. She loved it, so we played for hours on end. She was no longer angry and I was no longer afraid of her. I'm grateful for this time together. It didn't heal her, but it healed me. I showed up for her and when she finally left us, I had no regrets that I'd let her down or been too busy or unavailable. I'd done the best I could at the time.

And yet, looking back, how different it might have been with what I know now.

My way to cope at first was to work. On the evening after her funeral I travelled to London to pick up recording equipment from the BBC. I flew off early the next morning to Stuttgart to interview the Director of Education. It was one of the bleakest experiences of my life. I can't imagine now why I didn't give myself any time at all to recover or take it gently. It seems that the only thing I knew how to do was keep working. Perhaps it gave me a sense of stability.

Six months later I needed help. I was so blocked emotionally that I couldn't go on any longer. A friend introduced me to acupuncture and in my first session I experienced something close to a miracle. In forty-five minutes, I went from feeling completely stuck to being happy and relaxed.

It was the beginning of a fascination with the deep, traditional culture of the Chinese and my first introduction to the concepts of *yin* and *yang* – the underlying duality of the world we live in.

In hindsight, this was my first introduction to a more feminine version of divine power, although it was never expressed that way explicitly. It's very hard for the western mind to comprehend *yin* and *yang*. *Yin* energy is associated with darkness, the feminine, the negative, receptivity, cold and many other qualities which in the western world tend to be seen as inferior to the *yang* qualities, such as light, the positive, the masculine, direction and movement, warmth and so on.

The Chinese, in their metaphysics, are very clear that **positive and negative are simply two qualities that coexist on a spectrum.** Neither can exist without the other. Neither is superior or inferior to the other. It's like the positive and negative aspects of electricity. They create balance and movement.

Interestingly, at a certain level the *yin* energy always overcomes the *yang* energy. Deep receptivity or relaxation – *yin* – creates deep surrender which takes you to deep emptiness. In any challenge, I learned the power of accessing a deeply *yin* state, to move beyond or transcend the problem. To this day, this is core to my spiritual practice. If in doubt, I always relax first, become receptive and open and **let go of the *yang* impulse to do something**. I allow action to arise from deep within the emptiness.

I learned this through twenty-two years of training with two Chinese Masters. The first was a man, but he was the essence of *yin*. He taught us a healing form of *Qi Gong*[43] which was gentle, spontaneous, flowing, creative and deeply relaxing. He talked to us for hours, as we sat cross-legged in silence, sharing the Chinese philosophy that was thousands of years old. I loved the simplicity of it. He talked about the five elements – wood, fire, earth, metal and water – and expressed everything in the language of nature. It was relatable and understandable.

He taught us how to dance, paint and sing in a spontaneous *yin* way. We tuned into the energy and let it move us and often astonished ourselves with what emerged. Eighty people danced in a room with pillars and not a huge amount of space with our eyes closed and we never bumped into each other. I painted and drew the movement of energy, and even my mother, who is a successful and discerning artist, was impressed by some of my creations. I developed a method of healing based on spontaneous vocalisation, that was powerful and cathartic,

---

[43] Traditional Chinese system of movement, breathing and meditation.

and shared it with others. It was a magical time for me that freed up a lot of creativity and enjoyment.

I spent seven years with that Master and then I bought a book which changed my life. It was called *Essence*, by AH Almaas. It introduced me to the spiritual concept of ego. I hadn't known about this before. I was shocked, not only to realise I had an ego, but to discover that it was a big issue for me. I recognised that I needed to do something about it, but I didn't know how. I asked my teacher some questions and quickly realised that he wouldn't be able to help me. It was as if he didn't know anything about ego.

I was devastated. It felt like the floor fell out of my world. I had believed I would find all answers to all questions in the knowledge he shared with us. I'd reached a point where he could talk for two or three hours and I listened, fully awake and alert but deeply relaxed, and could remember every word by the end. Others were falling asleep around me and losing concentration, but I had crystal recall. I was so deeply steeped in this beautiful wisdom that I couldn't imagine it was lacking something. But once I saw that it was, I couldn't un-see it.

A few months later, I was introduced to another Chinese Master. She was a radically different kettle of fish, and most definitely a male soul like me. She was immensely powerful, direct to the point of confronting, and exciting. And she knew all about ego.

As soon as I walked into the theatre in Zagreb, Croatia, where she taught several classes every day, I felt at home. The air was charged with energy, so it felt thick and potent. Her sessions were dynamic and challenging. Sometimes she appeared angry, but it seemed powerful rather than weak. I was fascinated by the possibility of being able to express myself so fully without having to be beautiful and nice all the time.

Over the next few months I learned about ego operations. This was essentially an experience of being told the truth about yourself in a way that was extremely uncomfortable to the ego but comforting to the part of me that craved the truth. She told me I was complicated. I didn't know what it meant but I knew she was right.

I arrived as a person who believed I could communicate very articulately. With my previous teacher I was frequently praised for the way I expressed myself and spoke with clarity and eloquence. My new teacher seemed to find it hard to understand anything I said. It took me many years to realise that my beautiful words lacked essence and energy. They were like a parcel that has nothing inside it.

She was a master of energy. For her I was nobody. The people she most respected were simple people who spoke with sincerity, usually about their experiences of healing. They transmitted an energy that affected all of us deeply, and often healed people there and then. This was a completely different level of communication that I didn't understand. I felt like a beginner in her presence.

In my first week she talked in almost every session about enjoyment. It was torture for me. I realised I had no clue how to experience simple enjoyment. Others in the room were describing how they were enjoying the energy in the room. They were laughing and joking and having fun a lot of the time. All I could do was cry. Tears rolled down my cheeks almost all day long as I contemplated the inner tragedy of my life. I was so serious and boring – my worst nightmare – that I couldn't even enjoy something enjoyable.

The night before I was due to leave it culminated in an attack of hysterical crying and shaking. This was an energy reaction and I knew it was a good thing, although it was scary as well. Luckily, I was with two more experienced students who helped me calm down. The next morning, I sat in the session and I felt as if I was in Heaven. It was beautiful. For an hour or so I enjoyed myself with no external stimulation. I'd made it. That was what I came for.

I went on to train for fifteen years with that teacher, and I learned more about energy than I could possibly have imagined. She was an extraordinary combination of a very masculine woman teaching a very feminine essence of wisdom. Sometimes, in the early days when she was working mostly with very sick people, the love that emanated from her as she spoke of healing and energy and truth was tangible. At other times, especially later when we were working with business, she could be terrifying in the demands she made of us that we knew we would never achieve.

Years after I left her world, I realised that one of the things I gained was spending so much time in an environment where women were in power. I became manager of her academy and all the other people with positions of responsibility were also women, except the team who were in charge of construction and building work. For many years I didn't have to face the usual challenges of powerful women in a male dominated organisation. It's possible that she went too far in her mistrust of men, but it was a good experience for me. I learned to put the principles we learnt from her into practice in daily life. We never separated our knowledge about energy and spirituality from our practical responsibilities.

In November 2010 I was in the extremely unpleasant situation of having to close down the business I'd started ten years earlier in London. My teacher had invested a lot of time and money into it, as had I, but when the recession hit in 2008, we lost around ninety percent of our clients, because most of them were big companies and banks that had been hit hard. We staggered on for two years, struggling to pay bills, until it became clear that we weren't going to make it. My teacher was extremely disappointed in us and made it quite clear to us in daily ego operations, which only made it harder. We no longer wanted to hear the truth about how weak and incompetent we were. We weren't supposed to fail and we had failed.

A few weeks later, I was in the unusual position of having time because there was no more business. I was sitting on my bed in an apartment I couldn't pay for, reading a book called *How to be a Money Magnet*. It had questions for journaling at the end of each chapter. One of the questions was *What does money want to say to you?*

I put my pen onto my notebook and it started writing automatically. I saw the words *I would like to tell you to love me*. I was astonished. I had no idea that money could speak and even less expectation that it would speak of love. I continued writing for a couple of pages and saw the most beautiful words flowing out onto the page without any hesitation. This was not my language. It spoke of opening my heart and allowing myself to accept money into my life. It described itself as a beautiful energy of light that connects human beings together and supports our creativity. It told me that there's enough for all of us to have whatever we want and more, and that I shouldn't wait. It ended with the words *I will love you*.

I read it back to myself and was moved to tears. It was so unlike anything I'd ever come across. I'd never associated money with beauty or light. I knew it was energy but believed it was neutral and I still had many subconscious fears about it that I'd never brought to the surface.

The next day I tried writing the same way again, and I received another message. This time it told me that we all need to relax about money, and that we've all got completely the wrong idea about it, even the very wealthy. I decided to write every day for a while to see what would emerge. Day after day it delivered a new message, sometimes short, sometimes several pages long. They were enlightening, sometimes funny, always fresh. The language was simple, almost childlike at times. Some of it was hard to believe.

It gave me a new blueprint for making money which started with the instruction *Forget everything you already know about money*. That didn't seem likely to be correct, but much of it was intriguing and appealing. It spoke over and over again of the importance of **enjoyment** and **relaxation** in relation to money – it's surprising how often these two words have been core themes of my life.

I ended up with sixty-nine messages about money which I published in a book called, *Love Money, Money Loves You*. Ironically, at the time, I had no money at all. I was broke, and a very bad example of what I was writing about. I found it embarrassing and didn't promote the book as a result. But a couple of years later I had to get to grips with this new knowledge I'd channelled into the world.

I left my Chinese Master and moved to Australia with my husband. We had just enough cash to buy a cheap car, put a bond on a rental house and survive for the first six weeks. I realised I had to get myself into business extremely quickly to be able to pay our bills. We didn't know anyone in Australia, so it was a tough challenge.

I attended a women's networking lunch called *The Enlightened Goddesses*. I'd never seen myself as a goddess-y type of woman and I'm not a natural networker, but I had to do something constructive. I was lucky to win a door prize of a free consultation with a local psychic. We visited her in the back of the local mystical bookshop in a dingy little room behind a curtain. I can't remember much of what she said, but there was an electric moment when I mentioned my book about money. She told me it was the key. I had to use the book and teach about it.

I trusted the information even though I was clearly not a good example of my own writing yet. I started teaching people how to get what they want, based on what I'd learned from twenty-two years of Chinese teachings and the new information in my book. We struggled financially and I often had to use the book's blueprint for making money for ourselves to deal with paying rent and other larger expenses. Amazingly, it worked as long as I followed the instructions. I can tell so many stories of how money came unexpectedly into my life during those first few years, always when I needed it, just in time, in perfect amounts.

It's strange, looking back, that I developed a very feminine way of teaching. It was always in the moment, in flow, spontaneous and unstructured. I'd learned how to transmit energy, once I got over being too complicated and serious, so I knew as long as I talked with my students they would heal and solve problems.

As my confidence grew and I left my Chinese teachers behind me, I developed my own style and deepened my knowledge. Whenever I was interested in a topic, I developed a course about it and learned more through teaching than I ever expected. It was as if I was being taught by a divine source, as I taught others.

I created a course called *2017: Let's Start It with Love*. We held our first class on New Year's Day 2017. It felt very brave as I never associated myself much with teachings on love but when I wrote or spoke about it, the power I experienced behind my words was tangible and beautiful and I couldn't resist it. It felt very important to bring in the message of love in a world that was crazy and disturbed a lot of the time.

That course changed my concept of myself. Speaking directly about love in a spiritual, non-romantic way is deeply challenging because I wanted my teaching to have integrity. In my marriage I was often challenged by my childish need to be right or to be the best, which got in the way of loving unconditionally. In fact,

I've come to believe love is the greatest challenge of human life, and the most worthwhile.

Since running that course, I've recognised that every human problem is essentially a call to us to expand our capacity for love. This includes health, relationship, and money problems, as well as legal and business issues, challenges with family members, political and global challenges and anything else you can think of.

Love calls us to be strong, wise, expansive and inclusive of all people. That's not easy for any of us. One of the things I learned, from teaching about it, is that I don't have to be perfect in my ability to love. It's enough to be willing to get better at it gradually, in real life, with real people, in real situations. That's where love happens, not in my mind or in my beautiful words, but in the times and places where love is the last thing I want to engage with.

Towards the end of 2017 I started to run retreats with my husband, Niko, and my friend, Jeff Vander Clute, on *The Consciousness of Money*. This was an astonishing upgrade for me. The energy that's behind this body of work is exquisitely beautiful. The very idea that in exploring money we would uncover and share such sweet, delicious energy was surprising to me, even after teaching it for several years already.

Gradually I came to recognise Money as a profound spiritual teacher. It seems close to heresy to say this, but the evidence has been the proof of it. It's allowed people to integrate their spirituality and their material life in a way they haven't experienced anywhere else. It opens up our deep life creativity, sourced in unconditional love, and gives us permission to call in all the resources we'll ever want or need in order to express our greatest vision of ourselves and our soul's purpose.

One of the most interesting things for me has been the combination of Divine Feminine and Masculine. My way of teaching became so feminine that it was hard for people to describe it. There was nothing to latch onto or get to grips with. It didn't have a clear formula or format. It was powerful and gave results. There's no question about that. People are very appreciative of what they learn and the feeling aspect of it is strong, but they couldn't put their finger on what was happening, even though I always share what's going on very openly.

We introduced into our retreats a system of mapping resonance in numbers. My business partner, Jeff, tells someone that their idea or business opportunity resonates as sixty-seven percent aligned for them. Then we tweak and adjust the idea until it reaches one hundred percent alignment, or way beyond a hundred percent. Sometimes he assesses each person in the group on a particular variable, for example, the extent to which they're afraid of money or open to access all the resources that are currently available to them. There are many possible variables and behind each of them sit numbers, percentages and measurements. This is truly a divine masculine influence and people love it.

The sense of relief and security in having a number or a formula has been fascinating to me. It's caused me to face the imbalance in being over-feminine. It's helped me integrate more masculine energy into my work and my business again, discerning where planning, form and structure have power, in balance with the flow and emergence of the feminine principle.

It appears to me that Money is the essence of the Divine Feminine. It's the aspect of life that gives endlessly and generously of itself in service to humanity. And yet, in order to interact with it, we must both ask and receive, be specific and be open, deal with numbers and let go of the numbers. And beyond all of that we need to trust, relax, enjoy and love. For this **we must be integrated human beings, powerful in both our feminine and masculine divinity** and able to unite with that which lies beyond duality altogether.

The mentor who told me I have a male soul assured me that I will be a man again in my next lifetime. I'm not sure how I feel about that now, as I've become used to being a woman. I find myself witnessing almost daily the emergence of women in a new form of power which is currently hard for most men to access, however much they try.

I'm experiencing a growing confidence as I grow my business in a very soft way. There's no room at all for hustle, force, pushiness or any of the traditional masculine ways of doing business. In fact, I'm amazed at just how *yin* it's necessary to be, to create the best results. It seems like we need to surrender almost everything we know, in order to stay right on the edge of the unknown. This is scary if you need to be in control, but it's the wildly beautiful territory of the soul that's leading the way in today's world.

Maybe, if I become a man again, I'll know this deeply surrendered place and be able to share it with my fellow males. I feel the pain of men as they struggle to succeed and know, somewhere deep inside, that they're out of touch with today's energy. My wish is that we can integrate the masculine and feminine this time around. It's clear that it will only possible if we can allow the *yin* energy full expression first.

Detta Darnell

Integration

I'm a writer and artist of Irish descent, born in England, and I moved to Greece in my thirties. I have always felt more Irish than English, even as a small child. Being brought up with the spiritual as a way of life, and listening to stories of Irish heroes and heroines, gods and goddesses, I thought I clearly understood the Divine Feminine, until I came to write this piece.

The more I tried to write about my take on it, the more it became a battle. I just wasn't getting it. Hell, I didn't even know what *it* was. Unusually for me, there was no flow, no words; only a blank page smirking at me. The more I stared at it, the angrier I became.

I'd sent in my initial draft months ago. That felt okay, but when I picked up the pen to deepen and extend it, I had nothing to write.

On the point of giving up, I tried one more time. I moved my writing spot outside. It was raining; I wrapped myself in a pink blanket and made myself a cup of tea. I scrutinized the questions I had been given to assist my writing. Trying to make a connection between thought and page, I cleared my mind. Nothing. Frustration, anger and a feeling of ineptitude washed over me.

Distracted, I read a Facebook post from someone I'd admired for many years. She posted about why she'd deleted earlier posts about some deep personal feelings. She worried she'd be seen as a *bad mother* and *someone with mental health issues* – the shame of it all. Her beautiful and authentic words had given permission to hundreds of women to bare their souls, to be seen and heard, but she had given into fear and removed her comments. She'd done the work, this beautiful woman, and almost as soon as she recognized what was happening, she began reposting her original feelings again with renewed energy, fuelled by her anger. I held my breath as I read her words, painfully aware that I was unable to connect with the soft feminine energy needed to hold her, and I replied in what I now understand as angry male energy. I couldn't connect with Divine Feminine energy. Instead, a train of angry words poured out, outraged as I was on her behalf. As I finished writing my response, I looked at my own blank page waiting for words to appear.

Then it hit me. I realized that in being angry on her behalf, and on behalf of all women who come to my workshops and retreats, I was blocking my way to claiming my own anger. Anger that had kept me looking in only one direction.

A message I'd had from a medium some days before kept running through my mind. *You're looking in the wrong place.* I'd thought the message was about the fabled and long-lost treasure buried somewhere in my old house here in Kefalonia. Hearing it again, I accepted that it could equally mean the treasure that lay dormant inside the deepest part of me.

I had never connected with that anger when I'd revisited my horrendous childhood abuse. I could look at it and feel nothing. I knew I had disassociated from the feelings, split off, buried my pain, stuffed it down, and I didn't know how to reconnect with it. The thought of losing control frightened me. I was afraid to open the lid and look inside the box. What would bringing my anger out into the light mean? Would it affect my standing as a healer, a creativity coach, a retreat facilitator? I feared I'd be perceived as flaky, unhinged, on the edge, unable to hold safe space, and worst of all, not good enough.

What if the women who paid to come didn't think I was good enough? Or worse, what if they thought I *was* 'sorted' enough, wise enough, clever enough? I never want to be judged. I had been judged as a child and I had not been believed. I hadn't been believed then, or later on as an adult when I spoke of my abuse. It was easier to keep a lid on my pain and claim anger on behalf of other women.

This was a huge realisation for me. Despite twenty-five years of intense training, I still didn't feel clever enough or good enough to inspire and deliver with authentic self-belief and confidence. I opened up to the reality that my inner child was still crying out. This beautiful kid who experienced vile abuse from the time she could walk and talk – the kid who saw ugly in every mirror and wore a permanent cloak of shame. This kid hadn't been held or heard for a long time. Not really. Why else would she cover herself in layers of fat as protection? The child who grew into a woman kept the layers of fat firmly in place, and added to them as a means of defence against shame, vulnerability and pain. Training programmes, courses, seeking information and gathering knowledge became the norm. Businesses and success, leading to exhaustion, burnout and failure, were established as a lifelong pattern. Do more, seek approval, not get approval, do more, seek out approval. More was never enough.

Friends and acquaintances in my circle don't understand why I need more, why I never feel good enough. They can't understand why I doubt myself. I don't bother telling anyone anymore. They don't believe me anyway. *You, scared? You, unconfident?* I hear disbelief in their voices. They never realise their tone only serves for more shame to seep out. Shame for daring to feel less than enough. I knew my constant course-taking and making notes and reading books were one way of hiding the festering wound that burst to the surface from time to time. Much as I love knowledge and learning, I also knew I was in a holding pattern to keep childhood pain at bay. The child within knows. The child who cries for approval knows. Her pleas weren't often heard, so intent had I become on saving others.

I have been led to look more bravely into the mirror of self, to witness what effect some of the events of the past few years have truly had on me; a new retreat guest, beautiful in her energy, reflecting back some things I needed to see; my need for approval; a friend's post; binge-eating; my mother's passing; unmet needs and a desperate feeling of loneliness that my usual activities didn't quell. Time alone sitting with pain and loss, grief and anger. My old friend, anger.

I see that for fifteen years, despite holding a safe space for my clients to enter, to sink into, to yield, to share, and to begin their healing journey, I haven't honoured myself with such a space. Honouring oneself was an alien language in my childhood world.

My first understanding about self-honouring, self-realization and enquiry, came to me in my teens when I started reading books that set me alight. Dale Carnegie, Carlos Castaneda, Pablo Neruda, and a host of others who spoke of thoughts becoming things and inner self-development. I grabbed at their wise words with both hands to help me navigate the long climb out of self-hatred into a popular, attractive woman; at least on the surface anyway. I thought I was honouring myself by becoming bigger, better and cleverer, and along the way I became tough and not to be messed with. My dad showed approval. My mum remained silent under his control.

It was male energy that got me through the hell of my childhood and teenage years, the business years and the *making a difference for others* years. I'd thought this was the best way to go; it did the job temporarily. What working this male energy hadn't done was allow me to give myself soft nurturing feminine energy to apply to the tender parts of my childhood wounds, which was desperately needed for me to step onto the next part of my life's journey. The Divine Feminine was being kept down and I needed to integrate it fully with the masculine energy I predominantly used. This is the way to true and authentic healing.

Since I began really exploring Divine Feminine energy, it has stunned me just how much anger I have been holding onto deep inside. I have an unheard voice that is so angry, so fucking angry that it has never been heard, let alone honoured. I was angry with how I perceived feminine energy had let me down, even though I'd had strong women in my life as a child and an adult: strong aunts, opinionated grandmothers, Irish women relatives who didn't give a fig about doing the right thing. They wore red lipstick, smoked like chimneys, swore like fishwives and drank in the afternoons. They seemed to do as they pleased. Or did they? Did these strong wild women not also iron their husbands' shirts weekly, run their baths, polish their boots, and have their dinner on the table at 6pm every night? I had thought their rebellious ways encapsulated the energy of the Divine Feminine. I thought that *was* the Divine Feminine. In part it was, but it wasn't authentic; it was a mask, taken off when the men in their lives showed up. They closed their eyes to the child abuse that was going on right under their noses – the awful, degrading, horrendous abuse that my cousins, my sisters and myself all experienced but weren't able to tell about. They never protected us. They never spoke out.

Did they know? Did they see? Were they abused by their father who was systematically abusing their daughters, their grandchildren? Surely this wasn't how Divine Feminine operated.

I used to read about strong, kind, gentle women in the world, women who protected the vulnerable, but I didn't know any of them. They didn't live on our road, that's for sure. Even my strongest, most supportive, favourite aunt couldn't protect me against the blatant never-ending cycle of abuse. Sadly, and so disappointingly, she was complicit alongside my mother in her silence. Fear is a great silencer. During my childhood days, silence reigned. Nuns, teachers, doctors and friends never 'saw' what was happening to me. Never suspected. I used to visit a beautiful life-sized statue of Mother Mary in the nuns' garden at the convent I attended. I wasn't supposed to be there, but I loved to sit at her feet and look up at her, beseeching her to rescue and save me. She was holy. I knew about miracles. My name was given to me after a saint. Bernadette. Surely Mary could make life better for me. It never happened, and the abuse continued.

One very old nun used to look at me knowingly. She was tiny. Her weathered, wrinkled hand used to take mine, and she'd whisper *if you ever want someone to talk to, you can come to me.* I knew the way she whispered it she was frightened of the other nuns, who could be terrifying. I never believed her. I was seven.

Looking at my childhood, I realise it was a double-edged sword being a young girl in our family. You had to have manners, take notice of your father, do the right thing, be a good girl, and don't upset anyone's apple cart. You also had to punch harder, drink everyone else under the table, be fiery and ready to fight for your rewards, and be like a son. Until your father told you to watch your temper, and then you had to show contrition. Was it any wonder the eldest girls in our family were confused, defiant and rebellious, and the younger ones got away with murder? Their path had been well trodden by the older girls, who were used to being punished for treading it.

Reflecting on all these realizations and feelings, I knew it was time to let the anger flow. I wasn't sure what to expect. Would I crumble or would I fall? Would I sink into a never-to-rise-from-again depression? I felt like shit. I self-medicated: chocolates, crisps, chocolates, crisps. Not that much, but having been free from processed food and sugar for three months, I was disappointed with myself and I couldn't look at the face in the mirror. I didn't however break my fifteen-year abstinence from alcohol or cigarettes, tempting though it was, so that was a positive.

Anger surfaced almost every day. Showing up in different ways. Numbness. Self-sabotage. Shame. Busyness and feeling very snarky and bad tempered, both with myself and others. I looked at the waves of different emotions washing over me during this period. I allowed them to come, I sat with them, and even put some under a spotlight. I became an observer and patiently waited for my Divine Feminine energy to rise up and show herself. I invited her in to share the platform with the ever-shrinking dominant male energy that I'd got so used to using. I asked her to help me heal my anger and disappointment with the women in my life who hadn't been able to give me the protective space that I needed and deserved, but who still taught me so much.

I read and re-read the deep and probing questions offered by my friend and editor Sue, who had invited me to share my story. Without judgement. An offer I took up without knowing why. The first seed of the Divine Feminine energy to assist me in my ongoing healing journey. I re-read her story and tried the questions on for size several times. I got to it and did my homework to help me process and understand the true nature of the Feminine Divine. I've tentatively unpacked what that energy means to me, how I see it, what it feels like, where it is missing, and how I can allow it to show up in my life. I want to learn to embrace it as a regular part of my daily practice.

My insidious gremlin comes barging in, uninvited as usual. Like all inner critics, its main aim is to keep me static, unmoving and unchanging. It wants to usurp my excitement. Change is definitely in the air. My old critic, who I affectionately call Arthur, wants to shoot me down in flames and he attacks me often.

Things do feel different. The energy around this feels different. Usually I fight Arthur with gusto and end up exhausted. I've been exhausted for too long. Taking a breath to look at this new feeling, I see that fear has been directing my show and has long had a habit of doing so. It's time to invite a softer, more nurturing, less battle-driven energy to assist me with the changes I want to make. I want to feel more compassionate towards myself. I am slowly leaving the need for others' approval by the wayside and I'm embracing the strength and the softness of empathetic Divine Feminine energy.

I know I already know enough. All the training, courses, and seminars had my knowledge banks stuffed so full I couldn't see the wood for the trees. I am learning to create a clearing to sit and allow gentle guidance to appear. For years I have operated using an uncompromising, masculine, *kick up the arse* self-talk to guide me. Now I realise why.

The male voice was the voice of the first man I met and loved. It was the voice of my father. When this realisation came, I saw how for the whole of my life I'd been trying to rewrite my life story with male energy. Probably from birth; certainly, until now.

I was so busy trying to make my dad notice me, seeking his approval in order for him to protect and guide me, I had no time to trust or allow any softer energy to help me. My father gave crumbs of approval, disguised as love. If you did what he wanted, followed what he said, and loved him above all others, he would offer kind words. Looking back, I can see how confusing that must have been for me, a small abused child who thought everything bad was her fault. Too knowing, too wounded and vulnerable, used by whoever chose to use her.

From this unhealthy platform I grew into a dutiful daughter, shining my bright light over my whole family, *a good clever girl*, a product of my father's making, enabling my father to step out from his own shadows and into his daughter's light, where he didn't have to look behind him anymore. I was his beacon of hope. I became a massive disappointment to him though by becoming fat, not going to university, leaving home at seventeen, working in a factory, and not following the carefully laid out plan he had mapped for me. In his eyes, I had pierced his heart and he would never recover. He began to drink heavily to escape the disappointment with how his life had turned out, refusing to take responsibility for his own choices as a young man. I tried even harder to please him, while still doing my own thing. The more disappointed he became, the more abusive he was towards me. He refused to let me speak out about my childhood abuse, even when I worried about the safety of my much younger sister being left with the grandfather who had abused me and my other sister and my cousins when we were small. This was the nail in the proverbial coffin. I felt devastated that once more I wasn't believed or championed.

It's funny how a lifetime's story can hit you, like a dam bursting, in just a few seconds. In the blink of an eye, unseen words swirl through your head, hurtling towards you with unstoppable urgency, desperately searching for a place to land, a place to be seen, a place to be witnessed. I didn't have any great spiritual awakening with this profound realisation. I'd heard the soul whispers often enough but never let them out into the light to be properly examined. I've had lots of *Aha!* moments but never stopped long enough to process what they were, not in any great depth.

I've been too busy seeking approval from a father long gone and a mum who has since joined him. Perhaps this has been the catalyst for the slowing, the pausing, despite fear never being far away.

As I read over this piece, I catch sight of my clenched fist, and **I know that in opening up to be vulnerable, fear is lurking, waiting to taunt me with scary thoughts. I have written it anyway.** I've slowed down long enough to allow more of the Divine Feminine energy to be felt, and to witness how that really feels, without judgment or attachment. I'm genuinely interested in seeing how this will impact the next part of my life journey and I'm looking forward to the synergy of both male and female energy working in balance, which can only serve to nurture and enhance Divine Feminine healing.

I've come a long way since the days of my childhood being brought up on a tough council estate and I have had to dig deep to find my true and authentic self. I have had to become vulnerable enough and brave enough to embrace who I truly am, without alcohol to act as a bridge to confidence. It was ropey at the best of times! If someone had told me twenty years ago that I would work with women and women's issues, I wouldn't have believed them. But I am, and I know this to be an integral part of my life purpose. I am deeply honoured that I can be a voice for those who cannot be heard. I still have a long way to go. I know there is more exploration and excavation to do. There are still gaps and wounds to heal, **I am a wonderful work in progress.** An unfinished woman who climbs up the spiral to wholeness and falls down it from time to time. Each time climbing back up with more clarity and vision.

I have a much clearer understanding about the voice of the Divine Feminine now. I love that it can be both male and female, strong and soft, wild and gentle; not black or white, more a beautiful shade of divine grey, strong in intensity yet gentle in appearance. I can embrace the notion of the Divine Feminine with a deeper authenticity and truth. I know this is just the beginning of my exploration into the next part of my healing and purpose. It is an accumulation of past learnings, synchronistic happenings, and inner introspection, shining a light on the path ahead of me. I'm stepping into its brilliance, safe in the knowledge that it has been waiting patiently for me. It will take work and regular check-ins with my wisest self to ensure I am still on the right path and not dropping into fear or lower energy, just as I know it will take a lot more small steps to say *This is me* without having to use the voice of male anger to feel heard. I can quietly remove the mask of the funny one, the hilarious one, the crazy lady, whenever I choose, and step into a sacred confident energy more in line with who I truly am, and who I am aspiring to be. **My gifts of humour and joy won't go to waste; I just won't be using them to hustle for approval or ego strokes.**

We know we know our stuff inside out; we teach it, we talk it and we walk it. Yet, if we are honest, often we don't truly feel it from the depth of our soul. We sometimes become so used to the hamster wheel we forget to get off and reconnect with the forgotten parts that hold the most healing.

We forget about embodying a sacred way of life and we jump into the next thing that brings recognition in the outside world. Is it ever enough? Not really. Eventually we are forced to ask, is this it? When we feel this, what we most need is to reconnect with our soul and heart energy and allow the truth to guide us forward, healing as we go, allowing ourselves to find balance.

Writing this part of my life story, an image comes to mind: a child's see-saw, neither end up in the air, but level, with a book resting gently in the middle. I can see where I have been writing the same pages over and over: writing, erasing, writing, erasing, with each up and down of the see-saw. It's time for me now to embrace balance long enough to get more than a few pages written. By strengthening my foundations, I can return to balance more easily when the dips come, and they will. I can write the next chapters in strength, and with integrity for what holds true here and now. My mantra must be **My toolbox is full enough. I am enough, I have all the tools I need.** My journey, like many other people's journeys, is a healing one, and I feel safe in the knowledge that Divine Feminine energy will guide me well; sometimes gentle, sometimes strong, at other times with a wild roar.

I now know how much Chiron energy has touched the souls of those who have come to me for therapeutic guidance and healing. In Greek mythology, Chiron the Centaur is half-brother to Zeus. In astrology, he is a planetoid that orbits between Saturn and Neptune, symbolised by the wounded healer. It represents our deepest wound and our efforts to heal it. Chiron was ironically a healer and teacher who could not heal himself. It's no accident that my true-life purpose has always made itself known: healing others, and through others healing myself.

As I grow and heal, I feel confident in trusting myself enough to surrender to the Divine Feminine and allow my deepest wounds to heal as I embrace my Libran principles of mirroring and objective observation. Integration into the light is something I will remember to remember. **It's okay for me to be 'less than' and to share that.** In doing so, it makes me more than the person I was, who expended so much energy hiding my perceived lack, and overwhelming myself with ever more information to fill the gaps I thought were there.

Spirituality for me is a connection to something that I don't have all the answers to, something that waits patiently for me to ask for its guidance and healing light. I've made many journeys since that seven-year-old asked Mary for guidance and felt let down when no help came. No doubt I will make many more, accepting and using what is offered by my angelic and earthly goddesses, instead of trying to go it alone.

It's not only important to do the work I love; it's vital. Using art and words as healing tools, I can find depth and clarity. I also heal myself and I help others to do the same. Embracing the wisdom that comes from deep listening, my heart centre overflows with new-found soft feminine nurturing. I believe in holding space that is non-judgmental, wise, sacred and loving. A space that is profound and one that offers deep healing for those brave enough to enter its energy.

We don't have to be perfect. We don't have to know it all. **We are already good enough.** We already have the answers. We are on a pilgrim's journey and the wild, gentle light from our Divine Feminine Energy can help dissipate the ugly shadows of shame, assist us to climb our mountains and navigate the rocks in our way. It will save us from drowning in a pool of despair and will offer a healing balm for our jagged bits, our raw parts and our hidden wounds. We are, after all, just walking each other home.

As I move now into my crone years, thinking about everything those years are bound to bring, I can confidently assert that I am not damaged, I am not broken. I have the salve to heal the wounded bits, and the polish to make me shine. It comes in a tin marked *Divine Feminine Energy*, and now that I've found it, I will have a great time using it.

Sue Fitzmaurice

Heaven and Hell ~ Softness and Fire

I was born on the evening of 9 October. My older brother was born a year earlier on the morning of 10 October. My mother hoped I'd hold on so we had the same birthday. No such luck. I wanted my own day and pushed my way out. I've been pushing ever since. At fifty-six, I'm learning how to stop doing that.

The eighteen months from January 2018 to mid-2019 were heaven and hell for me. I knew going into 2018 that I was going to be taking some big new spiritual step up, but I couldn't have imagined in my wildest dreams or nightmares that it would have manifested the way it did. Through various parts of that journey, I struggled with grief, shame, depression, and thoughts of suicide. At various points, I thought I was losing my mind. It was horrific, but I knew all the way along that it was the culmination of a change that had been coming for ten years, if not my whole life.

I was born in Wellington, the capital city of New Zealand, and brought up in a town north of there called Palmerston North, generally considered by those who don't live there to be one of the most boring places on earth. It was very ordinary. I had two parents. I went to school. My father had a temper, and I bore the brunt of it. As a child, I wet the bed, and I was always walloped for it – for years and years. No other solution was ever offered. By puberty I grew out of it, but I was always afraid of my father and resented him most of my life. My mother was very loving, and when she died when I was only twenty it felt like the end of the world. She was forty-six. I was left with a father I was not fond of (I later forgave him and learned to love him) and a brother who had become a fundamentalist Christian, quick to judge, both of them in their own ways. We had no first cousins and only one dotty aunt. My mother's father died a year later from a broken heart, followed soon after by my father's father. The only grandmother I'd known – my mother's mother – had never been one to hug or teach me anything that I now imagine a lot of grandmothers do. She was a selfish and envious woman who, when my mother – her only child – had told her she was dying, notwithstanding the obvious horror of losing one's child, responded back to my mother with *what will happen to me?*

So whatever link I had to the feminine was, at that point, cut off. My mother – tall, beautiful, elegant, affectionate, funny, warm – had been my only connection to it. I looked to some of my mother's close friends for that influence, but it wasn't really forthcoming. Raising my own daughter, I made sure there were a myriad of mother figures around her so that she always had that support and comfort and influence.

Religion and spirituality had been part of my life since I was small. As a very little girl, I would dream of flying around the sky with God. My brother and I went to Sunday School, and at around thirteen we were both confirmed in our church, *All Saints*. Both of us went on to serve at the altar; I enjoyed the ceremony of it all. For a few years, through my early teens, I thought I would like to join the Church and be a priest. Spirituality for me then wasn't what it is now, not by a long stretch, but God was there and very much alive to me.

All Saints is an Anglican Church, a sort of poor cousin to the Church of England. We didn't have religious icons about, and so despite the name, saints weren't part of my world. Oddly, it was the movie – and later the stage play *Jesus Christ, Superstar*, released in 1973, that first really engaged me in the world of Jesus, Mary Magdalene, and the apostles, although then we all understood Mary to have been a prostitute, of course. Otherwise, despite a firm but relatively unformed belief in God, I found it all pretty boring after a while. I engaged very briefly with my brother's Baptist church, and I could see the attraction of the emotional highs that were stirred up by their way of doing things, but all the *Praise Jesus* and *Pass the offering plate* wasn't for me. When I saw a young, poor, single mother put a hundred dollars in the plate one Sunday, I turned my back on what I considered a hypocrisy.

A powerful spiritual experience occurred on my twentieth birthday, when my great aunt – the family matriarch – presented me with a gift from the grandmother (her sister) who I'd never known. In that moment, my father's mother, who had died a few years before my parents met, was standing next to me. Wide-eyed, I told my great aunt she was there. *Yes*, she said. *Of course.* When my mother died a few months later, my interest in religion and spirituality became a passion as I was desperate to find meaning in my grief and to know that she was somewhere.

At twenty-one, I discovered the Baha'i Faith. It was the culmination of an investigation into all the major world religions, where I'd come to the view that all had their good points and oughtn't to be considered mutually exclusive. The Baha'i view was more or less this: each of the great prophets had been sent at different times by the same God, with an underlying philosophy that was the same, and social teachings relevant to the particular period in which they appeared. At twenty-two, I signed up, which is literally what one did to join the Faith. I remained a steadfast and committed Baha'i for the next twenty-two years, serving the Faith both locally and nationally, proud to belong to what I considered a very progressive religion. Among the Faith's many pluses was its principle of the equality of men and women, and the notion that God was both feminine and masculine.

A little later on, in my early twenties, I found Merlin Stone's *When God was a Woman* (1976). As an art historian researching depictions of the Sacred Feminine, Stone's premise was that a dominant matriarchal society with a Goddess-based religion had been destroyed by those – Jews and early Christians among them – wanting to position the Masculine as the dominant power, ruling over women. She asserts much of holy scripture – e.g., the Torah and Old Testament – is a re-writing of history and society, giving ancient feminine symbolism a masculine interpretation. My world changed overnight. I felt validation as a woman that I'd never experienced. Wow! I hadn't consciously seen myself as *less than* as a woman, but I realised I had just the same.

Around this same time, also in my mid-twenties, I learned *Transcendental Meditation*, beginning an engagement with consciousness that hadn't been part of my world before. I spent many weekends in retreat, taking additional courses, and advancing to the TM *Sidhi* programme.[44] This was the beginning of a spiritual life that went beyond the religious one I'd experienced in one form or another most of my life. I began to understand consciousness and experienced it in different forms and at different levels. I felt myself without boundaries in meditation and as one and the same energy with other things around me. As I watered the garden, I was the water and the rose; as I breathed in, I was the air.

Mid-twenties through to mid-thirties were focused on career achievement and making money. I'd been a registered nurse but left to join the medical industry. I was successful, owning my own multi-million-dollar company. I married at thirty-two; our son was born as I turned thirty-three, and my daughter followed a few months prior to thirty-six. Becoming a mother was a massive connection – as it is for many women – to my own feminine power. Birthing and raising a daughter connected me back in some divine circle to my mother that was more beautiful and powerful than anything I'd ever experienced. I felt part of a female lineage then that stretched for millennia, both into the past and into the future.

I left my business behind and focused on raising my children and returning to university to complete an undergrad degree in political science. I went on to complete an Honours year, achieving a First, for me the pinnacle of academia. An MBA[45] followed. My marriage began to fail; it would take several years of leaving and returning before finally calling it quits. I returned to the business world at age thirty-nine, as CEO of a large, national not-for-profit. Several years as a business consultant followed, with another CEO stint in my mid-to-late

---

[44] An extension of TM that accelerates growth towards higher states of consciousness. One of the aspects of the programme is yogic flying, a technique where a mental impulse causes the body to rise.

[45] Masters in Business Administration

forties. A disastrous stint as a senior exec within a large tertiary organisation ensued before I ditched the corporate arena for good.

Meanwhile I had been an active Baha'i and loved the Faith very much, but over the years my frustrations grew at the dominance of middle-eastern[46] Baha'is within the New Zealand (and international) community, not ethnically but 'politically', shifting it away from a liberal Western culture to a more conservative, literal, and slightly fundamentalist one, in my view. In my early forties, a chance consulting contract brought me into the sphere of energy healing and the opportunity to explore who I was and why I was here in ways I never would have otherwise. My awareness of, and need for, a different spiritual world, wider and deeper than I felt I could gain within the Baha'i Faith, led me to resign. I had no regrets and have none now, and I still hold the Baha'i Faith in the highest regard, as I do my many friends within it. I consider it a religion for the times.

After exiting the corporate sphere, I had the good fortune to not have to work for the next few years. It gave me time to consider what I wanted to do next. I wrote a novel. It had been sitting in me a long time, so I knocked it off. I loved writing. It was hard work, but extremely rewarding. I felt sure there would be more books to come, and I began researching and writing a second novel. That remains only partly written several years on, but it's high on the list to return to. In the meantime, several non-fiction works followed, most particularly on the topic of purpose, for which I became known. I coached on the topic and ran courses online. As I developed more knowledge of it, I became clearer on what my own purpose was, which for several years was purpose itself. I worked with women who were becoming their new selves, after divorce, children, career burnout, and other life changes. They were all hearing a call from the universe towards a new path, new meaning, new careers, and fresh purpose. It was fulfilling to be a part of supporting this creativity in their lives.

After I turned fifth-three, both my children left home. I'd been anticipating it for some time, and knowing that I would find it difficult to cope with my empty nest, I prepared myself to travel. These have been the years of the most growth for me, much of it extremely painful, much of it very beautiful, almost all of it unexpected.

I visited friends and places throughout the United States, England, Wales, and Ireland, visiting Scotland many times, India and France several times, Spain, Greece, Morocco, Australia many times, and back and forth a few times to New Zealand. I sailed the Scottish Hebrides, rode a camel through the Sahara, sat in

---

[46] The Baha'i Faith was born in Persia – now Iran – and is still the largest community of Baha'is in the world. They have suffered horrendous prejudice there, particularly following the Islamic revolution in 1979, following which thousands were executed and the community remains without many fundamental human rights. Many Baha'is left Iran prior to this, and many more have left, or escaped, since, settling throughout the world.

prayer and meditation with Tibetan Buddhist nuns in the Himalayas, co-hosted a retreat on an island in Greece, and climbed a lot of mountains. In 2017, I discovered the joys of house-sitting and now have dozens of dogs and a few cats added to the list of wonderful new friends made all over the world.

More than a few miracles occurred.

The first was the discovery at the beginning of 2016 of an older brother I didn't know I had. Ross was the product of a relationship my father had prior to meeting my mother a couple of years later. Dad hadn't told anyone. I suspect he'd never even told my mother or his own parents. Ross and I met in person in November 2016, and it changed my life. We hit it off like a house on fire. We had four or five days together in Wellington, and later I spent time with Ross and his wife and son at their home in Western Australia. I'd noticed many things about him that were very like my father and brother – gestures, physical features – and then realised he was also like me! In some ways, he was *more* like me. He wasn't angry like my father, he didn't judge me as my other brother did, and he accepted me for who I was. **I no longer felt like the black sheep** in my small family. It was liberating. Suddenly, I was normal. I was okay.

Dad died soon after, and since I then had a small inheritance, I allowed myself time to focus on my writing. I'd not been without plenty of time to write, but like most artists, it's hard work switching headspaces from a 'day job' to one's art and feel as productive as one would like to in either. I knew from previous experience that it was better to immerse myself in one thing, so I did that. It was a relief to give up coaching and running courses. It wasn't that I didn't like doing them, but the distance afforded by the inheritance allowed me to view them as not part of my purpose any longer. By the end of 2017, I was aware that something new was coming. I also had some notion that it might be huge. I'd felt a pull to some higher spiritual level, whatever that meant. I expected it might be a little bit challenging. That was an understatement.

I was in south-west France in early 2018 and took a day-trip to Lourdes. I hadn't been there, and it held quite a lot of appeal – I've always liked visiting centres of religious and spiritual significance. It was a beautiful sunny day, and it was also out of season for tourists, which is really the best time to visit.

Lourdes became prominent in 1858 after a peasant girl, Bernadette Soubirous, claimed to have seen the Virgin Mary a total of eighteen times at the Massabielle grotto. Mary instructed Bernadette to dig in the ground at a certain spot and to drink from the small spring of water that appeared there. Soon after this, cures were reported from drinking the water, and tens of thousands have occurred in the hundred and sixty years since.

Above the main church – *the Basilica of our Lady of the Rosary* – is the *Basilique de l'Immaculée Conception*. An icon of the Madonna rests above the altar, which itself is directly above the *Grotte de Massabielle* several metres below where Bernadette received her visions. As I sat there, I felt a profound energy – it was obviously maternal, but very no-nonsense, and hugely embracing. I'd never felt anything like it before, and I wanted to stay in it forever. I wondered if this must be what the cult of Mary was all about, although it had never seemed to me that this was the nature of the image of Mary cast by Catholicism. Had I misinterpreted that depiction, or was it true that Mary was portrayed as something less than this powerful but that there were those who knew better? I bathed in that feeling that has stayed with me ever since. As it turned out, I was about to spend the next year or more following her, and her sister saints, around Europe.

I drove into Spain, and as I passed through this smaller end of the Pyrenees, I heard for the first time the story of the goddess sisters Sekhmet and Hathor and understood their resemblance to Mother Mary and Mary Magdalene, and the recreation of these twin female divines across innumerable cultures and traditions throughout history.

I came across a glorious cathedral dedicated to Mary in the back streets of the old town of San Sebastian, and a more purposeful mission of supporting women to tell their stories was placed before me.

I went on to the exquisite mountain town of Segovia. As I enjoyed a cold beer in the beautiful piazza, I found her again in one of Europe's largest cathedrals, and I started to think I was being followed.

At Malaga Cathedral, I was told to write as though I was writing for God, and I was struck by Light and Energy from several icons and chapels.

Over several weeks through February, March, and April, I experienced the presence of women saints, goddesses, archangels, Avalonian priestesses, lights, energies, dreams laden with purple, and my connections through the ages to other women close to me. I heard untold messages from the many guides who seemed to be with me, and literally saw and felt Light touch me. I began to be drawn to examining who I was as a woman and my own particular balance of softness and fire. I was immersed in the power of the Marys and surrendered to them, to be led wherever they took me. They filled me with their powerful, feminine, healing energy, and I was aware of being cleansed of things I no longer needed.

After visiting the Calanais stone circle on the Isle of Lewis and Harris in the Outer Hebrides of Scotland in June, I received an evening visitation in my ship cabin from a goddess-like woman, blonde, but dressed in Native American attire. I was mystified by such an odd combination. Surely a Native American would have dark hair. She appeared again many times after that and remains with me.

In July, I was in a remote and peaceful valley in Wales, enjoying a month-long respite from a great deal of travel, but it wasn't all roses. By now, I had something going on in me that I was struggling with. There was an emotional vulnerability that had been brewing since the start of the Marys' pursuit of me. I felt like I was in the middle of birthing something huge – some new *me* – and I felt quite lost in it some of the time. I often didn't recognise it or myself, and there was nothing I could grasp hold of and say *That – that thing there – that's the problem* as I'd done before. It was a mystery, and I could only say that it was 'the Marys' – my euphemism now for the general Feminine Divine – pushing something out of me I no longer needed. All I could do was go with it. But I felt raw and exposed and vulnerable most of the time.

Six months into this pursuit of the Marys, there was an obvious reconsideration of my spiritual Self and, consequently, other parts of me, too. I was unsettled. I was vaguely aware of very old insecurities rearing their heads – things I'd thought I'd dealt with decades before: my appearance, my weight, my hair, the clothes I wore. I lacked confidence in who and what I was. I felt clumsy, unsure of myself, even stupid. I ignored it, mainly because it made no sense. I was looking in a mirror and seeing the worst possible me. The discomfort was massive. But I assumed that whatever it was would find its way up and out. There seemed little point in analysing it.

I was conscious that things were changing for me internally as a woman, that there was some new dichotomy of softness and fieriness that I was being called to, which seemed entirely at odds with the very unpleasant way I felt about myself at the time. Above all, I trusted in a process, which I felt sure had to do with the Marys.

Eckhart Tolle describes this experience of **being minutely and intensely caught up in feelings and memory and story as a manifestation of ego and its fear of dying.** The idea of *the dark night of the soul* is where **the ego is fighting its last fight before giving way to the clear light of day.** Our perception of who we are gets turned upside down and every tiny and historical element of our entire inner story whizzes round in our consciousness like a never-ending round of pinball. That's what my mind felt like.

What made it so bizarre was it was also interspersed with many, many moments of exquisite joy.

As I felt nearly ready to explode with unfathomable emotion and distress, I visited the medieval church of St Mary in Totnes, in Devon. I felt awful! I waltzed in and plonked myself before a Mary chapel, and I *begged* for it all to be forced through – whatever *it* was. *Open my heart,* I beseeched with every ounce of sincerity I had. I knew as I did it that it might not have been the best idea.
The next day I felt like utter crap. I thought my emotions were about to detonate. The timing was way off as someone else's needs were front and centre at the time, so I sucked it up as best I could. I can barely explain the angst, the disorientation, the feeling that I was about to birth an alien through my chest wall. Every inch

of me felt ugly. My filter was skew-whiff. I wasn't myself, but I didn't know who I was. I truly wondered if I was going mad.

The next day I felt more myself.

The day after that, though, I felt even worse. I cried off and on through the morning, trying to hide it from people I was with. They noticed, of course, and offered help. I said I thought if I let it out I'd make a very big mess, and now wasn't the time. It felt huge. I wanted to crawl into a dark room and never come out. Every bit of energy I had went into holding on and not letting it all flood out. I felt I'd sweep everyone away if it did. I knew in a few days I could escape to peace and quiet, and it seemed as though then it would shift. *Those Marys!* I kept saying. *It's all their fault!*

At this point I was running pretty much on prosecco, coffee, and chocolate. There was a lot of talk about future plans, but I didn't know what I wanted. It all felt terrifying.

Shattered, I trained back across Devon to a solitary house-sit for a quiet month, in a small and very pretty town near the south coast, with two lovely dogs I'd met before.

When the dam broke, I cried for two days non-stop. I shut myself off. Increasingly, I didn't know who I was, and I continued to wonder if I was losing my mind. I felt completely annihilated. Any ability to function at all was purely instinctual for some weeks.

It's not easy to comprehend one's own unravelling, and I searched desperately for the meaning of it all. One after another, a myriad of friends stepped up, offering genuine understanding and kindness, and reasserting to me my own value and worthiness. Three or four I credit with saving my life more than once.

> *It is an absolute human certainty that no one can know her own beauty or perceive her own worth until it has been reflected back to her in the mirror of another loving, caring human being.*[47]

I felt my task was to go within, feel the pain, and allow it to take me to whatever it was I needed to learn about myself. Things were being pushed up and out that were beyond recognition or understanding, and my own Higher Self was calling on me to examine the deepest levels of my own self-loathing.

Thus began a journey – my dark night of the soul – that took me high and low, then higher and lower, then higher and lower still, and then really bloody low.

---

[47] John Joseph Powell.

I met one of my best friends in Glastonbury, Sarah McCrum, a colleague and coach of many years. *Your job is just to connect to your own soul. Focus on the Light and only the Light – explore it – that's your one job. Don't waste time trying to figure out anything else. There is no explanation, and there is nothing you can do.*

My *Mary Pilgrimage* continued, and I climbed the hill in Abbotsbury in Dorset to Saint Catherine's Chapel and asked her to take away my fear – and she did. I was starting to grasp the value of appealing to the Saints' intercessional power, and I began to invoke whichever female Saint or Deity might be around. I was extremely fragile, and a big part of that seemed to have to do with some re-balancing of female energies. Appealing to the divine and semi-Divine Feminine seemed apropos.

I went to France, this time to a whole series of new and powerful places. The messages I received from each were forceful and instructive. Every one of them had to do with love.

At Vézelay, I felt whole for the first time in months – light, and with a full and open heart. I went to the crypt of the *Abbaye Sainte-Marie-Madeleine* where Mary Magdalene's relics rest. I sat there for several hours during the few days I was there. I felt a golden beam of light run through the crypt from one end to the other, several inches in diameter, in a straight line, from the crucifix at one end, to the Magdalene's relics at the other. It felt like love. It was one of the most supreme opportunities ever to sit and *be* in this glow.

East of Marseilles, I sat in the *Grotte de la Sainte-Baume*, up in the hills, which legend says Mary Magdalene lived in. I knew I had been here before. Everything about it seemed familiar.

At Rocamadour, I had a beautiful experience in one of the several chapels. I suddenly had so much love for myself! I thought *Oh! So this is what that's supposed to feel like!* It made me wonder if I'd ever loved myself before. There was a clear instruction to love the God that was within me, because that *was* me. I felt *so* happy! Joyful! It was one of those messages that shows such a clear path that if you do only that then you'll need nothing else.

At the *Basilique de Sainte-Anne-d'Auray,* in Brittany, I sat in the presence of Saint Anne, the grandmother of all grandmothers. Not quite the same no-nonsense maternal of Lourdes, it was complete acceptance and utter safety.

These experiences are very simple and clear. They are what they are and nothing more, but they are the ultimate expression of whatever it is that they are. The purest form of something. My experience at the basilica in Lourdes was, as I always describe it, 'maternal, embracing, and no-nonsense.' I'm sure there are other sacred places in the world where one can experience 'maternal, embracing, and no-nonsense' just as powerfully, but probably not *more* powerfully. The experience of Mary the Mother as these things is the experience of the most divine expression of these things. Mary is a gateway to them. Which is not to say she is the only gateway to them; there will be other divine figures that provide the same, and other entry points to the divine. And in the end, it is any connection to the Divine that feeds our soul, whether it be via a maternal energy or some other.

It is the feminine energies that open our heart, and it is in the opening of our heart that we grow and expand, connect more readily to the Divine, and thus to our purpose and its unfolding.

One of the great gifts of these many sainted women is the reality of the shame they resisted as opposed to that both imposed on them and given to us in the traditional (i.e., patriarchal) stories we're told of them. Mary Magdalene, for example, was branded for most of history as a prostitute. What a difference it might have made to all of us had the western world been raised on a steady diet of women who truthfully had rejected shame.

Some days my own shame threatened to overwhelm me. It was only as I came to what was ultimately its nadir that I realised the extent and seriousness of it. It didn't relate to anything in particular – it was an accumulation, both from my own life and seemingly from the lives of women before me; it was in my DNA.

Months later, as I thought I was emerging, the Universe stepped up to say *Not yet, you don't.*

I was in Ireland. The scab from a wound I thought healed was ripped off, and shame descended in torrents. I wanted to die. How was this part of my growth? What did this have to do with being more spiritual, being a woman, softer, fiercer? This was shit! I felt hollowed out, gutted, stabbed in the heart, worthless, shattered. I thought I'd been to the bottom. But, oh no… *this* was the bottom. And it was crap. I thought about throwing myself off the Cliffs of Moher. I wondered if the light fitting in the ceiling would hold my weight. A few weeks later I left Ireland, spent a week in London, and then I was off to India. Distance and a whole other cultural divide seemed like a good idea.

For a week I drowned, dying every day, wondering how many of which drug I could take to end it all. Each day, India saved me. I meditated as much as I could. I sat with a Buddhist friend. I pitched up at my guides and said *Oi! You want me to go through this?! Give me some bloody answers, because I swear…!*

Answers came:

Stop pushing.

Those two words shone a light on the last ten years of my life, if not my entire existence.

On and off through my adult life, I've raged, bemoaned, grieved, despaired, and immersed myself in a long list of pains I believed were inflicted upon me by others – lovers, friends, employers, fathers, brothers, sisters – waiting for apologies, resolution, or someone's return to my life. **I wanted to know why!** Why had those things happened? Why was that person so cruel? Why did they do that to me? Aren't I a good person?

It took a week. Shame sloughed off, bit by bit. Calm like no other descended. Light shone, lighter and clearer than ever. And I was that Light. Power – a different power, something I struggle to put into words yet – became who I was.

There weren't answers to the *whys*. There didn't need to be. I could choose immersion in the pain or the light. It was that simple. Pain didn't have to be got rid of – perhaps *couldn't* be – but I didn't have to inhabit it.

Without *the Marys*, I would not have taken this crucial journey through and beyond my own shame, my darkness, my shadow. **I was hit so hard that I had no choice but to surrender.**

I emerged – into softness and fire. I'd wondered how I would know when I was through the other side, if indeed I would ever get there at all. Energetically, now, I'm a different woman. Stripped bare by *the Marys*, but held in the collective palms of their hands throughout, I fell into my own darkness, eventually accepting it, and with that it turned into light. Everything in my life now vibrates with the power of the Divine Feminine – the people I meet, the places I go, the work I do, the clients that come my way, the projects and ideas that flow through me. The masculine was always there, albeit not always divinely so, but I was disconnected from the feminine. As she blossoms and emerges within me, the masculine around me is allowed now to just *be*. I don't need to fight anymore, least of all myself.

This isn't an end though – it's another beginning. There'll be more. So much more. There'll be blissful highs, but I hope fewer lows. I remain saddened by the loss of two friends unable to stand by me, no doubt due to the burden I now see I had become. They were soul sisters, and I feel their absence still. When they come to mind, I imagine them sitting across from me in a noisy café; I smile, and my heart fills with love. In the here and now, though, it is no mistake that I place my story in between those of four women who saved my life more times than I can count, and among others who have also held my heart in their hands for a moment or a while, who've listened and not judged, who've understood that to *allow* is one of the greatest gifts any woman can give another – any human can give another. If I've been able to do the same for them, that too is their gift to me.

I don't know when I'll stop travelling. It's not on the cards yet. The more you see of the world, the more you realise there is to see, and the more you want to see it. It intrigues me how places and things can hold particular energies, often powerfully so. Certain mountains and landscapes, buildings and even ruins – the Himalayas, the Scottish Highlands, Celtic Ireland, cathedrals, stone circles, and icons. These are the places I want to go. When I pilgrimaged to Israel twenty years ago, a wise old man said *You don't come here to be a sightseer; you come here to soak up the Energies of the Holy men and women who walked here.* I still want more of that. There are depths to plumb, and as a Seeker I will continue to dig for them. I'm a Finder now, too, though. I've found so much; I've been *given* so much. I'm deeply, deeply grateful.

Besides that, my purpose remains to write – and to that now is added the role of midwifing others' stories into the world also.

I haven't always succeeded in being a voice for women – my own noise has been known to quiet others, often in ways I'm not proud of. Like everyone, **my past must remain unchanged, even as I endeavour to cast my mistakes in a new light, as lessons,** hopefully learnt, forgiving myself and sending love to those I've variously shushed and stifled. Healing is a habit requiring daily practise – it's not a magic that suddenly appears. It's hard, and it's not always pretty. It also needs *allowing.*

Allowing is a distinctly feminine quality. It's new for me, and it's very sweet. As I head into my crone years, I'd like to think it may become a signature of mine.

Stacey Phillips

Divine Me

Writing this has been, like many things in my life, a kind of haunting; something that I have been so conflicted over, yet something I wanted to do. For months and months, I have struggled to commit. I have fought myself, and given myself every reason not to do it. Eventually, and like most things in my life, I took a long hard look at why? The title is what irritates – *Journeys with the Divine Feminine* – I struggle to know if that is a thing, something I don't know that so many others of my gender do? I haven't found the answer to that, but perhaps that is just another part of my complex and peculiar character. In any event, I was nudged and cajoled, time and time again to contribute. *Contribute* – there is a word that perhaps answers much of my resistance. Do I actually have something to *contribute?* I'll leave that aside for a while. Journey to the divine feminine…

It's a weird thing about life: you spend your childhood being grown up when you're not really, and then in your adulthood, actually trying to do the growing up you should have done at the time you were busy faking it!

I have an issue with the notion of Divine Feminine. I've spent my life struggling with gender bias and battling to retain my femininity, whilst competing within a male dominated working environment.

My life was fast, fierce, and some might say totally fabulous. Oh, what a fall I had! I did everything on my not yet invented bucket list. I mean, really – bucket list? I throw shit into buckets, not dreams, desires and aspirations. I guess I was always hungry. Hungry for... everything! Love, knowledge, adventure. Life, I lived it big. I lived it real. I clawed to the top of the mountains and the depths of the oceans. For life, for love, to feel – to truly feel. I kept going, I held my breath, I jumped, I learnt how to land; other times I was lucky to find someone to catch me.

I was born to what seemed on the outside a normal middle class family, rich some might say, a bit posh and kind of normal.

No one understood why I used to say the things I said. I was dramatic and attention seeking. It must have been the youngest child syndrome. But when the school suggested that *this is really an establishment for refined nice ladies, and perhaps she needs a little bit of a freer environment* they knew I was not your average ten year old. Bringing up a spirited, untrained, untamed race horse, with no experience, when you don't even like animals, was never going to be easy.

Raised in a Jewish family, heritage and tradition were key factors. We lived in a predominantly Jewish area and thus school and friends were also mainly Jewish. Yet my family was so different. My parents where complex people. My father had two daughters from a previous marriage and my mother was twenty-two years his junior. I became an aunt at age two, and my father's love and attention for me was swiftly and painfully transferred to the new born granddaughter, the child of his first born, who moved into our house with her foreign crazy boyfriend, having left her foreign respectable husband.

I recall being somewhat ashamed of my 'old father'. People would often mistake him for my grandfather, and after all he did have a granddaughter just two years younger than me. My eldest half-sister was only five years younger than my mother, and so my mother was often looked upon as the 'bit of fluff that married the old wealthy man.'

With hindsight (what a wonderful thing), I think I was raised with ever-pressing, strict, almost Victorian moral values, in some vain attempt to keep me from falling into similar disrepute. I was staunchly wilful, and my mother's mantra was *I will break you!* Did she succeed? Never, ever, ever. That's the wild in me – the part of myself that I cling to – that did not and will not conform.

The female role models of my mother, grandmothers and aunts, were, in the main, very traditional: homemakers, cooks and housekeepers. Later on, after the kids had grown, they may have had jobs, but nothing needing much skill or intellect.

My eldest half-sister was estranged in quite traumatic circumstances when I was five. There were ghosts – so many ghosts – in my family's closets. It was a carpet with many lumps, formed from all the shames hidden thereunder. I accept secrets in my family as much as I accept inequality – not at all. I am driven to know as much as I can – to not get tripped up by the unexpected.

My mother's younger sister was my idol as a child. She was a little wild and no one seemed to object to that in her. There were excuses for her that I didn't know till later on. My eldest half-sister was hardly ever talked of after the 'incidents'; my other half-sister, thirteen years my senior, was a teacher, but this was undervalued as she didn't 'earn good money' and was 'never going to be a great success.' So the message I was given was: be a good wife and mother but we won't really respect you, or be a successful business woman and then you will have achieved and we will be proud. All of this programming led to an internal battle: follow the role models and accept the disdain at the perceived lack of success, or sell my spiritual soul to the perceived successes in consumerism and materialism. This split in values fuelled my need to find my own way. I couldn't find a way to live the dichotomy I was raised with, thus I battled for what I wanted. I got my first weekend job at thirteen and planned my escape at fourteen. The biggest lesson I was taught – which I am grateful for – was to ensure, at all cost, that the roof over one's head is safe. With a roof you can grow; without it, it is so much harder. Perhaps this is why, in later life, working with the homeless became my passion and a saviour of sorts.

As the nurturers (the women) were not financial providers in my world, it is no wonder I found myself completely torn as a working mother. I became a mother fairly late in life as I had convinced myself I did not want children. My parents had died in quick succession, leaving me with a baby and a business, and no hierarchy to answer to, to lean on, or to learn from. How to be the mother I wanted to be *and* run a successful business was a huge struggle. There became less hunger for the business successes that I soon understood were in some part tied to the parent approval I was still so desperately seeking. The mental and physical shift in roles was harder than I could have imagined – work became untold stress and pressure when all I desired was to hold onto the precious child I had birthed so soon after the loss of my parents. Grief turned into many things, as circumstances denied me the opportunity to grieve naturally.

My parents became functional alcoholics early on in my life and exceptionally *non*-functional by my late teens and twenties. I developed a highly attuned hypervigilance in order to firstly distract them and others from their imbibed behaviours, and then later to take control of more menial things like cooking the dinner for the extended family due to arrive shortly for Jewish High holy days, after putting my mother to bed as she was 'unwell.' I had to hide and later on confiscate car keys from their home. I never questioned any of this. I was a doer, born or bred. Nature or nurture? A strong dose of both, I suppose.

In my family, children were to be seen and not heard and that went deep. I mean, we were never, ever really heard; we did not have the right. We were children and therefore knew nothing. From a young child, my brother, the son and heir, was the prince who sat beside me, seemingly always doing right. He could not do wrong, yet I could do no right. His path seemed to me to be straight and easy, defined, and cushioned in red velvet; whereas mine was covered in glass. It seemed I had so much more to conquer and achieve, so many more pitfalls and so many more mountains to climb. I raged at the expectations that were placed on me merely due to my sex. *Clear the table* I would hear them say. *He has the same number of hands as me, Why?* Why? Why? This continues today with my partner and my two sons, all of whom still try hard to choose which stereotypical roles they are prepared to partake in and which not.

So you see when one is impeded by the need for gender equality, the Divine Feminine has been, and to some extent still is, a difficult concept for me.

143

I grew up in a time of the ultimate feminine dichotomy – as a woman you must be a) feminine; b) a carer and homemaker, a lady, a wife, a mother; and most of all you must be c) independent, physically and financially. You can and will have it all; in fact, you must! The overriding feeling for me was that if you don't, you will be a failure: to yourself, to your parents, to the female gender as a whole.

My masculine energy abounded as my path had been created to chase the dreams, the financial and physical successes, for approval – always deep down for approval. My innate sense of self, or some might call it my Divine Feminine, was tenuous in the extreme, derived from success and thus approval, be it from others or self. Everything was a challenge to be conquered. I held my breath with each challenge, and with each victory came a gasp of air to heal and grow from.

I embraced spirituality in mid life. I had touched upon my search many times in my youth, and had often been told that I had 'powers' and 'should learn more'. I spent my youth knowing this was true in my soul, yet waiting for the calling, the flashlight, the thunderbolt from the universe. I guess it came, in a way, quietly and persistently. I didn't go looking for the channelled connection, but the universe kept nudging me with messages that became more and more difficult to ignore. I suppose being a mother (and no one's child) had taught me to slow down, to become gentler and more inquisitive, and to listen and hear rather than hear and do. I came to realise that for me, in my world, there is a higher power, a god, that dishes out challenges upon challenges, lessons to learn or relearn. I believe the challenges are in an endeavour to improve me, in order that I may have an easier journey in the next existence: a demi-god or Archangel if I'm lucky and do well this time.

Spirituality helped me understand the innate complexities of each of my children, especially one who saw and communicated with spirit before he was even fully verbal. Perhaps that was the catalyst that pushed me towards a more spiritual life. Was it my father, in spirit, pulling me? Or was it the universe using my father to draw me in? Would I have found my way there had it not been for my son's connections to him? The most important tenet was and still is that my children feel listened to, supported and loved, and this I try to extend to all I meet.

I became a healer, a spiritual channeller and a medium, not for financial gain but for the benefit of those I love. I listened and followed the messages that presented themselves to me. I became interested in the connections between psychotherapy, hypnosis and spiritual mediumship. It was via these messages that I was led to work in the soup kitchen. I was probably the most fulfilled in that role, as I was able to utilise both my masculine and feminine skills for the greater good of others. I took my (masculine) business skills and turned a small kitchen running on a tiny donation into a large kitchen with free abundant food donations before supermarkets ever considered donations. Yet, I also cooked, nurtured, organised clothing collections and sales, put on Christmas lunch for two hundred people, with gifts for all: socks, soap, sleeping bags – all for zero cost. It made my heart sing – my *yin* and *yang* were at last aligned.

In my forties, I developed fibromyalgia and Chronic Fatigue Syndrome/ ME, and later on a plethora of other autoimmune diseases, one of which – ironically since both my parents were alcoholics and I don't drink – is a rare autoimmune liver disease. I was initially told I would require a transplant within five years, a diagnosis that hit me like a fifty-tonne truck. I detached myself from all things spiritual for a long time. How could I be connected and working for the greater and higher good if I was paid back like this?! I still struggle with this and try to find a balance somewhere with living my values and beliefs and my own sense of it all. Whilst I still believe there is a higher purpose, a higher meaning, a higher force, **I no longer reach and follow for anything externally, and find more peace reaching within, back to the essence that has always been in me,** before parental and societal indoctrination dulled the connection.

I believe in the mind body connection to some extent, and as a highly sensitive person, I am mindful of how much this is an aspect of my many diagnoses and ailments. What I do know is that I know so very little, and that what I know today may be irrelevant or inappropriate for tomorrow or the next day. Life is a constantly evolving landscape. When I stop and allow it all to just be, life is calmer, more peaceful and often times less painful.

My journey with the Divine Feminine is more a journey to the divine within me. I still and always will endeavour not to divide the sexes. **We are all a part of both the masculine and feminine.** I grew up in a time where women were fighting for equality and it seems to me that there is a growing emphasis on dividing the genders yet again, albeit from a more powerful female platform. For me, equality rules, and I hope and pray that that tenet will gain more and more traction as time goes by.

Swati Nigam

The Warring Goddess & the Archangel

I have always seen the Divine as one unified force. Not as masculine or feminine. Sure, I have acknowledged and loved the feminine and masculine forms of this unnamed, formless Divine, but when I think of God, God is not feminine or masculine.

As I struggled with writing this, God asked me to take a walk and talk to him (*him* is a neutral gender for me when talking of the Divine because writing *he/she* all the time is tiresome).

I went outside and looked at each flower in my garden and soaked in their beauty, thinking of how I could recreate them in watercolor.

A gentle voice within said, *This, my precious daughter, is your Journey with the Divine Feminine.*

I asked, *What do you mean? Painting?*

She replied, *Yes, and everything else. **Everything you see, everything you do, everything created is a function of the Divine Feminine. You are Divine Feminine in motion.** So is the flower. The seen is Divine Feminine. The unseen observer is Masculine. Remember your roots? Go back to your roots.*

I said, *I understand, but what can I write about my Divine Feminine journey?*

She said, *Your entire life about finding your path, your evolution, re-discovering your likes and dislikes, everything is your journey of the Divine Feminine. Because everything seen, done, and experienced is a function of the Goddess. Therefore, life itself is the journey of the Goddess.*

Ah! I see, but where do I begin?

The roots, my daughter. Go back to the roots.

So here I am.

I was summoned into this world by my mother through a special prayer to the Sun God. My parents had a son – the apple of their eye – but for some reason, they wanted a daughter too. There is a festival in India called *Chatth* where people pray to the Sun God. My mother asked him to send a daughter. And I was born soon after. I see the sun as masculine energy. So, in this case, an aspect of the Divine Masculine sent forth a ray of the Divine Feminine to my parents.

I was not a very happy child. People thought I was happy because I laughed and smiled all the time. It is a habit I have inherited from my mother. But there was always a deep inner sadness. I was not happy with many things. I felt like I didn't belong, and often looked into the stars hoping my real family would come rescue me. Not because I was ill-treated or anything like that – I don't know why, but I just didn't feel at home.

Also, when I looked at life around me, I wondered what it was all about? People were born, they ate, worked, slept. Rinse and repeat, till they are old and feeble. Then they eat and sleep. And then they die. What was the purpose? It seemed pointless and depressing to me. In other words, I was looking for the meaning of life.

Another thing that upset me a lot was the inconsistency between what my Hindu background talked about the Goddess, and how women were really treated. As a Hindu, I have grown up with the idea of the Goddess. The Goddess is the Power. She is sacred. She is worshipped. God (masculine) is the observer. He reflects, he observes. He plants the seed. After the seed of an idea is planted, the Goddess does it all, because She is the Power. She is the Power behind everything – creation, destruction, knowledge, art, wealth, beauty.

Yet, women were treated as *less than* compared to men. And I saw that inconsistency at every step. I was a prayed-for daughter, but my brother was more important and held a higher status than me at home. My mother was the uncrowned ruler of the home, but she believed that men were superior. For her, household tasks were too menial for my brother and father. It was beneath their dignity. But she often told me to do things at home *because I was a girl.*

When it was time to marry, the family of the girl is considered of lower status than the boy's family. The girl's family had to give huge amounts of gifts and money (dowry) to the groom's family. Why? I couldn't understand the logic at all. The girl was supposed to leave her birth family and accept her husband's family as her primary family and serve them, and yet she was the one who had to pay them to get married? Many women were ill-treated if they didn't bring enough dowry.

Women all over the world often get lower salaries than men. Why? None of this made any sense to me. Especially not in India where the Goddess was worshipped.

I was outraged by all of that. I picked up the sword and became the warring Goddess from the time I was little. I was not the sweet, docile girl I was expected to be. I was the fierce one, always ready to strike down any mention of male superiority. So I was labeled rude, heartless, and spoilt. Which made me angrier. And the war continued.

I did all other things expected of me – to study well and get good grades, etc. But the deep discontent within grew. I needed to know if this life was really so meaningless.

When I was in eighth grade, I learned meditation for the first time. I learned because I thought it would help me feel at peace. But when I started practising, I experienced all kinds of things that no one had prepared me for. There was a whole light and sound experience with meditation. Lightning bolts coming into the top of my head with the hissing sound of electricity. It did not hurt, but it was scary.

After the fear died down, I realized that it meant that life was not just what I was seeing. There was much more to life than what we saw. There was life and magic beyond the mundane.

I started to read and learn everything I could to understand what was beyond.

I taught myself to meditate in another way too. This was by focusing on my third eye and repeating *Om*. Later I learned that this was a well-established way to meditate and I was quite pleased that I came to it by myself.

When I started doing this style of meditation, I had my first full-fledged out of body experience. One day I was sitting and meditating, and suddenly I was out of my body. I found myself hanging in what looked like deep space and in front of me was what looked like the sun. Or a huge ball of rotating light. I heard a deep rumbling sound with it – it felt powerful beyond imagination. I was terrified. The ball of light sent me feelings of love, kindness, and humor, but I was still terrified of its power. I struggled to get back to my body, and soon I was back.

There were many experiences after that. But they were not terrifying because I asked God to make it gentler for me. And he did just that.

When I got married, I came wielding my warring Goddess sword. I was used to fighting for women's rights all through my life until then, and I looked at each experience with the eye of *Is this unfair to women? Do I need to slay this?*

And the first morning after my marriage was when this warring Goddess lay her sword down. I was sitting in my unmade bed when my new husband walked into the room and asked, *Why is the bed not made yet?* And I jumped up to fight. Was I supposed to make the bed because I was a woman? Why not him? Why couldn't he make the bed? Who is he to order me around? I asked him, *Why **me**? Why can't **you** do it?* He looked confused, totally unaware of the fight I was fighting. He replied *Yes, I will. But how can I do that if you keep sitting on it?* To him it was not about who did the work, it was about getting the work done, whoever did it.

And with that, I realized that my war was over. At least in my little household, I did not need to fight for women's rights – big or small. My husband did not see us as unequal.

It reminded me of a Hindu mythological story when the demons were causing havoc on earth. The Gods summoned the destructive Feminine Power – the Goddess Kali – to end the problem. She did that, but she was power untamed. She went on a rampage in her fury, destroying all in her path. Then her husband, the God Shiva, lay down in her path to stop her. When she stepped on him, she realized where she was, and her fury died.

I didn't grow up with just Hinduism in my fabric of mind. India gives you the opportunity to be as divided and fanatic as you want to be about religion, regions, castes, and languages, and she also gives you the opportunity to be a person who is a mixture of all the various cultures and beliefs, and carve out your own path and beliefs from that.

I chose the latter.

I had Christianity, and Islam too, molding me as I was growing up. I was sent to Catholic schools and colleges. In India, Catholic schools do not put down other beliefs and religions. We were never coaxed to convert. Every morning we all gathered together in the assembly hall to pray, but other than that we were not given any religious instruction. The Catholics went for catechism class, while the non-Catholics went to Moral Science class where we were taught to be good humans. Because I went to Catholic schools, Jesus was always a big part of my life though. He was my teacher, my friend. He was the one I talked to when I felt no one else would hear me.

Likewise, our family had many Muslim friends. We celebrated Eid with them with as much enthusiasm as they celebrated Diwali with us.

I grew up, not a religious Hindu, but a person who was a mish-mash of different religions, and a person who picked what she liked from each.

When I moved to the United States after getting married, Christianity was not something new for me. I was already part Christian, part Hindu, part Muslim, and part nothing at all.

When it was time for me to think about having my first child, I talked to my teacher and confidante, Jesus. I said to him that I would try getting pregnant only once because I wasn't sure if that was the right time. I applied the same method of meditation, except this time I chanted *Jesus* in my mind instead of *Om*. And I had another full-blown out of body experience. I was scared at first because I was half out of my body and thought I was going to die. Then I was fully out and face to face with Jesus for the first time. He said he was sending me a soul, and that I should take care of it. With that, I was unceremoniously dumped back into my body and I was quite stunned for a while. I found out I was pregnant three weeks later.

After my daughter was born, I stepped further into my spiritual path, the journey I now recognize as the journey of the Divine Feminine. I learned Reiki, and then went on to learn many other healing modalities.

I became interested in angels. Earlier I didn't believe that they existed but one day I saw them. They appeared when I needed them most, and that's when I realized they really did exist and that they were powerful beyond belief.

I began developing my communication with the angels with the help of angel cards at first, and soon realized that I didn't really need the cards – they were already talking to me through my mind.

I felt especially drawn towards Archangel Michael. When I was new to angels and wanted to know all about Michael, a fabulous angel channeler told me Michael had said to him, *Tell Swati,* **I am that part of her that guides. And she is that part of me which is sweetness.** And that was another way to show how the Divine Masculine and Feminine work together as a whole. He was the guide and observer (masculine). And he showed me that I was sweetness – the nurturing side of the Feminine.

Since then, I have chosen to work closely with Archangel Michael, whether it was with angel readings I was doing, or with healing, teaching, or life coaching. I consciously made him a part of my life and work. He said he had always been a part of me and my life. But as for me, it was a conscious choice to acknowledge that.

Acknowledging his presence brought its own problems, which led to my further spiritual development as Divine Feminine.

I wanted to see him. I could see the non-physical as a 'knowing' always. But not as images, in my mind or with eyes open. So I requested, demanded, pleaded that Archangel Michael show up to me. He didn't. And I got really mad. The sword was picked up again. This time to fight the divine. I now find it funny. But at that time, I didn't. It was a very serious business for me, the business of seeing Archangel Michael. I threatened him that if he didn't show up, I would not work with him. He still didn't show up. And my tantrums continued. He silently and patiently explained this was for my own good but I couldn't see why this was for my own good. So he, the Masculine, guided the Feminine Power within me. He said *Because if I just show up, you will not learn to develop your clairvoyance. Stop asking and begging.* **Do it.** *You have the power to.*

And I got it! Yes, of course! I didn't need to beg him. **I had the Power of the Goddess Shakti within me to do what I pleased.** So I taught myself clairvoyance. And with that, I saw him clearly within my mind, and then I saw his beautiful colors of sparkling cobalt blue all around me all the time. He was ever-present. I didn't even need to call him. It was so beautiful that he was always around me. But now I wanted to see him in a human form. You know: a man with wings. So I talked to him about that, and he said I was seeing him as he really was. He was not human. I said, *But seeing just colors is boring. I want to see you how we imagine you to be – a gorgeous man with wings.* As I continued developing my clairvoyance, that happened too. One morning I woke up to see him standing near my bed. In all his blue-winged glory! Mission accomplished. The goddess within triumphed.

Angels and other non-physical beings are not really humanoid. But they will take on the form that we will be comfortable with. If it is wings that will please us, they will show up with wings.

I wondered about all these different beings. The gods and goddesses. Angels. Archangels. And so many other divine beings. They all had names and forms according to various religions. And that did not make sense to me. Religion is man-made. Divine is not man-made. So how come all religions have their own set of divine beings? I came to the conclusion that God is as I have always imagined him – formless, indescribable. These various forms of him, these divine beings, are more relatable because they have forms and names that we have given them. And yet, they can't be different beings because different religions are not made by God. The conclusion: these beings are the same being. They are called by different names in different parts of the world, by different religions as per their ideas and beliefs.

As I sit here and bring it all back to the roots as the Goddess asked me to, I see that the idea I started with is the one I still have. If I were to divide the force we call God into feminine and masculine, we are both. Our subconscious mind is the Creative Power (Divine Feminine) that creates everything. Our conscious mind is the Observer Guide (Divine Masculine) that plants the seeds.

We, as the Divine Masculine (conscious mind), observe, examine, reflect upon what is, and what we would like created or destroyed in our lives. We then plant that idea within our Divine Feminine Power – the subconscious mind. And when an idea is planted well and received well by the subconscious mind, she creates that experience within our worlds.

Because everything in our life is created by our subconscious mind (the Divine Feminine), everything seen, experienced, and done is a function of the Divine Feminine. Therefore, life itself is a journey of the Divine Feminine.

We work together as one human unit – the Divine Masculine and the Divine Feminine. And when we work as a balanced force as a human or a society, peace and order prevail.

It is all about the balance. We are the Divine Feminine. We are the Divine Masculine. We are One.

And what is life about? My original question was what is the meaning behind it all? This was answered through a beautiful book I read – *Conversations with God* (Part 1). In that, God says that **God is everything. But God needed to experience what God was. So creation came into being.**

I also received this answer through a meditation experience. In one of my meditations I suddenly experienced what this One-ness was about. Everyone talks about all of us being one, but that day I experienced it. I transcended the limitations of being Swati, and felt and knew through experience that I was everything. I was Swati. I was every other human. I was every animal and plant. Every planet and star. Even everything we call inanimate was me. I experienced being one. Just one. It lasted two or three hours where I felt I was All. Along with it came an extreme sense of bliss, love, humor, and so much more. But most of all, Bliss!

Towards the end of the experience I felt a bit sad. I was thinking *I am All. I am Love. But there is no one else to love. There is no one else to be loved by.*

There was no one *else*. There was just me. There was just One. *I* desired to love and be loved, to *experience* love, and not just *be* love.

And then came the realization – the biggest reason for creation, for existence, for all of life is: To Love, and Be Loved. And it all made sense.

To love, and to be loved. To experience love. That is the point of life.

Deb Steele

The Rising of the Divine Feminine and the Feminine Divine

I was raised in an atheist and socialist family in the 50s and 60s, though somewhat paradoxically was also sent to Sunday School as a very small child. The beautiful pictures of Jesus that we were given on stamps to stick into our own little books filled me with a joy and delight which lingered. I grew up to become a teenage hippie who rejected the established church but was drawn to the peace and love ethos of the era which echoed with something in my heart from those Sunday School days.

When I was twenty-two, I gave birth to my first child and it blew away all my understanding of the world as it had been up until then. The chemistry, physics and biology I had been taught at school, and the sociology and psychology learned at university, went nowhere near explaining the wonder and mystery of the creation and birthing of a new human being as I experienced it. It was too huge for my limited self to understand and it led me on a journey, seeking a framework to help me make sense of this expanded experience of reality, which I framed then as either mystical or madness.

For ten years I worked at the hard end of mental health, during the 80s and 90s, the time of closure of the majority of the old psychiatric hospitals in the United Kingdom. As a community development worker for the charity *MIND*, and later as a visiting member of the Mental Health Act Commission, I saw clearly that I was not mad (variable and unreliable a term as that is), though had I shared some of my experiences with some of my colleagues they may have disagreed!

It was a rich and rewarding and frequently challenging path for coming into deeper ownership of my own spirituality. Alongside this were the experiences of being a counsellor, psychotherapist, and counselling trainer and supervisor, experiences where transcendence of the usual consensual notions of reality were tangible and undeniable.

In the early 70s, when I had my son, there were few markers, and very few explicit explorations, of the Divine Feminine. There were some feminist critiques of religion, and some explorations of personal experiences of the embodied divine, and of being a woman in the Christian, Jewish, Buddhist, Islamic, Vedantic faiths, but even these were few and far between. We mostly had no name or home or language for what spoke most deeply to our hearts, those of us who were experiencing these embodied senses of an imminent divinity beyond theology.

Before the age of search engines and social media, arcane knowledge and wisdom was much harder to come by. Monica Sjoo, Mary Daly, and Carol Christ, among others, were writing feminist deconstructions of the traditional religions and reclaiming notions of aspects of the feminine, yet these didn't speak to my heart. Time spent in the women's movement, especially in the early 80s at Greenham Common, when there would be spontaneous actions, a sense of something co-arising, gave me a feeling of the power and depth and potential of something potently 'other' and mystical that could emerge through women connecting in conscious co-operation. But it took my receiving *darshan*[48] with Mother Meera in Germany in the early 90s for me to experience what I would call the Divine Feminine, or the Feminine Divine.

I had been drawn to her since reading Andrew Harvey's *Hidden Journey*[49] about his time spent as her devotee, and travelled to see her with two friends to explore for ourselves the power of her silent teachings. She lived in a small unremarkable house in the dormitory town of Thalheim in Saxony, and we queued outside for entrance, then waited on the stairs before entering the sitting room where all was silent, and we waited our turn to kneel at the mother's feet. The sense of an alert and profound stillness pervaded the room, where Mother Meera sat in a wooden armchair on a slightly raised dais. The protocol is that as you kneel, bow your head, and hold her feet, she places her hands on your head as she unties karmic knots and then, as she removes her hands, you raise your head to look into her eyes. As I was kneeling, I had a surging energy racing through me saying *beloved mother I have been searching for you for so long, for so long I have been a seeker, I have searched everywhere ...* and so forth. As I looked up into her eyes, I heard her within, saying simply in the silence, *So?* It makes me smile now to recall that moment, though I wasn't so amused at the time. So? **Don't take yourself so seriously, no need for urgency,** it's all ok, I'm here now, what's the problem?

In a four day visit we were allowed two darshans. On the second occasion the words that arose in me were ones that have also stayed in my heart ever since, with a different resonance *Mother, the beauty of your Love fills me in its warm embrace.*

Though there are many aspects of the Divine Feminine, and many faces and qualities given to her in different religions and spiritual traditions, that of the Divine Mother is perhaps the aspect with which I resonate most deeply, and these words speak the essence of what she brings me when I connect deeply with her, whether in heavenly form or as our Mother Earth.

---

[48] The viewing of a holy image. It is also reciprocal: seeing and being seen.
[49] 1991

These knowings of the Feminine Divine are often numinous, mutable, changing; and yet they are also in our blood, our bones, our ancestral DNA. As we share our stories of her with each other, in all her wonderful forms, we build cairns to mark the sacred sites we are re-membering and creating, and bring through transmissions which spark ever deeper connections to each other, to the Divine Feminine, to all that is. These are some of my stories of connection.

I'm standing on the beach at Daymer Bay in Cornwall, late September, watching the sunset. As the sun goes down, the almost full moon rises, as though they are in choreographed movement. As a slight breeze stirs, I see that the tide is coming in. We are at the mouth of the estuary of the River Camel and the tide comes in in that particular way where a river meets the sea: rapidly, in swirls and eddies and strong currents. Everything is in motion, and deep in my heart and belly I experience that this is the underlying truth of the natural world. The underlying order of a life which we divide into segments, control by structure, build straight roads and high walls upon, is actually in constant flux and motion. Waxing, waning, ebbing and flowing, cycles and spirals – this is the true nature and order of life that at an animal, creaturely, instinctive level we know in our bodies. As women, particularly so, as our own bodies ebb and flow, wax and wane in synchronisation with the moon and the tides. **This is where the truth of our nature resides, this is what holds, sustains, nurtures, challenges us – these sacred rhythms of our Mother Earth.** And the clouds and the skies and the stars – by which for aeons we have navigated our ways upon the land and the seas – guide our way home. This is the Love in which we are held, this is the way that we are loved, unconditionally every day as the sun and the moon rise and set.

Another beach, another time – this one on the shores of the Red Sea, at the edges of the Sinai Desert. A fierce storm rages from the sea – everything on the beach laid horizontal – either by the wind or by hotel staff trying to protect people or objects from it. An electric storm rages in the sky unlike anything I've ever seen – thunder claps that make the ground beneath my feet tremble, sheets of light across the sky which illuminate the clouds and seas and sand as if it were daylight, all in play with jagged forks of lightning which seem to pin sky and earth together. It is magnificent! I have to use all the muscles in my body to stand upright against the wind and I am enlivened and invigorated and yet so deeply still that I feel as though I could stand here in this elemental tumult for infinity. And in this stillness, I realise that this day is *Imbolc,*[50] festival of Brigid, Celtic goddess of fire and sun.

---

[50] Traditional Gaelic festival held on 1 February, marking the beginning of Irish spring.

The day before, I had been at the foot of Mount Sinai in the monastery of Saint Catherine, an early Christian martyr. Within this holy place, built around the site of the burning bush from whence Yahweh spoke to Moses, there is a synagogue and a mosque – one of the very few places in the world where all three branches of the Abrahamic faith co-exist in peace and harmony. This place touched my heart so deeply that I feel my heart open and tears flow just in the writing of it. Century after century of devotion permeates the structure of the buildings, the land beneath our feet. As I sit in prayer I feel as though I could sit here eternally, in this place of love and grace and veneration for the Christ/Mary consciousness. The power of this devotion, of here and now, transcends all of my doubts and difficulties with the established church and my sense of exclusion as a woman. It feels like a place of pure spirit, and the awareness of it being a man-made building, imbued with the masculine, detracts not at all from the felt sense of its holiness: in such close proximity, in time and space, this experiencing of the masculine and feminine faces of God/dess in all its paradoxes. The monastery full of stillness, quiet prayerful peace. The elemental roaring of the seas, the winds, the skies, Mother Nature. Monastic contemplation and devotion, elemental rhythms, pulses, forces. All manifestations of the divine beyond any division of masculine or feminine. The stillness and the dance.

The Divine Feminine is not solely a female province – largely so, but not exclusively.

Carl Rogers, the founding father of counselling, was raised in a devout farming family in the mid-west. He'd enrolled in seminary until, at age twenty-two, a six-month trip to China with the YMCA shifted his career trajectory to psychology. Although he came to reject Christianity, these two formative aspects of his upbringing – religion and rural life – infused his work with a distinctive spiritual dimension. He specialised initially in working with children, which also involved him working with their families, and it became clear to him that there was great wisdom in what patients were saying to him, if he could truly listen. At a time when psychoanalysis was the only talking treatment that held any sway, this was radical.

As Rogers' practice and experience developed so too did his clarity about what it was that most helped people in their desire to change. Paradoxically this included **deep acceptance of people being exactly where they were,** offering them what he called unconditional positive regard (acceptance), empathy (understanding the world of the other as if it were your own) and congruence (alignment between what the practitioner is feeling, thinking, and being). The latter is also sometimes termed authenticity or genuineness and requires high degrees of self-awareness in the practitioner, which is why person-centred training is focussed very much on personal development as well as on skills and theory. *Person-centred* is the term Rogers used for this approach that became increasingly widely applied to group work, education, social and health care. In the year that he died, 1987, he was nominated for the Nobel Peace Prize for his work with the approach in Northern Ireland, South Africa, and within what was then called the Iron Curtain.

To borrow from the *Tao*,[51] this is an approach which can be seen as being based on yin (female) qualities of receptivity rather than yang (male) qualities of transmission. Much of Rogers' language about the approach is lyrical, and magnified by references to the natural world. He talks about feeling as though he is a midwife, attendant at the birth of clients, as they emerge into their wholeness, hearing someone's deepest truth as like listening to the music of the spheres. He moved in the world of soft facts, in a modality that in its time was the most intensively researched of any therapeutic approach.

For nearly twenty-five years, I worked within this approach, as a counsellor, psychotherapist, trainer, supervisor, and group facilitator. Many times, with clients or in groups, I experienced a reality that transcended the consensual norm. The particular one that I want to share here was related to an eight-day residential, personal growth intensive held in Scotland. In groups such as these everyone undertakes to offer to each other the qualities referred to above – known as the core conditions of unconditional positive regard, empathy, and congruence. The facilitators are, ultimately, holding the space, but there is an expectation that we are also doing that for each other, and that we will together design the content and the shape of the week. This particular group proved deeply meaningful – indeed, life changing – for several of us involved. Such were the connections formed that two of the participants, P and J, offered to host a follow-up at their home. Fourteen of us duly arrived at theirs a few months on. Again, we spent much of the time in circle, and again as we shared and interacted with each other deeply, a powerful trust developed and an opening of the communal heart space occurred, which is rarely found in a secular setting.

During the course of the weekend, P had been in regular contact with his adult daughter who was having a traumatic time in her relationship with the father of her six-year old son. P had shared some of this with us, and it meant that his daughter and grandson were also in the group 'field'. As we approached our final session, I mentioned that I had brought my angel cards with me – small cards with qualities and drawings on them that had originated in the Findhorn spiritual community – and suggested we could use them as part of a closing ritual. Given the go ahead, I shuffled them and lay them in a circle face down around a central candle. When we came back together everyone drew a card and spoke of what the image and quality meant to them. When it came to P's turn, he felt strongly

---

[51] Literally 'way' or 'path'; within Eastern religious tradition it has to do with the body of philosophy encompassing much of Zen Buddhism and Confucianism.

that he would like to draw two cards and the two he chose turned out to be *Patience* and *Play*. He spoke for a while about the particular significance these had for him.

Later, a crisis call came from P's daughter and he went to collect her and his grandson to come and stay for a while. P had talked to her in the car about the cards he had picked, and she wanted to do it with her son. Those of us who were still present sat again in circle and witnessed as P's daughter drew the card *Patience*, and her son, sitting separately, drew the card *Play*.

The realm of synchronicity, of meaningful coincidence, of grace, is available for us to access, or comes to us, when we are in open-hearted relatedness. This could also be said to be the realm of the Divine Feminine, the underlying order of the natural world, of profound interconnectedness. It seems to me that **when we are able to go into deep open-hearted connection with each other our humanity is transparent in its inherent divinity and magic.**

Circle has long been the way of indigenous people and is inherently a form of the feminine: no hierarchy, no tiers, no steps – non-linear. There are many forms of gathering to connect in circle and one is called *The Way of Council*, which draws on teachings and methods from first nation, Native American traditions. In this tradition the speaking stick is used to hold the space for the person speaking at any one time, along with different forms of circle used to facilitate communication and connection with each other, with the ancestors, and with the spirit of the earth and all her relations.

We sit on the ground to participate, surrounding ourselves with beauty gathered from the surrounding landscapes. Again, during the course of a weekend spent together the interconnections with all realms and each other deepen. One of the rituals we are taught in this particular training event is to walk into nature, to identify or create a gateway, and to consciously expand our awareness as we walk through it.

During the days following the retreat, I practise this as I enter an ancient deer park that I've walked in many times over the years. I feel my heart and my consciousness expand as I walk through a particular gateway between two much loved beech trees. And then I find myself walking automatically, as if I were being led, on a route that I have never taken before, or even thought to take – across the field, through the trees, to a boggy copse filled with willow and alder. As I enter the copse for the first time, I see hidden there a single ancient blasted oak, many branches lost, the remaining ones twisting and turning up to the sky.

As I stand and feel her presence, I hear loudly within the word *Ysgradil*. I have no idea what that means – I think that it sounds Welsh or Cornish and maybe is a place – all I know is the power and presence of this tree, which feels as though she has called me here. I approach her and lean against her trunk, giving her thanks, honouring her age and beauty, saying to her the blessing that came to me as I touched an ancient Dragon Tree many years previously in the Canary Isles *Spirit of the tree I ask of thee, give me thy blessing, as I bless thee.*

I feel filled with the presence of this old, old being, and when I am ready to take my leave, I find a different route out through the copse. As I stand in the fringe of trees at the perimeter, I see two buzzards slowly circling overhead and I hear more words: *Woman Standing Still,* and I know this as the name that I have been given. I am transported through time, to fifteen years earlier, on my first ever visit to Findhorn, when in a *Council of All Beings,* the being that came as the one for me to speak for, and from, was Rock.

Once home and able to search online, I discovered that *Ysgradil* actually seemed to be *Yggdrasil*, one of the world's *Trees of Life*, found in the creation stories of so many traditions. The trunk and the branches represent the intersection of the horizontal – the temporal, human, material realm – and the vertical, the celestial, starlight heavenly realms. Each equally divine. This initiation of the name, for that is what it came to seem to me, is still alive and at play in my consciousness, still teaching, still mystifying.

I am sitting in one of my most beloved sacred places – the shrine within the Anglican chapel in Walsingham. I'm sitting at the back, before the wall which contains a huge icon of Mary holding the infant Jesus on her lap. On either side are ranks of shelves of votive candles, each with a named card listing those individuals and churches to whom the candles are dedicated. It was a source of delight to me, the first time that I ever sat to pray in this chapel, to see that the name card closest to me was that of the parish church hundreds of miles away that was the church of the girls grammar school I attended in the sixties.

Despite being raised in an atheist household I have long had a powerful affinity with empty churches – on the whole it is only when services are being held that I have difficulty. Though some cathedrals or churches have repelled me, those which connect do so very deeply. It is as though the years of prayer and devotion have become part of the very air of the building – and in some the presence of the Divine Feminine, in the form of Mary, is powerfully present. Nowhere have I felt this presence as strongly as I have in Walsingham.

Although this is an Anglican shrine (the Catholic one is a mile or so away) it is very 'high church',[52] clergy in full regalia, services often conducted in Latin, complete with bells and smells. Parts of me feel called by the theatre of this, but my major sense is disconnection. As I sit with closed eyes, opening my heart to the beloved Mother, I can hear a priest, his gown swishing, taking a group of visitors around the wider body of the chapel. This jars with me, but I sit with that feeling. Simultaneously I hear a woman enter the shrine and begin to sweep the floor quietly around me, and proceed to dust and to refresh the candles. Meanwhile I can hear the cleric portentously intoning in the background and suddenly I am filled with the sense of this as a microcosm of the established church. The quiet background devotional, unseen, unheralded pastoral and practical care of the women, and the 'front of house' power and visibility of the predominantly male clergy (many of whom in the high church would still prefer to have a solely male clergy). And beyond and above it all, the transcendent power and glory of the birther of God on earth: Mary, the Mother.

---

[52] Anglican in name but Catholic in ritual and practice.

Mary is said to have promised Richeldis, the local noblewoman wh. of Her in the eleventh century, that if she built a chapel to replicate the Annunciation in Nazareth, then no pilgrim would leave without b by Her presence. That's been true for me every time I've visited presence every time. And yet that feels only to be an amplification of th of her in my heart.

Many years ago, I instinctively learned the catechism, purely to enable me to tune into the stream of her energy in that very particular way. My home has several images of Her, and there is a statue in my garden. Hers was the energy which came through Mother Meera (which is Hindu for Mary), and hers was the prayer or affirmation that came through for me in darshan: *Mother the beauty of your love fills me in its warm embrace.* She is also the origin of the prayer I woke up with one morning, which has never left me:

Beloved Mother, let the beauty of your love fill my heart, that it may radiate with grace and humility to all beings, that we may know the truth of our own Belovedness.

Martrice Endres

Celebrating Sisterhood

On Sundays, my family went to church. The Methodist church was where my grandparents went and their parents before. There was no question about why we were Methodist. We just were. From Massachusetts to Florida and eventually New Mexico, my journey takes place in the United States. I didn't think of my family as religious or spiritual. Those were not words used in our house. We went to potlucks and pancake breakfasts. We dressed up for church. We sang and joined the choir, and then we went back to our lives. I remember the music the most and the bond it offered our family. Eventually each family member playing a musical instrument, we would gather for family band night. My parents loved to dance and shared their love of that with us as well. My first memories of learning to dance were standing on my father's feet. I saw our family as typical, not recognizing its dysfunction and focus on alcohol until many years later.

I was the first of three children born to my parents. My half-sister, nine years older than me, left when she was 18 and did not reconnect with the family for many years. I became the oldest, next a brother, and then a younger sister.

A violin belonging to my great grandfather was produced when I was ten and my music education began. First in public school, then private lessons, taking me to music festivals around the US, and in high school to the *Festival of 3 Cities* in Vienna, Budapest, and Prague. As a teenager, I experimented with religion and continued my love affair with music. Both were supported by my mother as socially acceptable. For a time, I was a 'holy roller', a Jesus freak, meeting friends after church carrying our bibles for everyone to see; I loved the passion and excitement of a good old-fashioned revival. **The spiritual journey begins way before you know what a spiritual journey is.** I seemed to be searching for something.

My mother was extremely controlling, and seemed to need to check all the boxes. You know the boxes: church, choir, youth group, appropriate clothing for a 'young lady'. Later, I recognized her need to control something, anything perhaps. My father, the life of the party, was the buy-everyone-another-round fun guy. Our family dynamics were probably typical for the time. My brother, as the only son, was rewarded for behaviors not allowed by the girls. When he snuck a few cheerleaders in through his bedroom window, my dad laughed and said *that's my boy* out of the side of his mouth. When my sister snuck out to meet friends, my mother said *she's a tramp*. I learned to stay in control at all times, be perfect, deny any negative feelings, and not talk about what went on in our house.

By my late teens, I stopped going to church, eventually returning after marriage and children. Back to the Methodist church and Sunday school and children's choir. I'm not sure why in retrospect, other than it seemed like the right thing to do when you had children. I was trained, after all, to be perfect and check all the boxes. The violin was put on a shelf after I married and began motherhood.

The marriage was, like many I assume, a fairy tale; until it was not. The marriage began a downward spiral and my days were filled mostly with survival. My husband began to sink into depression after leaving his job, and vacillated between hiding in his cave, to verbal and psychological abuse. I went from second income to bread winner. It began to feel like I had become an old woman and yet was still in my thirties. Maintaining an air of 'our life is perfect' is exhausting. I had been trained for it in my family of origin, but this was a new level. I learned to make myself small. When small, I was almost invisible and wouldn't stir any dust or make anyone angry. **The thing about living in a toxic relationship is that you slowly begin to believe there is nothing you can do.** As you believe it, you become powerless. You become smaller.

I maintained an arm's length relationship with my sisters, not wanting them to see my darkness. Several times I did leave with my children. During the ugliest times of my marriage, I let my sisters in and they formed a circle of support. Their fierce protectiveness helped to save me. My early experience of being nurtured and protected was my sisters' strength and compassion for me. It was as if they circled me with love. Today I would describe them as surrounding me with Divine Feminine energy. Called by many names, the energy I have learned to embrace as I have grown, is beautifully healing, protecting, and balancing. I was embarrassed to share each time that I went back to the relationship. My childhood training served me well. Of course, everything was going to be okay. Just be more perfect and deny any negative feelings. Stay small.

I made my way back to church during the dark years of marriage. My safety zone was in a large non-denominational church with live music and singing. Music, singing, moving has always been part of my soul. There I could pretend my life was just like everyone else's. Whatever that meant. The words of the pastor resonating in my ears – *in sickness and health, 'til death do you part* – a vow made before God. I kept praying.

Life keeps moving. I cried and prayed and sometimes laughed. Keeping my children's lives as normal as possible was my goal. As my children started to grow up, I went back to school to pursue a degree. I began to see the world through new eyes and recognized that I had lost myself. The marriage fell apart both suddenly and finally. Scared and relieved, it felt as though I was walking out of darkness into bright sunlight. I experienced a sense of freedom that surprised me. Small and perfect, I wasn't sure what to do next.

My older half-sister had been in and out of my life over the years. More out it seemed, and then we came together. Three completely different sisters, now in their forties and fifties, getting to know each other, what we valued and loved, who we wanted to be. We began the process of acceptance over a history of judgment. My older half-sister, the wild one; the goodie-two-shoes (me); and my younger sister, the army veteran. The oldest sister, always a free spirit, had lived an unexpected life and helped us stretch our imaginations in many ways during her time on earth. Most of the time I was shocked by her outrageousness but admired her courage to be unapologetically herself. My younger sister, my hero, returning from the army in a stronger physical body, with a battered soul as the result of her time in the military. A new and deep bond had been cemented. Sisterhood.

Again, I walked away from church. They preached to me of being a submissive wife and other doctrines I no longer felt true. I had not honored my vows. Being treated as though I was wrong when they knew nothing of my life surprised me. I didn't know if I should be sad or angry so I felt both. I started to know what resonated with me and what didn't. It was amazing the thoughts I had once I was out of survival mode. In many ways, the air felt fresher, the sun a bit brighter, my steps a little lighter. My younger sister supported me through grieving and then celebrating the losses. Imagine drinking a potion that allowed you the power to speak or act on what was in your mind or heart. That was the freedom I was tasting. Suddenly, I started to become visible and not so small.

We found a tribe of women or they found us, and they too helped me on the journey to myself. No longer just my sisters supporting me, but a new family circling me with love. I started to recognize the power of women and of my own power. **The loving power of women became part of my healing and feeling of empowerment.** I often wondered how they knew just what I needed. Later, I came to understand the empathic connection. The concept of spirituality began its climb into my reality. Recognition dawned that I was still a spiritual being, regardless of going to church, and I searched for where I belonged in this realm. There were no sets of rules or commandments or religious leaders telling me how to live. I read books about spirituality and karma. My spiritual journey took on a new pace as I searched. My mind was opening past the doors of the churches and I took what I needed with me. This was the start of what I call *Life Part 2*.

My new home became a place of healing. This was sacred space. A place to heal, infuse with new sparkling energy, and to begin again. I walked around the space thinking how important it was to not have to worry about making too much noise or coming home a little late. How had I stopped dancing? Popcorn for dinner now, then singing as loud as possible when I knew the words, and sometimes when I didn't. I wondered how I had become a woman who walked on eggshells and pretended it was okay, who left the abuser and then went back. Strong female warriors gathered in my new space and I was surrounded by their energy. They had fought their own fights and lovingly shared their wisdom. We gathered here together and I declared it heaven. We laughed and cried and sang and danced. Dancing is magic.

In many shamanic societies, if you came to a medicine person complaining of being disheartened, dispirited, or depressed, they would ask one of four questions: When did you stop dancing? When did you stop singing? When did you stop being enchanted by stories? When did you stop finding comfort in the sweet territory of silence? ~Gabrielle Roth

I had daydreamed about yoga all the years of what I call living in darkness. The postures seemed so beautiful and I could imagine them in my head to music, as a dance you would want to watch again and again. A beautifully choreographed dance that flowed with energy – that was my vision. I had learned through my reading that the postures were only a piece of the story. The eight limbs of yoga sounded like something so special. Yoga was a way to live your life. The first time I tried yoga, the words of my childhood came back loud and clear. Awkward. Clumsy. Skinny. *It's okay, your brother's the athlete of the family. You're really good at the violin.*

In *Life Part 2*, I didn't give up so easy. I went to a couple of workplace wellness events. A co-worker heard me express my disappointment in the classes and invited me to go with her to a yoga class. It turned out that yoga wasn't horrible. I was so happy to meet the teacher, who had the most calming voice and presence. The class was meant to be intermediate level but she guided me when I needed more from her. Even though we were doing yoga in an elementary school gymnasium with full-on fluorescent lights, I could see why people liked it.

The sisters continued to gather. The outrageousness of my older sister was fully embraced when we were together. For me, it was the opening up of my newfound joy in life. We would meet for an evening to celebrate the full moon. Sisters playing drums and singing silly songs and, of course, dancing. Sometimes my patio became the gathering space and we would sit and talk for hours, usually ending up with the music on and someone, or all of us, dancing. I talked to them of the yoga journey I was on and we practiced *Warrior II*. *Warrior II*, a strengthening posture that improves physical and mental endurance, embodies the warrior spirit, with a deep lunge and open arms. Balance is also learned here. While I felt the sense of how out of balance my life had been in many areas, this particular posture reminded me that I was a warrior. The sisters' unerring and unconditional support nurtured me into continuing to find my voice. I was beginning to have something to say and needed to share it. The concept of the Divine Feminine filled me with purpose and passion. Women needed to hear my story and know that they could overcome being small. I felt sadness, compassion and empathy for my old self. How many other women had become small and lost their voice?

My older sister loved playing her drum and voiced a wish to participate in an organized drum circle under a full moon. A drum circle was found in our area and we waited for a full moon event. The event was to be held at a National Park outside Albuquerque. At the last minute, my sister's health didn't allow her to attend, so little sis and I promised to go in her place. My older sister advised that the moon called us to embrace our goddess energy. We laughed at that, but felt powerful and understood the importance of this trek on her behalf. The unconditional love, support, and joy of sisterhood bonds driving us, sis and I hiked into the park a couple of miles to find the group. Armed with a drum, folding chairs, and water bottles, we found the gathering. People of all walks of life, already drumming, some dancing, some chanting. Two sisters out in the darkness with a drum. We should have been scared, but instead we felt empowered. Drums and other percussion instruments were shared. We watched and listened, and then joined in. People expressing pure joy began singing. This experience took us out of our comfort zone, but we were there on behalf of the sisterhood. As darkness began to fall, we realized that our research on the full moon had not been complete. This was a blood moon eclipse – it would soon be completely dark. As the darkness progressed, we realized we were miles from the city armed only with a cell phone flashlight. We hiked out and went straight to the arms of our sister. Celebrating the power of our sisterhood, we hugged and danced in the dark.

During this time, I was delving deeper into yoga. No longer just a physical practice, I embraced it for all of its eight limbs. Reading everything I could get my hands on about yoga and its history and philosophy became my focus. I went to as many yoga classes as I could fit into my week, finding my way to a small studio with a focus on spirituality. I felt as though I had come home. My yoga practice blossomed here in this safe place. I finally felt what I expected to feel: a sense of coming home. I opened my soul on the mat and found myself crying as I let go of the old lady I had been. The need to be perfect began to fade. Diving into negative feelings and living through it left me feeling powerful. My children living their own lives now, I continued to work in my career as a subcontract manager at a large corporation whose focus was on engineering and research and development. I recognized the imbalance of my work life with my personal evolution. A need to use my creativity and personal power in that setting began to unfold.

I had never really believed I would be in a life that included going to a yoga retreat. A Buddhist retreat center *Bodhi Manda*, (Sanskrit for *Place of Enlightenment*), was my first yoga retreat in the little town of Jemez Springs in New Mexico. Nothing is taken for granted in this new life. I tried to fully experience each moment, as though too much time was lost and I must make up for it. I feasted on the beauty of the forest, breathing in the mountain air, connecting to myself. Oracle cards, tools to learn to trust your intuition, were produced and shared. Intuition was at first a bit scary to me. Trusting it in the past had been a painful experience. Survival dulls your senses as you begin to let go of dreams. So many new experiences and it left me feeling exhilarated. Chakra balancing? Sure. Chanting? Okay. During the day, our schedule included yoga, helping around the center *karma yoga*, and soaking up the energy of the hot springs. One afternoon my job was to help in the kitchen with a group of other women and the abbot, a woman who was the administrator of this temple. It was a special afternoon of community and getting to know each other, everyone sharing their story, feeling a bond when we left.

The final morning, we were invited by the abbot to the temple for Sunday meditation. Each was led to a small wooden stool to kneel on; we sat in silence for thirty minutes and then recited the *Metta Sutta*.[53] The end of the meditation was signaled by a bell. As a group, we rose and walked outside single file in silence, learning to experience sounds of nature around the perimeter of the temple – mindfulness in its simplest form. I gained more understanding of my personal power in learning to meditate, and of myself. **I learned that my power was my choice.** It seemed a shocking epiphany at the time. I learned to breathe and how to focus my mind. Was I still searching for something or had I found it? I left the retreat feeling that I would never be the same. My heart and mind were opened to all possibilities.

A Sunday morning restorative yoga class replaced the ritual of church. A warm, ninety-five degree class with a gentle nurturing teacher. I made my way there every week as I continued to transform. I connected to community and music in the same way I had years before in church. Most of the yoga teachers were female. While powerful, they were intuitive and able to be gentle and non-judgmental. A feeling of relief comes to me as I write these words. I remember coming to class one morning a bit out of sorts at the craziness of the world. The teacher came to me with compassion in her eyes and let me know I was not alone. I don't remember the words, but they were just what I needed to hear. The Divine Feminine was alive and well here in the shape of nurturing, compassionate healers. I saw that I had that same power.

Our beautiful, free-spirited sister died unexpectedly. Devastated by the loss, we spent months trying to wrap our heads around it. Finally, several months after her passing, we realized that the remaining sisters needed to let her go. A

---

[53] Metta Sutta = Buddhist Loving Kindness Meditation

celebration was planned. Day of the Dead, *Dia de Los Muertos*, a celebration of the life and loss of loved ones is usually celebrated on November 2nd. The idea of the celebration is to help support the spiritual journey of those who have died. The sister community was broken and we needed to heal it by honoring her in the most outrageous, free spirited way we could dream up, as befitting her beautiful spirit. During a full moon, a lunar eclipse, and even a comet, the two remaining sisters celebrated her life. As is traditional, we set a place for her at the table, and dined on her favorite food and drank her favorite drink. (Jagermeister. *Yuck.*) We ended the evening singing at the top of our lungs, dancing, and beating her drum. We felt she was with us and we finally completed the sister drum circle. A year later we sprinkled her ashes in a garden near the Eiffel Tower in Paris.

According to Hindu mythology, Durga[54] is a warrior goddess known for combatting demonic forces that threaten peace. I was introduced to the Goddess Durga during an Indian festival known as *Navrati*. I was the only blonde head in a sea of dark after my Indian friend adorned me with traditional Indian garb and jewelry, including a bindi. When you need to ward off evil or even destroy it, you'll want to call in the Goddess Durga for support. Women, a few men, and children, all danced in a large auditorium for hours and celebrated the goddess, friendship, and community. A beautiful experience in my journey of recognizing feminine energy, Durga embodies the force I dreamed of being in my days of feeling hopeless. While I don't participate every year, I continue to recognize this festival annually. This is a celebration of recognition for me. I, too, have combatted demonic forces.

Yoga led me to writing classes focused on spirituality and intuition offered at my yoga studio. I found writing to be healing and was at times surprised to find words on paper I hadn't planned on expressing. A connection with an author led me to a retreat in northern New Mexico focused on writing, using our intuition, and yoga. Nature was calling my name again. Yoga and writing began each morning in a yurt in the forest. Our pens flew over the paper as we were led through exercises, finally looking down and seeing a piece of ourselves on the paper. Writing was shared with each other by reading aloud, then tears or laughter, and a community was born. When the energy in the yurt became heavy or the day was feeling long, we re-energized. Music was turned on. And yes, we danced. We danced and laughed and ended by throwing our hands in the air and cheering.

We had in our midst a wide variety of healers. From yoga teacher to medicine woman to physician. Beautiful souls each in their own way sharing words and gifts of healing. Artist, author, life coach, therapist, seekers of truth. I felt humbled and honored to be in their midst. Breaks were guided nature walks,

---

[54] Durga = In Hindu mythology, Goddess Durga is a warrior who symbolizes positive energy used against the negative forces of evil.

including once to a labyrinth. Small cabins and dormitories surrounded the main house where meals were served and the evening gatherings were held.

The retreat had filled up. My friend and I were asked to take a more secluded cabin about a mile away from the center, mostly because the leader knew us well and that we would not refuse. At night, after evening meal and yoga and writing, we made our way driving and following the headlights to the cabin. The forest at night is dark, and there was no electricity or plumbing at our cabin. Time to face my fear of the dark it seemed. A fellow retreat goer gave us mini flashlights and mine stayed on the first night. I shared my fear of the dark and we talked through it. If I can do this, I can do anything! I was becoming larger and stronger. The days were filled with writing and yoga and hiking and nature. In the evening, drum circle and singing bowls, and dancing. My sister would have been so happy here. The last evening our medicine woman held a fire ceremony for us. We pulled oracle cards and used essential oils. As lovely as it was, by the final day of living in such rugged accommodations, I was ready for civilization. My friend had shared that she had never been on a road trip by herself and was not comfortable driving in the rain. The universe gave us rain and she drove us home. We had both felt safe enough to face our fears. A new circle of sisterhood, nurturing and supporting each other. We had a new tribe.

Last year, at age sixty-two, I completed a two hundred hour yoga teacher training – ten months of study – taking me further on the path of what had become my passion. Philosophy, asanas, chakras, the Bhagavad Gita and the yoga sutras all fueled my thirst for knowledge. I opened my mind and heart even further to the concept of holistic wellness: body, mind, and spirit all working together. Using spirituality, meditation, and physical movements designed to keep us healthy, I embody strength.

My days start with meditation. I express gratitude out loud as my mantra. While still working in an almost thirty-year career, one evening a week I share yoga at a local studio. Yoga and I battle demonic forces in a different way than Durga. I greet students as they enter the studio. Most of them I see regularly and have connection with. My role as yoga teacher is to share yoga asanas, as well as give them tools to take with them into their lives. I make my way to my mat and settle onto a blanket. We begin class with meditation, focusing on the breath. *Your breath is your super power* I say gently, *the most powerful tool you have to enhance your physical, mental, and spiritual well-being.* I guide them through breath and movement for the next hour, helping them focus on their progress and power. *Remember your value and importance to the universe.*

Namaste.

Dianne Graham

Finding My Voice

My Mum was born of a Scottish mother and a German father in 1935 in New Zealand. War was brewing in Germany and the Depression continued with unemployment running at twenty-one percent. They were tough years to be a child of a German parent. Her family were fervent Lutherans and she reconnected with that faith after the birth of us five siblings. Mum gave birth to me in 1955, her first baby, when she was twenty. My grandmothers, one English and the other a Scot, taught me home skills like handcrafts, sewing, preserving, cooking and gardening. Although I spent a lot of time with them during school holidays, I don't recall hugs and kisses.

Mum, Benita, named after her father Benno, who'd been named after Benito Mussolini, was born and raised in Greatford, a small town near Palmerston North in the North Island of New Zealand. Dad was born and raised in Gisborne, a farming town on the East Coast[55] of the North Island. They met at a dance at Ohakea airbase where Dad was a telegraphist in the Air Force, and married on June 2nd 1953, the same day as the coronation of Queen Elizabeth II. When my sister was born and I was eighteen months old, they moved to Dad's hometown, Gisborne. Dad's Mum had put a deposit on a house for them. Mum speaks of this with anger as she had no choice in the matter, the house or the move. It was decided for her.

I was born Dianne Kape. Kape is a Maori name. Dad's Mum – an English nurse – had come out to New Zealand on one of the nursing ships in 1915. She became pregnant to and married a Maori man, Jack Lewis Kape. He was a caretaker and congregant at the local Protestant church. Dad was their second child of five. Nana was ashamed of *having* to marry and would have preferred to marry a white person, and I sensed her powerlessness in this as I got older. I recall her using the word *nigger* often when referring to Maori. Pop was shamed for being of colour and it was never talked about. Our name was usually pronounced *Cappy*, rather than the correct *Kar-pe* (the *e* as in *pet*). One of my aunties pronounced it as if it was a French word, *Car-pey*. Once I'd learned how to say Kape correctly I'd

---

[55] In New Zealand lore, the East Coast is different from the east coast. The East Coast is that part of the North Island running from roughly Wairoa to Te Araroa, depending on who you talk to.

often be corrected to say it the Pakeha[56] way. Maori culture was looked down on and my first schools forbade the language being spoken. We siblings learned not to ask questions about Maori, and to keep quiet about it, and so we took on the shame of the past generations.

Around my twelfth year, Mum insisted I do confirmation lessons and then be confirmed into the Lutheran church. All twelve year olds are becoming aware of where babies come from and I recall asking the Pastor teaching those lessons *If Mary was a virgin, how did she get pregnant with Jesus?* He turned pink, stuttered a few times and said *It was a miracle and you just have to accept that.* I'd wanted some glorious answer so any vague interest in Jesus dissolved about then. Some Hare Krishnas had been handing out pamphlets and singing in town. They were far more interesting, as was a book on the basics of Buddhism a friend lent me.

Also in my twelfth year, I became curious about my family name and researched its origins in the school library. I found it has several meanings. The verbs *to eat, to reject, to copy;* the nouns *eyebrow* and *a stirring stick*. It made no sense to me for any of these to be family names. Except perhaps eyebrow, if we came from a lineage of ancestors with prominent eyebrows. We don't appear to. My friends thought it hilarious and called me Dianne Eyebrows for a couple of years. It wasn't until I was in my mid-forties that I found out the name had been shortened five generations back by English speaking people who couldn't pronounce Kaperiere. This means Gabriel and was taken from the early missionary teachings of the archangels, as Gabriel had appeared in a vision to one of my ancestors.

As Mum turned forty, I turned twenty. She was pulled between compliance with the dogma of the Lutheran church and the rising tide of the feminist movement, all while enduring an abusive marriage. I could see she felt powerless to change things. Dad didn't seem to believe in anything. He had no strong values or beliefs except sport and drinking, although I think he was afraid and angry with people believing in things he couldn't see or touch. Some of my worst memories are from the days Mum had been to church. I was enjoying the hippy years, smoked lots of dope and slept around. Mum was emotionally unavailable to me as a teen exploring my sexuality and pushing boundaries. I see now she was frying bigger fish and was at the forefront of huge changes for women in New Zealand during the late 60s and early 70s. As a unionist she fought for changes in wages, working conditions and maternity leave for women. She spoke out about the attitudes of a lot of men (many of which were in my dad) toward women. She broke the chains and yelled her way out of her marriage.

I was leaving school and beginning work. I'd successfully applied for a position as a telecommunications technician trainee with the New Zealand Post Office, until that time considered a man's realm. I didn't have to fight for the position, I

---

[56] European or white person.

got it on my own merits, and worked for a boss who appreciated what women brought to that world. I was a bit numb to what was going on in Mum's world as my own had become very exciting.

Telecommunications in the early 70s was reliant on crystal radio sets, especially for remote areas and intercity or international calls. Six months of my engineering studies was about the ability of crystals – in particular, clear quartz and rose quartz – to transmit and translate pure frequencies. Here's where my love and appreciation of crystals began. Knowing the science of them is why I know the healing gifts crystals bring to our world. It's also where **I learned that there is a measurable energy to every single object on this planet,** and I understood the world in a language of frequency.

So, growing up, my experience of woman or feminine anything was of pushing or fighting to make something happen. Years later I came to know this as the Undivine Masculine, that aspect of us we all visit at times of pushing or forcing to make something happen.

At twenty-three I married a man a lot like my dad, emotionally (although not physically) abusive. I didn't see it at the time though. When he proposed to me, I remember thinking *I'd better grab this. No-one else will ever want me.* I gave birth to a daughter when I was twenty-seven and a son when I was twenty-nine. I experienced severe post-natal depression after both births and struggled to get through days. I wasn't in paid employment any longer and all sense of purpose or belonging disappeared. I felt powerless to make my life any different. My mother-in-law would say *What's wrong with you? You've got a home, a husband, two lovely children and money. What more could you want? Pull your socks up and get on with it.* There were days when deciding what to wear was more than I could bear and I'd still be in my nightclothes at 3pm. Any decision was a nightmare.

After our daughter's birth there was some pressure from his family to have her christened. I wasn't keen on the idea and felt they could decide at a later age if they wanted to be christened. I preferred that concept. But I chatted to a pastor at a local church and arranged a day for the ceremony. Our families all went along one Sunday. The ceremony was lovely and we were welcomed like long lost friends. I felt very comfortable with these people. A week later I went back to a service on my own. I experienced a power that evening that literally knocked me out. I thought I'd fainted. They told me I'd been filled with the Holy Spirit and that the experience was called 'being slain in the spirit.' It happened many times over the next seventeen years. It was deeply healing every time. I committed my life to Christ and chose to be baptised. It was in this Christian Church community I first experienced a group of supportive, friendly, inclusive women. I taught Sunday school and managed a clothes bank delivering clothing for low income families. I could spill my heart to other women and even shared the secret of the mess my marriage was in. I'd found a tribe and sense of belonging that had been missing since I'd left work. My husband, who believed very much in sport and drinking, seemed to either be afraid of, or angry at, people who believed in things he couldn't see or touch – just like Dad.

At home I felt I had to conform but in the outside world I could be myself. I was afraid of my husband, and I was unhappy and felt powerless to speak about it. I was never sure who he was going to be each day. His personality altered depending on stress at work and how much he was drinking. But I stayed, because that's what good girls do. When I realised he was an alcoholic, I spoke with counsellors at church and went to *Al Anon* meetings. I learned to put on a happiness mask for the rest of the world.

When the children were toddlers, I trained as a colour and image consultant after experiencing my own transformation with colour and style in my wardrobe. I excelled at this. I was a natural at talking to women, encouraging them, and helping them feel great about the way they looked. I was interested in clothing and style, having always made my own clothes. Wearing colours and styles that complimented my body colouring and shape was life changing for me and I discovered a confidence that hadn't been there previously. I was great at helping others achieve this. There were regular breakthrough moments when a client would weep as they recognised their own beauty, often for the first time in their lives. I revelled in the intimacy this work allowed with women, and was driven by the transformation it brought to their lives.

Mum left Dad and they had several years apart, but they eventually got back together. It was always rocky but it seems they couldn't keep their hands off each other. Dad became unwell after he retired. He'd always been active – a keen jogger, a rugby referee and golfer. His limbs were tingly and numb and he needed surgery to remove calcification along his upper spine. Nerves were accidentally severed during surgery leaving him unable to toilet, dress himself, or walk unaided. As a result of a deceptive experience with a doctor many years earlier, Mum chose to avoid many services available to her and Dad. Our lives changed dramatically as we siblings rallied to support them. Dad was hard work, and his fiery temper didn't suddenly leave him just because his body was a bit damaged. Mum needed time out, so one day every week she had a day for herself. She's a writer and poet, so this time in her own space was precious. Each Wednesday, after my kids left for school, I'd go over and get Dad out of bed, shower and dress him, and take him to my home for the day. Showering and toileting my father was extremely difficult the first time I did it. It got easier. The first time I ever recall him telling me he loved me was when I was showering him in those early days. I realized in that moment how vulnerable he was and just how much he appreciated me being comfortable with his vulnerability. It allowed a whole new space for me to have loving conversations with my father. In one of these conversations I learned Dad was a water diviner. He'd shut the gift down years ago. I learned years later that this is a mantle passed down the generations.

The shame of being Maori ended abruptly when my brother John, my youngest sibling, spent time working with Dad's second cousin who had been researching our ancestry for decades. John arranged for Dad and us to meet many of these people. It was deeply moving, particularly for Dad who at seventy-eight finally embraced aunties, uncles, second and third cousins, all much darker than us. The shame dissolved that day. We began to learn more about our heritage, our ancestry and our land, the land we all come from. Our lineage goes back to Ngati Kahungunu,[57] the tribe we *whakapapa*[58] to. There were many healers, diviners, and *tohunga*[59] in my bloodlines. I was forty-three when I finally felt I'd found my roots.

I felt like a tree that had a place to grow, with roots that ran deep. I had visions of thousands of strong women who'd come before me and sensed my soul united with them all. It was as if my body and soul had a whole new understanding of the eternal feminine spirit and I felt the blood of these women run in my veins.

I'd often felt a part of me was missing, but not anymore.

I did the *Landmark Forum* that year, a three-day personal development course. It's a deep exploration into what it is to be a human being and is designed to bring about permanent positive shifts in your quality of life. A couple of dear friends had made huge changes in their lives and were so much happier than I'd ever seen them. I'd been going to counselling, and moaning to the rest of the world about my marriage, but not actually doing anything about it. After the course I had some meaningful conscious conversations with my husband and realized he wasn't prepared to make any changes or go to counselling with me.

Twenty-three years married to a deeply wounded man was as much as I could stand, and in 1999 I chose to leave him. I heard of hundreds of relationship breakdowns in that year. It was a powerful astrological time of endings. It took a huge amount of courage to leave, and at times it took even more courage to stay left. It would have fixed everyone else's world if I'd gone back, but not mine. The pain and shock in both our families was huge. They were devastated. The unconditional love proclaimed at church turned out to be very conditional. I recall one woman saying *Oh, this is just the devil. You must go back to him.* I didn't. I began to explore what was really true for me and chose not to return to church. It was interesting who was there for me at this time, and the women who really cared with a softness and generosity I'd never known before.

---

[57] Third largest of New Zealand's roughly 20 iwi or tribes. 'Ngati' is pronounced *nga-tee*, 'Kahungunu' is pronounced *ka-hoo-ngoo-noo'*, 'iwi' is pronounced *ee-wee*.
[58] Descend from. Genealogy.
[59] Spirit doctors, medicine priests.

I was financially destitute before settlement two years later. My children, then thirteen and fifteen, chose to stay with their Dad so I didn't qualify for government support. I got a job as a disability information consultant with a social services organisation. I was well qualified as I'd been helping Mum care for Dad for ten years. This is where I began to grow a sense of the Universe having my back, of something bigger than me leading me in the right direction. Our office was in a space shared with several community organisations, all managed and peopled by women with what I now call Amazonian strengths. They had a strong sense of who they were, advocated for the down-trodden and disadvantaged, spoke out at injustice, and helped write policies that made the world a better place. They'd kill to protect their cubs and have a good laugh after the battle. It was the perfect space for me to heal, learn new skills, connect with a different community, and stand tall. These women unknowingly taught me how to drop my fear of being strong, that it was possible to have a voice, be staunch, have boundaries and not be put down for it. When life was challenging, they'd reminded me of why I'd left him. They held me gently and watched as I had a rebound fling with a man who turned out to be another control artist, helping me laugh about it when it ended and I saw the lessons in it.

A friend introduced me to a clairvoyant medium who was running spiritual development classes. Influenced by Christianity, I'd always considered anything spiritual outside the church to be dark, bad, evil or dangerous. So this was new ground for me. It took some bravery on my part but I wanted to learn more about using colour intuitively and about crystal healing, so I began attending her classes. It was in one of these classes I first heard the terms Sacred Feminine and Sacred Masculine. We spent time in meditation, connecting with our sacred feminine, and sacral chakra. I learned to connect with the earth and to see her as 'the mother' and myself as an aspect of her. I came to know that **regardless of gender, we all carry aspects of the Divine Feminine and Divine Masculine within us.** Masculine aspects lead to public power, security, territory, social identity, and the capacity to meet one's needs, while the feminine aspects lead to unconditional love, creativity, nurturing, and emotional and spiritual connection with self, body, others, children, community and nature. When these are out of balance or shut down, we forget to take responsibility for our actions, get lazy with life, or push to make things happen with little regard for others. I now call this the *Unsacred Feminine* and *Unsacred Masculine* but have seen it called the *hyper* and *Undivine* of each too.

In 2001, I started seeing a man who'd been a good friend for seven years. We both had wounds from our previous marriages, and in many ways set ourselves up to fail. Because of our past experiences we both unconsciously looked for ways to sabotage our happiness. At the core of this was the belief that we didn't deserve to be happy. He did the *Landmark Forum* and as a result we were able to have powerful conscious conversations. We dug in to what we were doing and worked through it. He is not afraid to cry or be vulnerable, and he's willing to talk through the tough stuff and not walk away. It was all so refreshing and liberating. He has consciously and unconsciously allowed me the space to become all of me. He has embraced feminine qualities, which creates a space for me to live mine.

We bought a house together a year after we got together and three of our four children lived with us until they went flatting or moved to other cities with work. We married in 2006 and made plans to take a year out to travel around Australia in a caravan. We'd had four close friends die within a few months of each other and it was a wakeup call that had us look at the things we really wanted to do, so we decided to get on and do them. We travelled up the east coast of Australia with a caravan for eighteen months. We found work and settled on the Sunshine Coast in Queensland.

I've since trained in many energy healing modalities. My intuition and ability to read people and their bodies is powerful. Without fail, every time I do the work of helping others, I'm compelled to do my own inner work. In 2012 I was fifty-seven. As part of a visionary intuitive training, we delved deep into our childhood wounding. I observed the beliefs I'd carried forward from my childhood experiences. The main ones were *I'm ugly* and *No one wants to hear what I have to say*. There's always a story behind these beliefs, why they're there and why they're so strong. They were still influencing my life, sabotaging decisions, relationships and my business. The pain of recognising these lies was excruciating. I cried for days, screaming into the ethers at my parents, siblings, schoolmates, friends, enemies, partners, God, life. I got so bloody angry, I finally felt it all and was emotionally wrung out by the end of it. I learned processes where these beliefs, once recognized or brought in to the light, could be collapsed or deleted at their point of creation. This is deep healing energy work. After deeper exploration I chose to install a new truth about myself. I chose *I Am*. I love how unlimited this feels. It's a bit like deleting a computer program and installing something completely different. I saw the truth of me and experienced the rise of the Feminine Divine within for the first time: it was physical at times – a sensation of a power surge moving upward through me, and an awareness of being a part of the collective feminine. I felt new, unencumbered, light, fresh and free. If this feeling had a colour, it was red. I found a place to stand, started to own all of me, and discovered my voice. This sensation has never left me.

The same year I attended a three-day 'Goddess on Purpose' gathering. More diving into wounds and seeing how they stopped me from living a life on purpose. Several speakers offered their perspective, and on the third day we rose! We celebrated all aspects of the Goddess – life, birth, death, vulnerability, courage, strength, softness, power, rage, authenticity. We meditated, danced, sang and shouted. All those wounds – the beliefs about life that turned out not to be truth, the hurts and lies – and the profound healing and releasing them, have led me to offer the gifts I do today. Without full and intimate connection with my Divine Feminine I'd not be equipped to lead others to seeing the truth of who they are. Without unreserved reconnection to my soul essence I wouldn't have been equipped to experience the Divine Feminine aspect of me. It has nothing to do with my body and everything to do with my spirit and essence. It's ageless and timeless. **I came to see myself reflected in all other women.** All women who have been, will be and are now. And I see them all in me. I experienced my own limitlessness.

Interestingly, and vitally, the Feminine Divine has a dark side, a shadow aspect, a bit like the *yang* to the *yin*. The word dark had scared me away from my fullness. I'd been programmed to believe light is pure and dark is evil. Being a 'good girl', being quiet, being pretty and towing the line had been an integral part of my existence. It had stopped me leaving an abused, abusive, alcoholic husband because I didn't want to be the naughty girl. Good girls held the family together for the children. In the end I left for the children. I realized I was living a lie for them. The sorting of life into good and bad categories had flavoured my desire for acceptance. Because creativity and self-expression had been suppressed through my childhood and marriage, I'd developed a secret side of me – stuff I didn't want the world to know about me: dirty secrets, sinister thoughts and incongruous friendships. Inner child healing and the Goddess retreat led me to see this shadow and how it was created by the same lies. Untangling shame and guilt have been a heavy and necessary practice to heal my shadow self. Essentially **our shadow is that part of our personality we don't want to admit to having,** those things we're challenged by at varying levels, all our lives. My reconciled shadow is now an expert secret-keeper, trustworthy, recognising untruths in others easily and noticing when my thoughts are out of alignment with my own truth. The gift of the shadow as an aspect of purpose has been to liberate it, allowing me to lead others to see the gift of their own shadow and to master it. For years I'd secretly thought myself a fraud, a pretender, fake or a charlatan. Mastering these shadow aspects takes regular inner work and part of that is embracing the praise of others, another phenomenon I'd been programmed to turn down.

The following year, 2013, I attended a cosmic womb retreat. I'd become aware of my womb space as the core of me, and I was aware of the potency of the sha-woman offering this retreat. Twenty of us on the floor, heads at the centre of the circle, legs facing outward, all wearing long skirts, spent the day in ceremony, honouring the womb space, energetically feeling in to the shame, guilt, wounds, pain stored there. We cleared the bloodlines of these wounds, doing this work for our children and grandchildren and future generations. The shaman leading us energetically reminded me of who *I Am* at my most basic soul template, that part of me written in all time. I was reminded of the unlimited nature of my newly birthed self as we were led through a holy rebirthing ceremony where we tuned in to our births, connected to breath, earth, and sound, and saw the holiness of it all. **It was the first time I'd perceived myself as holy or sacred,** and I wept at the beauty of it. I felt as if I'd been to the centre of the Earth and the Universe and I saw myself as an aspect of it all. I felt expansive, expanded and infinite as I embodied the Divine Feminine. I felt myself in a realm where I got to see and embrace my uniqueness and loved what I saw. It was the deepest cellular and spiritual healing I'd experienced and I felt it all ground solidly into my being that day. It awoke in me a remembering of the female ancestral lineage that stands with me today, that contributes to my own Divine Feminine. I had a vision of all my female ancestors standing behind and beside me, thousands of them, and sensed them preparing the ground for me, clearing a path. I took on the healing mantle of several of the medicine women in my lineage that day. At times they speak through me and I often call on their wisdom when I'm working with others or making decisions. We ended the day around a fire pit in the bush, singing and laughing.

Following this retreat experience, I felt inspired to honour my body – my temple – with deeper integrity. I cleared our home of chemical cleaners, began using only natural hair and body products, chose to eat mostly organic and stopped colouring my hair. I'd been colouring it for at least twenty years and knew my natural colour was now grey. As the colour grew out, I moved through processes of vulnerability, feeling exposed and untidy. Embracing untidy was foreign and a bit exciting for me. For nearly thirty years I'd complied with the concept of an image consultant keeping up the image. It all felt a bit rebellious and thrilling. After eight months of growth I had my hair cut very short. No more colour. It was unexpectedly liberating. I wanted to create something to celebrate me. Not a birthday party or dinner. Something beautiful to honour my years, my wisdom, my journey, my body, my soul and my spirit. A close friend, a medicine woman, devised a croning ceremony with close friends who all contributed unique ideas to honour who I am for them. It remains one of the finest experiences of my life.

In 2014, my daughter birthed a daughter and I stepped onto the hallowed ground of grandparenting. I'd tuned in to this soul about four months into the pregnancy and felt a strong soul bond with her. I knew that this soul had mothered me in another lifetime. I felt she was coming back to teach me what she had run out of time to complete in our previous life together. She was waiting to share my breath. I was so excited to meet this wee soul and to *hongi*.[60] I'm a Maori descendent so this sharing of breath or life force was hugely significant for me. Watching my baby birth a baby was an exquisite experience, and I watched my granddaughter take her first gasp looking right at me. I held her, our noses and foreheads met, sharing breath, oneness. But her greatest gift in that moment was when I looked into her eyes. I believed that we move through life accessing different aspects of the Divine Feminine at different stages. What I saw in my first *mokopuna's*[61] eyes were all the aspects of the Divine Feminine present in that same moment. **I saw all aspects of the Feminine already present in her – child, youth, mother, crone – and I realised that that's true for all**

---

[60] Hongi is the New Zealand Maori word for the meeting of nose and forehead, the sharing of breath, the acknowledgment that we are all one.
[61] Grandchild.

of us. We don't age into those stages; they're all present in the now. Fully integrated and accessible. Maid, Mother, Crone.

It's been helpful to read about the many archetypes of the Divine Feminine and to see how each of them show up in me. The warrior, mother, grandmother, sister, secret-holder, creatrix, dreamer, sensitive, lover, healer, alchemist, priestess, crone, darkness. I've loved learning how each of these qualities correlates to an ancient Egyptian, Greek or Hindu Goddess, and I invoke those goddesses when I want to work with that quality.

I've found a deep soul connection with my mother, noticing so many of her qualities in me. In my sixties now, I see much of my strength and courage comes from my darling Mamma. She is in her eighties, and her voice to the world now is mostly through poetry, and particular Haiku. She and I have a wonderful relationship – she hears me now and I believe I can finally hear her.

My journey with the Divine Feminine has offered powerful experiences that have equipped me to support others as they explore and heal themselves. My life now is about making conscious choices and I love nothing more than to have conscious conversations with others willing to meet me at that level, without needing anyone else's approval. As an aware woman I feel a responsibility to hold a loving and safe space for others, to collapse their unconscious beliefs and move forward with a new belief in themselves.

Alison Smith

The Power of Three – a story of embodiment

I grew up in the 1960s on a housing estate in southeast Northumberland in the United Kingdom. It was a bland collection of semi-detached brick houses with gardens back and front, and garages – designed for the newly emerging house-owners, the lower middle-classes. My parents had both come from a working-class background, with their fathers having been in the coal mining industry while their mothers worked in the house, cooking, child rearing and cleaning. Both my mother and father were brought up in Faiths – my mother was a Methodist and my father was in the more militarised Salvation Army. The latter I did not encounter much, except in the annual May service, my grandad's brass trumpet, and copies of the *War Cry* which I would find in Grandma's newspaper rack. (I was always looking for things to read, and children were supposed to be *seen and not heard.*) My mother was a kind, sensitive woman; she was uneducated, having left school early under mysterious circumstances. My father had entered a career in the civil service, prior to which he attended grammar school, then the National Service. He was a scout master and hockey player. I was the oldest of three daughters, and we lived at number 3 on an ordinary street in an ordinary housing estate.

Each Sunday morning, we went to Sunday School which consisted of an hour or two of Bible classes and then we had to troop into the main church to sing with the adults. We had our own hymn book, which I enjoyed. Of those times I remember a book of Bible stories like Daniel and the lion, and the story of the crucifixion, and it came with a book of stickers which you had to match up with the stories. There were a lot of stickers with Jesus on them. He was handsome with long hair and blue eyes. I remember being haunted by the story of his betrayal and death by being nailed to a cross, which came up every Easter, along with cold winds, chocolate eggs and new dresses. *There is a green hill far away, without a city wall, where our dear Lord was crucified, he died to save us all* we sang, and I remember feeling sad and troubled by it. Why did he have to die for us? Why did we need saving? It didn't really make sense other than to instil a sense of not being enough. Couple that with being a girl, growing into a woman in the mold of Eve, who tempted Adam and was created from one of his ribs – I questioned all of this right from the start. There was more of it at school. There was religion, with its songs and stories and rules, but no spirituality. Jehovah's Witnesses would sometimes come to the door and my mother would buy a book from them or they would persuade us to take a leaflet; I'd look at the pictures of the world as we know it ending and being replaced by a paradise where lions slept with lambs.

I loved stories and books. We always got books at Christmas, and from the local library. Dad would tell us his own made up stories too, tales of magical happenings and girls going in the woods to meet various characters who turned out to be guides and teachers. At school I fell under the spell of teachers who could tell stories, and subjects where books and stories were important like English, drama and history. I had a vivid imagination and loved to read and draw, as well as write my own poems and stories. I remember in the first year of grammar school learning about the *Ziggurat of Ur*, and feeling some stirring, some interest that seemed to go beyond mere curiosity.

I was the second person in our family to go to university. Against my parents' wishes, and my careers teacher who told me I would make a good accountant (I think she told everyone that), I chose to study philosophy. Along with the experience of leaving home and also having started a regular poetry writing habit, the stage was set for an intellectual and creative adventure in late 70s/early 80s Liverpool. I became part of a small group of poets and philosophers, smoking cigarettes and going to the local greasy spoon a few hundred yards from our faculty for challenging conversations about Marx and to share our new pieces.

At that time, I felt my daily visitations from the Muse as a masculine influence. I actually believed that I was the reincarnation of Hermann Hesse; I spent hours writing my thoughts in a journal, and into poems, and listening to Roy Harper. God had been a man and all of the philosophers were male too. Right up until the age of twenty-four I did not experience myself as a woman at all. Despite having attended strange sessions at school on periods and sexual reproduction, when I was too young to understand it, I had no idea how my body worked. I preferred the company of men, experienced myself largely as a disembodied brain, and sometimes as a body without a brain. But I do remember strutting around the campus, my head full of questions, with a feeling that my body was buzzing with untapped energy. I had this beautiful lecturer, who used to deliver his lecture on Kant on a high stool, smoking cigarettes and drinking fresh orange juice straight out of the carton; he told me once: *Alison,* ***in philosophy there are more questions than answers,*** which nestled right down into my being.

After graduating, I tried psychiatric nursing (which was not for me, I hated it) and discovered through the nursing school the work of Rogers, Maslow and Donna Brandes. The human potential movement opened up for me. I attended a few workshops in growth at that time. There were trust exercises and circle work, games, and also a psychodrama group that I attended for a while.

Through my mid-late twenties, three pivotal events occurred.

First, I became pregnant while searching for a job and I had no idea how. It was a chance encounter with Paula Weidegger's book *Female Cycles* that opened my eyes and explained how. Understanding that the process of ovulation and what blood flow actually was, and how it was in time with the moon phases and the tides was a revelation to me. I did not really have time to fully assimilate this new information however, which was actually my first exposure to feminism, until after I had given birth. During my pregnancy I discovered Zen Buddhism and attended a meditation group weekly until it became too uncomfortable to sit on the cushion! My time with this group, and at the *Throssel Hole Buddhist Abbey* in Northumberland, had a profound effect on me.

Second, I gave birth to my son in a maternity hospital and experienced the medicalisation of birth. I am proud to say that despite immense pain and interminable contractions I found strength from I don't know where (following forty-eight hours of no food) and delivered him from my body without forceps or Caesarean. In fact, it was upon hearing the mutterings that this might happen if my son and I took any longer that was enough inspiration for me to push him out into the world naturally. In the early stages of this process of giving them my body, under the influence of gas and air, I was eventually violated without my permission by a male doctor who pushed an implement up my vagina into my womb to artificially burst the amniotic sac. How I didn't pass out I also don't know. But I felt violated. And for months after the birth I felt angry without knowing why. I had lost control of my own body. In addition to this I was shocked by the experience of antipathy in the maternity ward towards the physical contact I required with my baby and to breast feeding him. I remember being discouraged from sleeping with my baby, and even from carrying him around, which I loved to do. (In case I dropped him, I was told!) When the nurses were not around, I would take him from the plastic box where he lay swaddled next to my bed and cuddle him up to me and fall asleep. They also took him away from me at certain times of day and tried to give him bottled milk, to give me more rest time. The first time I saw my son's arms and legs was days after his birth when the time came for me to be taught how to bath him. Always trying to take away the control. I was reading *Breast is Best* by Sheila Kitzinger, and it was on my bedside table. One of the nurses looked at it scathingly and told me to *take that with a pinch of salt*. This whole experience taught me that in this reality my body was not considered a sacred vessel but was instead a battle ground to be conquered, numbed and tamed. It also taught me that the medical establishment pushed the idea that a mother did not know what was right for herself and her child. But I had a beautiful baby, and after a week of visits from friends and family I was expected to get on with it. **Anger was not appropriate, so I turned it inward and became anxious and depressed instead. This was much more acceptable for a new mother; it had a name: it was a clinical entity called post-natal depression.**

For years after my experience of giving birth in that hospital, I was inexplicably depressed. Now I hated symbolic 'men'. I became acutely aware of the fluidity of gender. I also started studying furiously, fearing that I was going crazy, and the courses I studied at that time kept me anchored. I studied sociology with the Open University, but it was a course run by the Worker's Education Alliance that really shook things up for me. It was called *New Opportunities for Women*, and the module that touched me the most was the literature that we read together as a group and then discussed while our babies were looked after in the free creche. The set texts were *The Bell Jar* by Sylvia Plath, *Hotel du Lac* by Anita Brookner and *The Awakening* by Kate Chopin. These three novels blew me away, opening my eyes and my heart to the possibility that there was a specific female experience, and it was one of oppression under patriarchy. They helped to explain why my son's birth had been so traumatic for me, why I hated working in psychiatric wards and why I did not seem to want or need a long-term relationship with one man. I was waking up to the oppression even within my own apparently loving relationships with men. Soon after, I started reading the magazine *Spare Rib*, and with some women that I met on the course we set up a consciousness raising group. One of the main topics of conversation in our group was the alienation we had felt from our body even from childhood, and that this was a shared experience was revolutionary for us.

While all of this was going on, I had begun a detailed correspondence by letter (pre-internet days) with an old friend from university and we started a relationship. In a life-altering moment, he persuaded me to visit the island of Crete. This was my third pivotal experience and a time when everything opened out for me.

Something told me to say yes to this idea despite initial reluctance, and several months later I found myself waking up in a world of light, warmth, expansiveness and beauty that I felt a part of, not apart from. As I wandered the ruins of the halls and chambers of Knossos, I felt a sense of myself as a unity in mind, body and soul. There was a sense of deep knowing that I had been here before. I discovered upon subsequent visits to Crete that I had a sense of belonging to the entire island, its mountains, caves, beaches and coves – a sense of being home in every sense. I became receptive to all that this land had to offer and felt the music of the wild lyra enter my soul one evening as we sat eating by the sea. And as I gradually discovered more and more about the Minoans I also found out about their worship and reverence of the mysteries of the Divine Feminine through the energies of the earth.

I discovered through their traces that there had once existed a civilisation that revered the earth through priestesses that were largely female. And once I knew that, I was able to understand why whenever I again visited the island of Crete, **I was at my most vividly alive and my most sensuously creative.** This was a peaceful civilisation based on the values of beauty, creativity, spiritual connection to the earth and delight in pleasure that make up who I am as a teacher and healer today. I was captivated by the notion that the ruins of Knossos, Malia, Phaestos and Zakros were, according to archaeologists, palaces, but which I intuited were in fact communities where all life was infused by the sacred and where priestesses lived alongside potters and poets in safe communities and where ritual and celebration brought all of them together.

Here was a land where I experienced true connection in every sense for the very first time, and I believe it is the legacy of the Minoans[62] that gives Crete, more than anywhere else in Greece, its special quality. It feels like a passionate love affair. I have been compelled to go back ever since, whenever I can, even going so far as to buy a little house there. **In Crete these things that are the domain of the Divine Feminine are felt and celebrated in the embodied lives of the people – food, beauty, sensuality and sexuality, music, dance, nature, community, interconnectedness, celebration, spontaneity and sharing.** Crete is an expression of the life force. This is what I had been missing, and I was reunited with it the moment I stepped off the plane in September 1988 and felt a subtle but nevertheless visceral shift. A thrill, a sense of adventure, that always waits for me there calling me like a siren song.

My spiritual search was accelerated further by the death of my mother just before I turned twenty-nine and I was thrown once more into questioning existence. I had joined a body work group well before going to Crete, taking up yoga and Reichian[63] release, discovered dream work and Jung (and the archetypes). When my son was about six, I decided a steady income was required and took up a career as a teacher, teaching English in secondary schools. I knew by then that even though I had made the sacrifice of working for the still patriarchal hierarchical system, swapping hospitals for schools in order to earn money, **I wanted to work somewhere which honoured the feminine qualities of cooperation and collaboration.** I studied the teaching of sex education as my PGCE[64] dissertation topic and chose a school, probably the only in the whole of the North, that was based on wholeness, with circle time and experiential emotionally-based learning central to the life of the school. I stayed there for eleven years, honing my skills in circle work and guided journeys.

I was able to form deep relationships with young people through these methodologies and to have a transformative impact on their early lives. I discovered my real work, which was always central to my work in education – group work in circle where the leader is a facilitator and everyone's experience is equally valid. I created after-school writing groups, drama groups, a buddy-mentor group for boys with 'behavioural difficulties', conferences and trainings for teachers, and later in my second school introducing circle time and experiential group work into a tough inner city comprehensive school. **I can see now how this nurturing and egalitarian style of education stemmed from my immersion into the energy of Crete, but at the same time I also**

---

[62] A Bronze Age Aegean civilisation on the island of Crete and other Aegean Islands.

[63] Originating in the work of psychoanalyst Wilhelm Reich.

[64] Postgraduate Certificate in Education

see how every experience I have had has led me to experience immanence,[65] which for me is the heart of the Divine Feminine. For this is not an unbalanced, head-based, sky-based spirituality with a white bearded man at the helm, but an earthy, embodied knowing that we are all expressions of the divine in both masculine and feminine aspects. The rising of the Divine Feminine is not a replacement for patriarchy but an urge to integration which will eventually result in the 'new world'.

I did my post-graduate counselling training while still teaching in schools, training in Rogerian counselling, which from then on infused all of my work relationships and teaching. Before he died, Rogers had been moving towards a view not fully articulated by him, that love was the curative factor. When I moved towards pastoral care because my interest lay in children who could not fit into the system it was because I also wanted the system to be better, to be more peaceful, joyful, loving and creative. I fully embraced the core conditions as an integral part of my being (a way of being, as Rogers expressed it). I supported many children labelled as disruptive and mentally ill to fit in, because they had no other option, by regarding them without judgement which is indeed the attitude of love. In my final role in the education system, I developed an affinity with teenage girls, struggling as they were with identity and a societal crushing of their essential nature, and latterly with young people struggling with gender identity. I worked for several years developing tailored educational programmes for these casualties and outsiders of the system – the excluded, the so-called 'emotional school refusers' and the pregnant – using language, communication, group work and the arts to free up their trapped souls. One such group of girls, who I was working with on a creative project, self-titled themselves the Mainstream Misfits, self-published their own poetry anthology called Open your Mind, which still sits proudly on my shelf, and then went on to a win a regional poetry slam competition. Poetry and self-expression – creativity – was their way out of various forms of self-harm.

Underpinning all of my work has always been a passionate desire to create a new world. I knew that education for young people was crucial in this, and my son grew up alongside this work. What was needed was something different, something creative, exploratory, something that honoured feelings and relationships, that united people and helped them to feel relaxed and valued, and also to enjoy life. I always enjoyed working against the grain of exam and assessment driven standardisation that were part of an outmoded system designed for the dying industrial age.

In 2017, I was forced out of education. When I could take no more of the insults to my integrity, I left and set up my own healing and therapy business, where I intuited I would be able to express all of my skills. It was a leap into the unknown.

---

[65] The idea that the divine is manifested in the natural world.

In 2016, I received my strongest message yet that the entire system had to change, when I learned about receiving, and how in the receptive state we can access a direct communication line to nature, of which we are of course part. Shortly after this, I experienced a shamanic extraction where the pain I had felt as a sensitive child was removed from my being.

I now specialise in guiding women through life transitions by putting them back in touch with their divine essence – their soul, if you will. **Women are receptive now to their emerging power but many, including me, need guiding through the challenging terrain of the potholes of the dying patriarchy.** We are doing this with the help of guides, and also with sisterhoods, tribes, circles. This truly is an exciting time to be alive.

The whole experience of writing this has been revelatory for me. It has been a consciousness-raising exercise in itself. In making the shift from disembodied purely head-based experience to an integrated, lived experience of wholeness and with the full unhindered expression of the life force as being also an integration, I can see how my very life story mirrors this process that society is currently still undergoing. The survival of humans now depends upon it.

Maddison Bee

Metamorphosis

There are three paths we walk in life. The physical path in which we feel, smell, see and hear; the mental and emotional path which defines how we interact with our surroundings, other people and our beliefs; and our spiritual path. This is our essence. Not all of us truly awaken to this path and yet it is our greatest trial and teacher. This is a story of how I found my spiritual path. I'm still walking it and making mistakes. I still feel anger and frustration, I still struggle and I still cry, but I have learnt how to overcome and persevere. Most importantly, I have learnt how to accept and honour all parts of the struggle; the fight and the glory. When I was younger, I valued the glory, all the while not recognising that I was learning more from the fight.

I believe we have to discuss the raw and unpleasant emotions that drive us, to accept that light doesn't exist without shadow, and that this process is **a journey of duality between pain and pleasure.** I'm not always sure where I am in my journey; some days I feel strong in who I am, and others I am drowning inside. This is my internal struggle – two strong forces of energy between elevation and destruction, the masculine and the feminine, the *yin* and *yang*, that I am constantly trying to balance in order to find my inner equanimity.

> *A human being is part of the whole called by us 'the universe,' a part of limited space and time. We experience ourselves, our thoughts and feelings as something separate from the rest – a kind of optical illusion of our consciousness. This delusion is a kind of prison for us, restricting our personal desires and affection for a few persons nearest to us. Our task must be to free ourselves from this prison by widening our circle of understanding and compassion to embrace all living creatures and the whole of nature in its beauty. ~Albert Einstein*

This quote is a reminder that all of the earth's inhabitants – you, me, the flowers and the trees, the rivers and the seas, and everything in between – are sacred and worthy. We need to harmonise our attitudes and behaviours to live in a state of equilibrium whereby all is one and one is all.

A misconception of the feminist movement is that in order to honour a woman's rights and place on this earth, she must be glorified in ways that exemplify and separate her from men. However, there is no *us* and *them*, no *superior* or *inferior*. Such schools of thought make young women, like me, feel wary of being remotely associated with the dogma that has slandered what it means to be a feminist. A true feminist knows that she is a divine balance of both the masculine and feminine energies within herself. She needs to nourish both parts to feel balanced and whole. It is equally important to recognise our divine masculine and feminine. Suppressing one leads to disharmony, and our own energy centres can become overloaded.

I have struggled to find this divine balance within my personal life and have learnt first-hand the dangers that come from ignoring calls to our feminine and masculine energies.

Before I share my personal journey to unravelling the Divine Feminine within me, I would like to talk about where my inspiration to honour and understand both these divinities within came from. As a disclaimer I would also like to note my hesitation in describing my experience of womanhood as divine. For me, the word divine implies esoteric revelations, and my reality is humbler. I haven't had profound moments of enlightenment arise through meditation retreats in Southeast Asia or shamanic ceremonies in the Amazonian jungle. I am however, deeply connected to myself and my environment. When you live in tune with the natural rhythms of life, experiences and events reveal themselves to you and you learn to live openly through these, by letting go and refraining from the initial instinct to try and control what happens to you. This is a fine art to master and has taken determination, discipline and devotion.

My inspiration for my spiritual practice stems from Gaia[66] and the Anima Mundi.[67] In contemporary thought, Gaia, as a philosophy and spirituality, encompasses a means of interaction with our world as a living entity, whereby every organism, animal, plant, landform or person has an essence rooted within it – a life force, a soul. Nothing is separate and all life co-exists. This phenomenon is easier to contemplate if we think of nature as a living, breathing organism. In Hindu philosophy, nature is an intelligent and conscious entity. The elements of earth, wind, fire and water have divinities intrinsic to them. The rain god Indra, the wind god Vayu, the fire goddess Agni, the earth goddess Bhumi, and the sun and moon goddesses – these deities are worshipped as part of nature, rather than separate, overseeing entities. Within these elemental forces there are both masculine and feminine energies that shape them. This is the anima mundi, or the soul of the earth. In connecting to the soul of the earth I learnt to connect to myself. My essence was in a deeply rooted connection I found with my landscape.

---

[66] In Greek mythology, the ancestral mother of all life, the Mother Earth goddess.
[67] The world soul.

I grew up in Australia where the landscape can be a harsh teacher, with floods, bushfires, and drought. You learn to exist in extremities. This taught me the appreciation of duality; the cycles of destruction and creation. Through these observations I was able to apply these cycles to my personal life and learn to honour the creative harmonies of my energy as well as the darker shadow sides. It was almost as if the landscape was ritualistically cleansing itself. After a particularly severe bushfire along the Great Ocean Road[68] – a place I would regularly visit to regenerate – I remember walking through the once glistening eucalyptus forests that I had visited only months before. Where there were once fragrant scents enriching my senses, all I could smell were the charred remains of the forest. Where there was once shining greenery stretching everywhere in sight, all I could see were burnt hues of amber and ash, and the husks of incinerated trees. Where I could once touch trees of paper and bark, all I could feel were blackened dusty remains underneath my fingertips. I sat in the middle of the burnt forest floor, where life once thrived around me. I felt a metaphor Gaia was trying to teach me about my own pain. I listened to her and I wrote:

When the earth burns,
There is a lesson for us to learn.
Her spirit yearns,
As vicious flames of destruction wipe her terrain,
It seems impossible to start again.

But she has a plan, for new life can't spring without her hand.
She burns to allow herself to heal,
As the cycles of creation begin to reveal,
You too can spring from the ashes of your pain
And allow yourself to bloom again.

At the time, I was experiencing a spiritual block. I was at war with myself. But a lot of this came from an overwhelming pressure I was putting on myself to rise above my experiences of anxiety and depression, because I thought these were negative experiences. I was trying to suppress a large part of my experience of living by denying its reality, because I had internally judged feeling angry or depressed or anxious as undesirable. I learnt that there were some toxic beliefs within this new age spiritual movement I was following. For someone that is already struggling but trying to improve themselves, hearing phrases like *you attract what you feel* is detrimental to well-being, and it's unfair. Everything exists within dichotomies. The philosophical principle of *yin* and *yang* is based on balancing the dualities between so-called 'good' and 'bad' – why would our emotional state be any different? If in nature I experience the parallels of creation emerging from destruction, and vice versa, or the abundance of spring after a perilous winter, why would I expect to feel whole and happy all the time? I was

---

[68] A 200+ kilometre stretch of National Heritage road along the south-eastern coast of the state of Victoria in Australia.

making myself suffer from this expectation. Once I learnt to release it, and accept these 'negative' emotions I was able to anchor myself a lot more stably, and once I was anchored, I learnt how to find the balance between feeling elated and feeling deflated. This was an important, rebuilding realisation for me. **I redefined my spiritual journey to open up and learn from my shadow self, rather than struggle by trying to block and suppress it.**

Sometimes the cages we feel trapped in are created by ourselves, by our own limiting beliefs. Self-doubt and self-criticism have been the hardest obstacles I have had to overcome, and I still feel that this is a process rather than a destination. Yet **warriors are not made without going into battle,** and it is with these internal struggles and releasing ourselves from them, that we are able to connect with our true life-force and creative power.

In my personal journey, to understand myself and my place on this planet, I learnt that there is a process of unlearning that I must embark on. Cultural conditioning, expectations and opinions of other people, and the conclusions I'd devised as a child to define who I was, had shaped my experience of what my life ought to be. Once I began to strip these beliefs from the way I interacted with myself and the world around me, there was no pressure to *be* anything; I simply was.

As you let life live through you, you become more of who you really are. ~Rodger Keyes

It was comforting to resist this process at first. It was easier to struggle, because the struggle was a familiar illusion. But I couldn't continue living in resistance. The more I resisted and challenged, the more I noticed those two forces flooding my life.

I remember my early childhood being full of inspiration, passion and creativity. I was an intuitive and highly sensitive child. I had a deep fascination with what I was told was fantasy, but I innately understood energy, spirit and other non-verbal communications. Though these interactions came naturally to me, I was taught to suppress them and this caused a lot of conflict and confusion.

I was raised by wonderful women who were intelligent and strong, and whom I adore. But they were fixated on reason and logic. No one in my family let themselves go, or let themselves feel deeply. Recognising this I would watch their struggles and carry their pain. I had one beacon of light, my grandmother. She was a rainbow amidst the clouds, who told me to believe in fairies, to listen to the spirit of the Earth and to honour my intuition. Her wisdom was often ignored and criticised, especially by my parents. I started to listen to them, and from that moment I felt my essence being drained, and for a long time I believed I had lost this forever. My journey is one of reclaiming my child-like joy and passion for life and relearning how to interact with the world from a place of feeling and instinct. I took back my personal power that was always there – I'd just got caught up listening to what other people told me I ought to be.

As I grew into a young teenager this sense of fragmentation caused me to resist. I began to resent the world and I indulged in that suffering by being careless. My relationship with my father collapsed when he realised I wasn't the quiet little girl that wanted to hide in her room any longer. No, I was trying on the kind of woman *I* wanted to be. I wanted to challenge! Challenge him, challenge expectations, challenge anyone. I wanted my presence to be felt. I defied and protested but my ultimate intentions weren't being met. I wasn't making the positive impact I wanted to make. I wasn't inspiring anything. I was actively trying to burn the pathways that shaped the bright future I had ahead of me because I was hurting and confused.

The irony of feeling defenceless in the world, was that I was at the time an exceptionally skilled martial artist. But I was only defending myself physically, when it was my mind and spirit that felt under attack. Feeling mentally and spiritually protected are lessons from my martial arts training that my younger mind wasn't yet ready to comprehend, although I now understand more deeply. This is why we meditated before, during and after each class. Meditation was particularly important in combat. I understood how to train my mind to mentally overcome an opponent before I physically met them on the mat, yet it took me years to apply this kind of focus to my life outside of karate. I was eighteen when I gave up karate. I was selected to represent my country at an international level of competition, and was mentally and physically beginning my preparation for my *shodan*.[69] All that I had spent ten years of my younger life working towards, I gave up. I'd mostly understood my training as a competitive sport rather than a physical and mental discipline and a profound spiritual teacher.

Behind all of this is a very raw story of being groomed by my martial arts teacher from the age of fourteen, being in a relationship with him, his wife finding out and leaving him, and finally quitting my training at the peak of my athletic career. What followed was guilt – guilt I placed on myself for my responsibility in the destruction of someone else's marriage, and guilt for losing something I had spent ten years of my life working for. The heartbreak is still real years later.

I formed a lot of fixed negative beliefs about myself during these years, that for much of my early adult life I believed defined me. These beliefs all had similar themes of inadequacy and disappointment. Growing up I felt my voice was consistently over-powered by my father. I never felt heard or understood. This got worse when I grew into a teenager. He felt he was entitled to my respect, but neither earned nor reciprocated it. Our relationship was very authoritarian and I felt I was spiritually suffocated by his domineering attitudes. I put excessive pressure on myself to appease him, not realising at the time that it was his own

---

[69] Black belt grading.

personal battle being projected onto me, and nothing I ever accomplished would give me the validation I was seeking from him.

This situation manifested in many crippling ways as a young woman. I didn't speak up when I was uncomfortable or felt something was immoral. I would agree to things I didn't want to do just to avoid the paralysing confrontation of feeling that I had to explain myself. This was particularly damaging in my personal relationships where for a long time I felt unworthy of respect. Seeking superficial connections, I enabled myself to be used and mistreated because I hadn't had a healthy relationship with my father that fostered self-respect and worth. My first experiences of romantic relationships were, unsurprisingly, violent, controlling, and detrimental to the sense of self-worth I was desperately trying to rebuild. By twenty-three, I had been cheated on multiple times, developed STIs from my supposedly committed partner, lied to, betrayed, verbally and physically abused. I knew this wasn't who I was, but I hadn't yet had the kind of awakening that would prevent accepting these volatile behaviours in my life. The inability to direct my own life and speak for myself lead me down so many false pathways that I ended up losing my entire sense of self.

At eighteen, after busting my butt to graduate high school with marks ranking me in the top ten percent of the state, I applied for a bachelor program, still unsure about what I wanted to do with my life. I had a yearning compassion and care that meant whatever the answer to that question would be I had to feel that I was making the world a kinder, more tolerant and peaceful place. I wasn't sure university was the best path for me, but at the time, being so caught up listening to what those around me thought was best, I enrolled in a liberal arts programme and was again presented with the feeling that I wasn't in the right place. My sense of disenfranchisement upon completing my undergraduate degree was immense. Why didn't I feel accomplished? Why was I still feeling lost? Was this not supposed to open up pathways and more directions? Why was I still working as a waitress, when my parents assured me university was the bridge that would give me a ticket out of the life that was their working-class experience.

After being passive for so long, I started to get angry. I had done everything I had been told to do and still wasn't feeling satisfied. I realised that what everyone else wanted for my life was just that: what everyone else wanted. I had ignored the calls to my creative passions in favour of the academic pursuits my parents assured me would build me a better life. I was twenty-five, with an undergraduate degree, no field experience in my area of specialisation, working in a café, and still feeling unfulfilled.

It was time for radical change.

My awakening to the Divine Feminine was more like an eruption in that I had repeatedly ignored her calls, but I could no longer continue on this path. It was uncomfortable and I was afraid. I knew it would mean letting go of comfortable habits, people and places. I was grieving the loss of the familiar. I had to learn that the people closest to me weren't necessarily the right protectors and guides I needed to be surrounded by. This meant losing friendships and lovers. It meant establishing firm boundaries from those who I couldn't exactly release from my inner circle but whose energy and effect on me I could redefine. This is a core-shattering process for a young woman to embark on. It feels like walking into the woods unknown, leaving behind the skin of what is known and comfortable to embrace the dark path that lies ahead.

As raw and painful as it was, it was also the liberation I needed to heal my old wounds and overcome my shadows of self-doubt and anguish, or at least learn to live with them in a more accepting way. It also meant it was time for me to be the driving force behind my decisions and to start carving the life that inspired me. For a long time, I believed that my insecurities and anxieties were harmful and hindering. Instead I have started to ask myself what I can learn from these emotions by allowing myself to tap into them and explore the lessons I had initially been repressing.

I learnt that I was yelling, and pushing those close to me away, not because that was what I wanted, but because I wanted to feel heard. Evidently being louder was not making me be heard any more clearly. I learnt how to talk again and express my concerns in a more meaningful way. It was hard to do, because it meant I had to expose my fears and insecurities, but this created a deeper connection to those around me and myself, which was the reassurance I needed.

I had to unlearn the beliefs I'd internalised about where I thought I should be in life. I had to unlearn and channel into my own inner guidance and wisdom, and listen to that voice instead. For a long time, this voice was a whisper; it was ironic that I felt I had to shout to be heard. But now that I have taken myself away from all the noise of what those around me were telling me, I am able to tune in and listen more clearly.

Through traveling and reconnecting with the simple pleasures I loved as a child, I have learnt to release many of the pressures I put on myself to please those around me. I have allowed myself to slow down and just be, and through doing that I found my path to learning more about me. This was my call to Divine Feminine. **It was about listening to and nurturing myself.** Having ignored these needs for so long – putting those of others above my own – it is no wonder her call manifested in anger. For now, it's about weathering that anger and learning how to redirect impulsivity towards intuition. Through listening to her call, and honouring my own needs, I have been able to turn tidal waves into a still sea. Through allowing the call of Divine Feminine into my life I am now learning how to love myself again, and through that journey I am finding a way to liberate myself from the prison of my mind's limiting beliefs.

It's been about getting in tune with my body, with what I feel and sense, and rebuilding enough trust in myself to honour these intuitions, rather than overthinking them and getting stuck in a loop of self-doubt. I've started to notice little reminders along the way, messages that some may dismiss as coincidence, but I know are reinforcing that I'm on my true path; a path to acceptance, accountability and authenticity. I have had to accept the shadow sides of myself, the less desirable parts of me and learn that healing does not come by erasing these elements, but rather accepting them so that they can be built on. For all the dark counterparts within yourself, there exists a mirroring light of that energy.

Which brings me to my next point of accountability. I had to be really honest with myself, and more often than not, I didn't want to hear the truth. **I had to recognise where I was actively contributing to negative patterns of anger, self-doubt, denial and guilt.** When I was operating from these places, I would be nasty to myself and those nearby. It's easier and more comfortable to ignore one's own behaviours and blame those around you. It was easier to be angry at the world, for the abuse I had suffered, for the pain, for not feeling like I had the autonomy to direct my own life. But if I continued to live in this narrative, I would be a passive observer for that which happened to me. Accountability means acknowledging that you have suffered and that you can't control the past, but you can control how you overcome that suffering, by keeping negative coping mechanisms and attachments in check, and by confronting and releasing them. Finally, we reach authenticity. After we have done the soul-searching work to accept both the shadow and light that radiates within, and we can be accountable for our actions, we are able to be who we really are, unmasked. I still find this overwhelming and treacherous at times – it's like posting a selfie on *Instagram* without the benefit of any filters. Each day is a journey of self-love and commitment. The more I practice this, the easier revealing myself becomes.

Accept that which makes you human, account for your actions and find your authenticity. May we all feel whole and loved in our unmasked selves.

With love and gratitude.

Tia Christiansen

Reclaiming my Connection to the Great Mother

I grew up in the countryside of western Massachusetts. I was a tomboy and spent my days outside playing with my dog Toby, who was my best friend, building forts and climbing trees.

My family never went to church or had conversations about God. My mom had a terrible experience as a child at Catholic school which left her agnostic. My dad, who grew up Lutheran, is a perpetual seeker of the Divine. We celebrated all the Christian holidays with my grandmother, aunts, uncles and cousins. We had a Christmas tree, presents, hunted for eggs, and received chocolate bunnies. I was always free to ask about God, church, or religion, and knew if I ever wanted to go to a church my parents would take me.

My family often spent time outside on long walks in the woods. One day I asked my dad *What is God?* Dad told me God was everywhere – in the trees around us, in the rocks, the sky, and the log I was sitting on. God could not be contained and was always present. This was a comforting concept and I remember it *felt* right. Plus my dad told me so.

At about six or seven, I remember thinking it was ridiculous that religions excluded people because they went to a different church or had a different way of connecting with God. If people were good and treated others well how could it be possible that they went to some place called hell? What was that place anyway? Real, or just made up to scare us?

I also thought it was silly that one group's idea of heaven or an afterlife was the only possibility. That didn't make sense to me. This God that was everywhere, that could not be contained, and was present all the time, surely would not be so narrow-thinking? **I crafted my own belief that whatever a person thinks is heaven, or exists in the afterlife, is what exists for them.**

I had a lightning bolt moment when I was fourteen. I was a sophomore and my English class was assigned Hermann Hesse's *Siddhartha*. This was my first introduction to Buddhism and it rocked my world. The search for Enlightenment. That we can find Enlightenment within us, no matter where we are; it is all-inclusive and all we have to do is be empty. This kicked off my thirst, my craving to understand more about our world and spirituality. I read books with messages from channeled guides, and tried to meditate like Siddhartha because that surely was the path to this peaceful existence.

Then Shirley MacLaine came out with *Out on Limb* in 1983 when I was fifteen. My mom read the book, then me. The conversation about reincarnation and aliens began to be more public than before, and it took over my imagination. I *knew* it was all true. I desperately wanted to connect with my past lives, find out what had happened, and learn how I could clear that karma. If only I could sit down with Shirley and figure it all out!

That year my mom gave me a chakra chart, that included affiliated stones, for my birthday. My mom was very open to conversations about new age things, and had her own fascination with Edgar Cayce, reincarnation, and all things Egypt. I loved the idea of being connected with these healing stones and having them as guides to healing.

When I was sixteen, I visited a friend of my aunt who was a channel, as I was sure she could help me clear my karma. It was a fascinating experience and I craved a deeper understanding. I tried meditation again, but still couldn't get the hang of it. There weren't any apps at that time, or any classes to take or yoga studios I knew of to visit.

I graduated high school and I was still the kid who was into all the new age stuff. I was aware of the Goddess, but did not feel a real connection with her then. After graduation I joined corporate America, climbed the ladder to the corner office and a seat on the board of directors for a fifty million dollar company – the first female to be on the board. But I was miserable, with no spiritual connection.

At twenty-seven, I quit my job, packed up and headed west to finish my undergraduate as a full-time student at the University of Oregon. I took a class called the Philosophy of Love and Sex and we had amazing conversations about Eros, the Greek view of love and sex, and the modern view of both. I became aware of the Age of the Goddess and the crushing of her worship with the rise of monotheistic male oriented religion (Christianity) during the Roman era. I was desperate for understanding and knowledge once again. My anger that the Divine Feminine had taken a back seat for centuries reawakened my spirituality. How could it have been stomped out? Why had She been forsaken for a male oriented entity? As humanity had reached the age of enlightenment, why was a gender attached to the Creator at all? I left the business school, declared a new major in religious studies and focused on Judaism in antiquity.

After completing my undergraduate degree, I received a scholarship to attend the *Oxford Centre for Hebrew & Jewish Studies*. I dreamt of bringing forth the stories of powerful Jewish women in the Herodian era. Salome, Herod's sister; Queen Mariamme I, whom Herod killed; and Cleopatra.

I buried myself in study, ancient texts, and words. I was thirsty to know Her, but never really found Her in the way I desired; it is not through the head but the heart that we find and connect with the Divine Feminine. That is where She lives.

The Great Mother.

I had been working with a life coach for six months and joined her retreat in Malibu on how to develop a connection with your Inner Guidance System (IGS). The IGS is your inner voice/wisdom that is always with you, and when you develop a deep connection with it you always know when you are on path. It is your personal GPS system powered by God/Goddess/Spirit, or whichever word most resonates with you. The thought of going made me extremely uncomfortable. Participating in a retreat with others, developing deep connections with their inner wisdom; learning about energy – how to sense it and play with it – and the art of manifestation, and sharing personal space with others in an intimate setting for multiple days, were not things I was accustomed to. I knew facing the discomfort would awaken me to something new. *The Secret* had been out for a while and this retreat was a deep dive into the heart of what the movie and book had made accessible to hundreds of thousands of people.

We spent the first day projecting energy towards each other while thinking of a specific word such as *love* or *compassion*, learning how intention and ways of being ripple outward from us and impact others. The second day we practiced sitting in deep meditation to quiet the mind and connect with our IGS. We practiced receiving guidance by *feeling* responses in our bodies. Did we receive a physical opening sensation or a closing sensation when we made a query? Opening indicates that what we are thinking is on path, whereas a closing indicates we are off path.

The last day of the retreat was when I first felt the Divine Feminine, or the Great Mother as I call her. I sat facing a fellow attendee in deep listening. The exercise was to connect deeply with the Divine and say whatever came up. No judgement, no thinking, just intuition and connection. In my mind I asked: *What needs to be said? What needs to be revealed?* There was a bubbling sensation from the top of my root chakra, a feeling of warmth, and a surrender of my ego and conscious mind. A voice came through me, and as I faced my friend, a message was revealed to her. I spoke automatically while still being very present and conscious to the experience. It was me talking at first, then I felt a power growing within and my speech shifted from first person singular to first person plural, eg. *We see your light and it will grow to heal others.*

I don't remember all that was said in that moment. I don't remember what is revealed to others when it happens, as the words are not for me but for the person receiving the wisdom. I do remember saying my friend's divine love and light would fill this world and heal others. When the message was complete, I felt the sensation of coming fully back into my body as if from a deep meditation: the heaviness of the body, automatic breathing, my heart beating. The voice, which for me is the Great Mother, said *We are complete.*

I was astounded and humbled and felt an intense love for others, feeling loved beyond words, in tears, rocking back and forth giving thanks for allowing me to speak Her words. After a few minutes our teacher asked if we would like to try again. Without hesitation, we both said yes!

Again I asked, *What needs to be said? What needs to be revealed?* The same bubbling sensation came, the ego was set aside, and Her voice rang in my mind. Again, She said *We are complete* when the message had been fully revealed. Tears of gratitude and deep love flowed. I opened my eyes and our teacher had tears. It was the first time in one of her retreats an attendee opened to the connection she had experienced since she was a small girl and had begun hearing God speak to her. My experience represented the ease (with practice) with which anyone is able to connect to the Divine.

The experience punctuated what I had always believed about spirituality since I was fourteen. Spirituality comes from within. **When we clear our minds, when we are still and set aside our ego, we are able to connect with the Divine.** I wanted to be within Her warm embrace all the time. To be of service, to help humanity, and do Her calling.

Now that I had opened to hearing Her, I began to receive information through clairvoyance and clairsentience. It could happen anywhere at any time, and I shared what came through with those for whom the message was meant. One night I was out at a bar with friends and went to the bathroom. As I was leaving, I felt Her presence. I turned to the bathroom attendant and asked *Would you mind if I share some information with you? Sometimes I receive information for people from the Great Mother, God, The Universe, Spirit, whatever you call the Divine?* She said yes, and I told her not to worry and that her grandmother was very proud of her. She was tearful and told me her grandmother had passed and that she missed her deeply. I saw her grandmother standing behind her and her grandmother asked me to tell her *I am with you all the time.* I felt myself come back to my body and the Great Mother's presence faded.

On another occasion, I was talking with a dear friend, Frank, who mentioned feeling restless with where he was at in life. Without thinking, and from a place that was not my conscious mind, I said *it's time to spread your wings and move away from your home town.* I had no idea my friend still lived in his home town, nor why I said those exact words other than they just came out of me. Frank was shocked and amazed. *How did you know I wanted to move?* I said *sometimes I just know things.* We continued to talk and the Great Mother showed me Frank's angel wings. They were tight and constricted and needed to be flexed, like stretching your muscles after a long hike. I asked if I could share some information that was coming through intuitively. Frank said *yes, but I have no idea what you mean by that!*

I had him close his eyes, take in a few deep breaths, and imagine he had a pair of wings on his back. Of course he opened his eyes and said *Are you kidding me?!* I said *Trust me. This will be amazing.* We began again and as Frank followed my guided words, I felt him open his angel wings and become lighter, and I sensed a shift within his muscles. When we were done Frank told me he'd bad back pain for years and that it now felt much better.

Goddess Codes.

I had been seeing an acupuncturist to support my body following a diagnosis of adrenal blowout four years prior. She also became my Reiki teacher and mentor, and activated seven of my ancient Goddess codes.

Every human has ancient Goddess codes embedded within their DNA which travel through each life time. These codes are our gifts, our powers, part of our identity, and can be activated. I cannot relay my mentor's process as it is unique to her, but my experience during the process was similar to the euphoric feeling sometimes experienced during massage, Reiki or acupuncture treatments. Sometimes I would sense a shift deep within my physical body, my energy body, or in the area around us. Sometimes I would have a greater sense of knowing after the activation, and other times it would take weeks for me to feel something different. Sometimes messages would come in deep meditation. It was very subtle; a sense that something deep within me shifted – woke up – that I was remembering and reclaiming knowledge that had been with me throughout time.

This activation, and becoming a Reiki Master, blew the doors off my perception of time and space, and gave me a deeper understanding of our relationship to the Divine.

I most often receive information visually (clairvoyance) or a strong feeling of knowing (clairsentience.) Sometimes I hear the same song over and over again or see the same number (usually 444) many times in a day. Often coincidences occur, like Mary Magdalene's or Isis' name being referenced multiple times in different circumstances in a day. These are all hints from the Great Mother to pay attention as a message is being conveyed.

My first experience with Isis was during a Reiki session. I saw myself in full regalia dressed with armour made of leather and metal much like a Christian Archangel in paintings circa the 1600s. I carried a staff and sword. My hair was long and black with loose curls. I wore a simple diadem with a green stone encrusted within that sat on the center of my forehead. I felt an unyielding power of Light and it was as if my heart grew beyond the capacity of my human body. I felt the presence of Isis – pure light, larger than the human mind can comprehend, and She reached out to touch me on the head. I knew I had been an initiate of Isis in a former life and that moment was my time to choose whether or not to continue Her work or decline. I willingly accepted. I have knelt many times since at the feet of Isis in meditation.

In 2018, I had a period of doubt and struggle with the new information of my ancient Goddess Codes. I questioned whether what I was seeing, hearing and sensing was true. Was I just making it all up? *Who am I to be a Warrior of Light?* I asked for help; help in settling my human mind, help to quiet the doubt. One day, as I meditated, Mother Mary and Mary Magdalene appeared. They embraced me and I felt that I was reconnecting with sisters. They were not separate from me, but part of my experience through time. We walked down a wooded path that morphed into a temple. We dropped to our knees and Isis appeared before us in pure light humanoid form. She handed me a scroll and I realized this was a graduation ceremony, a symbolic gesture to put my mind at rest, with Mother Mary and Mary Magdalene as witnesses. It was an experience I could grab onto to understand that I am a Warrior of Light with the mark of Isis.

I am encoded as Queen Maab of the Fairy realm. This still feels strange to say out loud for fear of judgement by others! There are many Fairy clans all responsible for protecting certain aspects of time and space and the planet. When I connect with the Fairy realm, the feeling I get is playful, as well as a sense of being home.

My first conscious experience with the Fairy realm was also during a Reiki session. I felt an energy that was ticklish! I saw a number of fairy folk and presumed they were guides revealing themselves to me. When the session was over, my Reiki teacher told me she had been tapped on the shoulder by a fairy and asked to tell me *Remind her she is Queen Maab.* I had no idea what that meant, and neither did my teacher at the time. I went home to meditate and research. If it was real there would be something factual to back it up, right? What I found brought me to tears. The first mention of a Queen Maab is in Shakespeare's *Romeo and Juliet.* Mercutio mentions a *Queen Mab* who rides at night in her acorn chariot across the lips of men who sleep, to pull their dreams from their minds and lay them on their lips. About four years prior, I had heard a loud voice in my mind during a time when I was not really asleep and not really awake. All it said was *dream sculpting.* I wrote down the phrase in my journal and forgot about it until my fairy guide appeared to remind me who I was.

I am Rose Sophia nourishment. Sophia is Greek for wisdom and the rose is the symbol for love. It is my responsibility to embody a way of being that carries divine wisdom and love forward into this time and place; to spread the nourishing wise loving energy of the Divine Feminine through Reiki, channelled energy healing, Her words, and my declaration to awaken a million hearts to their Divine Feminine power of love and intuition.

I am a Portal Shifter. I am responsible for the safe keeping of passages that lead to different portals, which are used for travel by all beings. Specifically, I am responsible for blocking unbalanced energy from taking over these passages or blocking beings of Light from using them to access different points of existence.

Mary Magdalene.

Four years ago, around the same time my ancient Goddess codes were activated, Mary Magdalene appeared to me in meditation for the first time. I was surprised, and more than once have told myself I imagined the experience. Who was I to see Mary Magdalene? Was it really Her? How could I be worthy? However, every time I told myself it was just my imagination, or it was just some woman, my inner guidance closed. This is how I knew that it truly was Mary Magdalene who had appeared. I was meditating and I saw myself in a busy village. I had the sense that someone was looking at me and a woman wearing a *peplos*[70] of natural colors turned her head to look directly at me. Her eyes were deep saucers holding much love and wisdom and I was filled with humility and love. She spoke directly to my mind: *You have my secret.* I was so startled that I opened my eyes. What secret? Why hadn't I asked?

A few years later Mary Magdalene appeared to me again. Again she said *You have my secret in your heart* and added *You will awaken to it when the time is right.*

I learned the meaning of this in June 2019 when I went to Sedona, Arizona. I had heard about the Sedona vortices, swirling centers of energy conducive to healing, meditation and self-exploration. Many people feel inspired, recharged or uplifted after visiting a vortex. They are places where the earth is especially alive with energy. My first stop was the *Chapel of the Holy Cross*, sitting high atop the red rocks in Sedona.

When I arrived, my first reaction was sadness. I looked out over the landscape and was struck by the beauty of the land and that it had once been home to the Apache, one of the most well-known tribes of indigenous 'First Nation' peoples.

---

[70] A heavy woolen garment.

You can hear the songs of the First peoples on the wind, hear their cries, and feel their pain at the loss of their home. You can also feel the Divine Feminine. As I sat in meditation outside the chapel, I sensed the strong presence of the Great Mother in the form of the Rose Sophia, along with many female maidens who are the caretakers of the area. The Great Mother's presence is of immense creative power. It took my breath away.

What I understood is it is time to unlock the Rose Sophia energy within us. *Sophia* is Greek for wisdom and the rose represents divine love. Thus the Rose Sophia is the Divine Feminine wisdom and nourishing love that lives within our heart. **It is time to let that energy blossom and flow through us.** This is where our true power as women lies. **Heart-powered leadership is our divine right** and gives us the strength and energy to lead.

This was the secret I was keeping in my heart for Mary Magdalene. It is the secret many of us have kept safe through time, and it is now time to spread the message.

Gaia is the physical representation of the Divine Feminine – the Earth – and it is time to connect with her: to feel her, hear her pain, and heal her. **Now is the time to feed her healing energy, see and preserve our natural resources, and increase our vibration so she may increase hers.** We are intrinsically connected like the roots of the trees in a forest. We must stop tearing her, ripping her and ignoring her. **Mother Gaia is speaking and now is the time to act.** Not tomorrow.

I have not shared my stories widely out of fear of judgement, and misunderstanding, and my own need to be accepted. But the Divine Feminine, the Great Mother, the Goddess, has told me it is time for me to speak up and out. It is time for me to put aside doubt and **get on with what I am called to do** as an energy healer and leader, to awaken hearts, and help women reclaim their Divine Feminine power of love and intuition.

Allison Gentle

A String of Jewels

I am trying to remember when I first became aware of the divine dimension, and I find myself going further and further back. Usually I place my first spiritual awareness at an experience when I was nineteen, looking out a window at a single tree, and seeing beyond its ordinariness, seeing that it was connecting heaven and earth, its roots reaching far into the soil and its branches reaching into the sky, just as I stand as a human being, feet on the ground, most of the time, and arms stretching up to the infinite.

But then I remember confiding in a friend after a night of drinking, a couple of years earlier, and saying, *Sometimes I feel this longing, and I don't know what for.* She said, *I feel that exact same thing.* Around the same time, I discovered the poet Tennyson, and his poems moved me in a new way, like a feeling, but more than a feeling, something that swept my consciousness away from the page to savour a kind of euphoria, then back again to the book, so that it took me two hours to read a poem. And in between reading poems, I was looking at the world differently, discovering the profundity of the night sky and its stars as if no one had ever noticed that before. In my senior school studies, we read a poem by Marvell, *On a Drop of Dew.*

> *Restless it rolls and unsecure, trembling lest it grow impure, till the warm sun pity its pain, and to the skies, exhale it back again.*

Though I wasn't connecting the dots yet, this was naming the nameless longing I had confessed to my friend.

And I hurtle back ten years earlier, to holidays spent on my grandparents' farm, my happiest days, loving the sights and sounds and smells of the countryside. Waiting in the morning for my grandfather to emerge from the house so I could ride on the tractor with him, watching the dew sparkle like jewels in the grass under the sunlight, imagining tiny fairy castles nestled in the grass, the only clue to their existence the turrets encrusted with gems that sparkled in the morning light. My grandparents were the only people in my world who were walking a spiritual path, and it was a traditional Methodist one, but it was expressed in care and love and a calm acceptance of everything that happened. In my Scripture book I pasted a picture of the famous praying hands painting, which reminded me of my grandmother's old hands, and created a link between what I heard in Scripture every week and those rarer times at the farm.

These early intimations of the divine were not gendered or even embodied. The spiritual world, in my first apprehensions of it, was a very lofty place, removed from this world, and even at odds with it, as in the plight of the drop of dew, wanting only to be evaporated back into the air. Learning to bring my sense of the divine into my physical being came later. After the experience with the tree, I found myself drawn to people who were practicing some form of spirituality. Living away from home for the first time, I met a young woman a few years older than me who carried around a copy of the *I Ching*[71] wrapped in a scarf, and used old Chinese coins to consult it. She showed me how to do it, and helped me to interpret the hexagrams I was led to. She lent me her book and when she saw how hard it was for me to give it back, she said I could keep it. I still have the same book, forty years later, and still turn to it sometimes.

I continued to be moved by nature, and often walked along a path by the beach at night, lost in contemplation, till I learned that a young woman needs to keep her wits about her if she is going to walk around by herself at night.

In my twenties I did a *Vipassanā*[72] meditation retreat. It was a revelation, as I discovered equanimity for the first time that I could remember. This created a radical shift in my deepest goals. Instead of seeking highs, I was seeking that centered, grounded feeling. Instead of excitement, I was seeking calm, I was seeking inner peace. Drinking and smoking dope lost some of their attraction, but not all. Then I became pregnant, and after cutting down and feeling guilty for not giving up altogether, after the rocky first trimester, I stopped. This was hard, so I resorted to yoga, which also promoted centering and grounding and finding that calm and peaceful inner space.

I could not abide the pre-natal clinic I went to, and their approach to my pregnancy as something routine, rather than something miraculous. So I found my way to a home birth midwife. She asked me why I wanted a home birth. I said, *I hate hospitals.* She said, *That's not a good reason. There are positive reasons for having a home birth,* and loaded me up with five books to look at. I read about natural birth, and that all female mammals, when it is time to give birth, look for a place that is quiet, warm and dark. When I went back to see the midwife, she could see that I had moved enough in my understanding that she could start working with me. She said I needed to get in touch with my instincts. I barely knew what that meant, but I started trying to guess things I couldn't know, and reach for some other way of knowing that might be instinct. The midwife could see I was not the most promising pupil, but I was moving in the

---

[71] An ancient Chinese divination text with over 2,500 years of commentary and interpretation.
[72] 'Insight', a Buddhist meditation practice.

right direction. During the birth itself, I found myself in a strange position, standing with one foot at an awkward angle behind me on the bed. I turned and looked at the foot, and started to take it down again. *No, no, leave it there, it's good, it's instinctive, it's asymmetrical, it's helping the baby to turn,* said the midwife. During my first days as a mother, the midwife kept drawing me back to my instinctive nature. *You know how to look after this baby,* she said. And I did.

I was looking forward to my first joint now I had no other bloodstream joined to mine, but the first time I smoked after that was my last. Somehow the grounded feeling had become my preferred state of being, and being pulled away from it into however pleasant a place felt wrong. I had the disorienting feeling I'd had when I was standing on a wharf and a ferry was pulling away. It felt like it was me that was moving, not the ferry. Now I was on the ferry but it felt like the wharf was moving away from me and I regretted leaving it and wanted to be back there.

By the birth of my second child, three years later, I was very confident in my ability to give birth. I sent my partner to bed, as he was tired and grumpy and I didn't want that energy around me. I laboured through the night by myself in the garden, leaving calling the midwife till I was well along. New place, new midwife. It was a warm January night in the country, with bright moonlight you could have read a book by. I had a herbal birth tonic a naturopath had made up for me, and when I started to feel weary, I walked through the dark, quiet house and had a drink of that. But mostly I sat on a garden bench between contractions, and during contractions I took up whatever position came to me, and some of them were completely painless. I felt wonderful, completely at one with the unfolding process. As the sky lightened and the contractions were getting close together, I woke up my partner and asked him to run me a bath. Then I rang the midwife and hopped in. She arrived about two hours before the baby came, and said she wished all her deliveries were this easy.

Around this time, I joined a group to study the *Course in Miracles*. I could never get very far with it and kept finding myself neglecting it, repeatedly longer than the time beyond which the course guide said you had to start over. I finally accepted it was not for me. I may have been wrong, I was in my thirties, which is young for a spiritual seeker. Most of the people I met on the path were women twenty years older. But the aspect of the course that **I could never resonate with was the idea that this world is not real, only the spiritual dimension is real.** Try as I might to decide that my sense of the world as real was an illusion, I never quite bought it. **To me the wonder was that they are both real.** I experienced the spiritual world as a shadow presence, that underlay and overlay and lay behind every aspect of the physical world. Perhaps my early experiences of the beauty of nature, and the symbol of the tree, uniting heaven and earth, led me to resonate more strongly with the message of the *I Ching*: as above, so below. And as we sang about, in the country church where my grandmother played piano: *let heaven and nature sing.* My spirituality was not disembodied, it felt at home on earth. Perhaps it was the experience of my mothering instincts that led me from being a drop of dew restless to return to heaven, to one content to live out my short life on a rose, or even on a leaf.

Through all the phases of my journey, meditation was a constant. Since learning how to meditate at *Vipassana*, I had learned other ways of meditating, and had become pretty blasé about mixing them up – whatever was working for me at the time. Then at forty, I started getting Christian content in my meditation. I heard a voice say *May the peace of Jesus be with you.* I was pretty surprised to hear that. The consensus of the people, books and speakers I had encountered on my journey was that Christianity had lost the plot, and enlightenment was only to be found in the religions of the east. But in meditation I was seeing a staircase of light, and Jesus – of all people – was taking my hand to lead me up. I thought of Jung's advice to the middle-aged, to return to the religion of their childhood. I thought of the praying hands, and my sweet Methodist grandmother. I decided to follow where I was being led.

The only place I could think of to learn about the Christian path was church, so I went. After working through a seismic culture shock, I found some gems among the dross. I developed a love of theology, because it united my spirituality and my rationality, which had become estranged in the new age milieu where if something boggled the rational mind it was probably true. I found the actual teachings of Jesus, stripped of their accretion of Victorian morality, rich in suggestive and symbolic truth. It didn't take long for me to lose a sense of an anthropomorphized God. I could see the appeal. *Human beings want a God with whom they can deal,* said Tillich. When I ended up with God as Love, Truth, Wisdom and Justice, it was hard to relate to a collection of big nouns. Anselm said that **God is greater than any idea we can have of God.** I started to relate more to the indwelling Spirit, the higher self, who was the spark of the divine in me, and therefore feminine. I read about Sophia, a figure who represented the Wisdom of God. Still, it was hard for me to believe in a superhuman being anything like a person. **I thought of God more as a pervasive force, spirituality itself, the power of love itself, a force that moves through and around everything,** always available if we can perceive it, tune in, open ourselves, flow with it. Easier said than done.

I still don't experience the divine dimension as gendered, but at the point where it intersects with my finite life, the point of spiritual consciousness in me is my Divine Feminine.

My main connection with the Divine Feminine continues to come through my sense of a higher self, who I always think of as female, because she is **my best self**. She is very wise. She is the part of me that has a direct link to the divine, and the closer I can stay to her guidance, the better my life is. She doesn't always make my life easier for me, but she is always with me to help me find the best course through the changes. Once she gave me an image, when life became very hard. I was looking at a river running between jagged rocky cliffs, and I was precariously navigating this river. There was no other way to get through this passage. It was not possible to get out and walk – the only way was through. I could accept the situation and hold on till it was over and then I would move on to the next stage in my journey.

The moments of my life when the divine dimension has broken through into my consciousness are precious jewels in a string, that make sense of other moments when I trust that the divine is still present. *Bidden or unbidden, God is present,* as Jung had inscribed above his garden gate. My sense of who God is may shift and change, but God remains a reality I have never doubted. *Be at peace with God, whatever you conceive God to be,* says the Desiderata. Maybe each jewel added to the string has marked a step towards that peace, like a divine Pandora bracelet. Sometimes I wear the string of jewels, sometimes I look at it in wonder, sometimes I forget it's there, and sometimes I am the string of jewels.

Melanie Toppin

A Witch without a Coven

Looking back on my life, I was always looking for something. Always searching, never finding. At least that's what it felt like at the time.

Growing up, I'd always felt out of sorts, like I was different from the rest of my family. I didn't understand it, and in a way, I always felt like my family didn't understand me either. Now, in hindsight, I know it wasn't so much a lack of understanding me but a confusion as to the outward signs of my spiritual journey. I was a rebellious child. I knew what I wanted in life and who I was at a young age. But I also wanted to please my family and belong, so as I grew older, I let myself become more and more mainstream.

The rebellious little girl turned into a quiet introspective. This happened so gradually that I hardly realized it myself until I was well into young adulthood. At the same time, I felt a conscious connection to the Divine Feminine.

When I think of the Divine Feminine, there are a few things that come to mind. For the most part I relate it to characteristics such as nurturing, intuition, empathy. The male counterpart, to me, is more the logical, practical energy in life and society. But in essence I believe it is a connection to life and nature. And that is something I only really found through my Wiccan, or rather Pagan beliefs.

I grew up in a more or less Christian family. Born in the Netherlands to a Dutch father and a German mother, I was baptized Catholic as a baby. Both my parents were officially Christian, but lived it in different ways. This influenced my spirituality growing up. While my mother would go to Church with us and her mother every Sunday, my father always stayed home. Though it wasn't something our community really cared about, it was also unheard of where I grew up as most people who didn't go to church were Muslim. In my community, you were either Catholic, Protestant, or foreign, the latter in the sense of being something other than Christian. Religion was an integrated part of the curriculum in school, so most of my friends would get a free period while the Christians were in class. That was when I realized that there was something more out there for me.

I had just kind of accepted that I was Christian because my parents were, and they had decided that I should be baptized. I didn't question that we went to Church every Sunday and on Christmas Eve (even though my Dad never joined us), and even went as far as becoming an altar girl along with some of my friends. I was never very good at it, and often forgot what I had to do. So I was always lucky to have a friend along with me who could help me to at least make it look like I knew what I was doing.

After a while I stopped being an altar girl, and we even reduced our time in Church altogether. My grandmother continued to go, but the older we got the less we went along. One year, I got sick on Christmas Eve before we went to mass. For some reason, and I never found out why, this was the end of even my mom going to church. After that, we never went again. In a way, I believe that also changed my outlook in school.

When I could decide whether to keep on going to religion class or switch to ethics, I immediately took ethics instead. I still had faith, but I didn't see the point of learning the Bible. Yet I still stayed true to the Catholic Church until my confirmation.

After graduating high school, and still feeling like I was missing something, I met a few Mormons while I was at college. They had me intrigued and for a while I joined them too, going almost every Sunday, even speaking in mass and going as far as being baptized again. But it didn't last long, and after a year I moved away and continued my search.

I still believed in a higher power, but I had turned my back on big religions. I wasn't yet what I consider spiritual though.

Before leaving Germany for the Netherlands, I had heard about Wicca, but wasn't very familiar with it. I was curious, as it seemed to be a very Earth-centric religion and I had always felt like Earth itself was my church rather than a brick building. But in the end what drew me most was that **at the core of Wiccan beliefs were the God and Goddess.** For Wiccans it refers to the all-encompassing life force responsible for all of creation.

Since I learned through my Christian upbringing that we were all created in God's image, this concept intrigued me, and I wanted to learn more. I had always found it odd that we had both genders if in fact God was a man. It made much more sense to me that God was both, and so I grabbed anything I could find to learn about Wicca. At some point I realized that I could only learn so much from reading and looked for other people following this belief. A small German Christian community wasn't the place to look though, so I continued to read.

I found out that there were varying Wiccan beliefs, and that Wicca itself was only the umbrella term. Just as in Christianity there is more than just Catholic and

Protestant. At this point, I had found a difference between being Wiccan and being Pagan. Pagans are usually Wiccan, but not every Wiccan is a Pagan. And though I shared the core beliefs that are true for every Wiccan – the Goddess and God working for the good of all, not harming others or the world – I felt a need to dig deeper into the Pagan side of things.

Unlike Wicca, Paganism has its origin in ancient and medieval times. It predates Christianity and refers to various beliefs practiced in Western cultures. Though I felt a kinship to today's version of Wicca, I was much more intrigued by what I found out about Paganism. The variation that interested me the most was Celtic Paganism. I always had a connection and fascination with anything Celtic, so it made sense on a subconscious level. I didn't understand how much until I found a Celtic Pagan group online. It was an international group with three leaders – one High Priest and two High Priestesses, referencing the Triple Goddess – the maiden, the mother and the crone. Each leader had a connection to one of the three and to one Celtic God or Goddess that in turn was represented by the three stages.

The Triple Goddess is typically viewed as a tri-unity of three distinct aspects or figures united in one being. These three figures are often described as the Maiden, the Mother and the Crone, each of which symbolizes both a separate stage in the female life cycle and a phase of the Moon.

To me that was always the essence of the Triple Goddess. Not simply the belief that some sort of Higher Power was behind it, but the notion that we all unite these aspects within ourselves. And even though the symbolism is inherently feminine, it made sense to also have a male leader. It was always about having a unity, and to me that also meant a connection to the masculine.

This was my first real connection to the Divine Feminine.

The High Priest took me under his wing and began teaching me Celtic Paganism. I believe he sensed something in me that he wanted to nurture, some kind of potential. He was an interesting person and had founded the group along with the other two High Priestesses.

I found what I'd been looking for. The group was in transition though. The other two High Priestesses wanted to hand over the mantle, and even though I hadn't been there long, I quickly rose up to one of those positions as the High Priest's acolyte because he saw a natural gift in me and sensed a strong connection to my Mother Goddess. I didn't know it at the time, but this was unusual and lead to some tension as the remaining High Priestess didn't quite agree with him, perhaps because he was teaching me something that he hadn't offered her. Most of the group was happy about it though.

There are many Gods and Goddesses in the Celtic pantheon, but the strongest connection for me was with Arianrhod, Goddess of the Silver Wheel. One of the things the High Priest taught me, was to call upon the elements. Each has a connection to a deity. I had an affinity for most of them and learned quickly, but calling Arianrhod's element was the easiest for me. In a sense it felt like I was coming home when I connected with her.

She's represented by an owl, which was why I was blessed with the Wiccan name White Owl. In terms of the Triple Goddess, she also represents the Mother, which seemed fitting as that was the role I eventually took on within the group.

As soon as I embraced her as my Divine Mother, which is what we always called the deities we were drawn to in this way – the High Priest felt the same way about The Morrígan[73] – I often heard owls in my vicinity, especially when I struggled. This may not seem odd to some people, but to me those were special experiences, especially as I lived in areas where there were no owls. To then hear one so close to me that I could almost touch it felt like a message from above to let me know everything was going to be okay, no matter what I was going through.

I learned to pay more attention to my surroundings and especially to the elements. It wasn't only owls, but I learned to listen to the wind. Even though Arianrhod is generally associated with water, I could always hear and feel her in the wind. Through that connection I discovered the Divine Feminine not only within myself but all around me.

I believe in the Triple Goddess, and although I have this connection with Arianrhod, they're all a part of me. But I also believe that I can find it in my surroundings. **The world is full of magic if we're open to seeing it.** That's why I cannot share individual spiritual experiences as nature itself became my church, meaning I felt it in everything I did and learned. And with that connection I rediscovered who I am at my core and what I'm here for.

Looking back, it felt like I was floundering before and letting my environment and society influence who I was and what I did. As a child, I knew what I wanted, but as I grew older and graduated secondary school and later college, I was more focused on what I could do to get by rather than what my heart and soul called for. But I wasn't happy as that version of me. I don't believe I'm all the way back to who I was before I listened to what the world wanted and expected. But since turning away from Christianity and embracing the path of the Celtic Pagan, I've rediscovered myself and gained the ability to listen to the universe. **I'm comfortable in knowing that I can be me,** and that is just what the world needs, even if it doesn't realize it yet.

---

[73] A great queen of Irish mythology, generally represented by a crow.

That doesn't mean that I've turned my back all the way on Christianity, but rather what it has been made into. I appreciate my Christian friends who don't just use their Christianity as a label, but truly live it the way it should be. And this appreciation is what leads most of my work and attitude today. The Wiccan Rede[74] states *An' ye harm none, do what ye will*. That is what I live by and hope to express through my work. To me, it is a statement and a message that should be part and parcel of every religion and spiritual belief: as long as you don't hurt anyone, do what you want and believe what you want.

---

[74] An ancient word meaning counsel or advice.

Mary Louise Malloy

Hail Mary Full of Grace

Growing up in New Jersey during the 40s and 50s, Mary was revered by the Catholic Church even more than Jesus. The Trinity was Father, Son and Holy Ghost, the all-in-one, and Mary was the role model of obedience and love of God. Even the local movie theaters featured movies about Mary. Our local theater featured the movie *The Song of Bernadette*, the story of Saint Bernadette of Lourdes. My sister and I were so emotional about it that when we got home, we knelt on the front porch of our house in front of our statue of Mary. We really believed that Mary would appear to us. *Our Lady of Fatima* was another story we heard while growing up. Lucia, the oldest age ten, Francisco age nine, and Jacinta age seven, were cousins. Lucia was the one who heard and saw the apparition of Mary in Fatima. To this day it still has its believers and skeptics on what it all meant.

Mary was put on a pedestal of perfection, and women and girls had to strive for that perfection in order to become perfect in their faith. She was always a part of that example of what being a woman was supposed to be. Prayer and petition to Mary was the way that we would find answers. It was through her intercession that we could approach God and his Son with our prayers and needs.

My belief in her was so sincere that I attended a Novena with an intention that my baby brother would be able to walk. He had gone through surgery, having had problems with his feet when he was born and so he was late learning to walk. At the end of the Novena, I went home and stood him up in front of me and told him to walk to me. Well, he did. And he continued to walk from the front of the house to the kitchen, back and forth, laughing as he went. My parents were astonished and told the priest that they believed it was a miracle. I believe the priest mentioned it at Church to the congregation.

That same 'baby' brother was a long-haired free spirit in the 60s. He came to our home for dinner with a girlfriend and he spoke of Jesus with familiarity, like he had a close, personal and rewarding relationship with him. No longer did we need to approach Jesus through his mother, Mary. He said you needed to ask Jesus to come into your life and your life would be changed. This was during a time when my life was filled with uncertainty and stressful responsibilities. That night, I stole a few moments away from my husband and children who were gathered in the living room watching TV, and closed the bedroom door behind me. In the darkened room, I knelt down beside the bed and began to cry. I pleaded for help and comfort in the days ahead, and when I got up to go back to my family, I felt that somehow things were different and more hopeful. It was after this incident that I was drawn to the parish prayer group. I would get up early in the morning before everyone woke, longing to sit quietly reading the Bible. When I read at home or when I went to Mass, the words of scripture jumped out as if to teach me and comfort me. This was during the time of the Jesus Movement. Reading the New Testament, especially the words of Jesus in the Sermon on the Mount, filled me with peace and grace. It was also where I encountered some of the women in the Bible. Mary Magdalene had been previously caste as the duality image of Mary. She was the shadow side – the less perfect side – of womanhood. Later we recognized her as a part of us too. We began to see a more human side of Mary that we could relate to in our everyday lives as women. There was Martha, whose purpose was to clean and cook and provide for the needs of others. There was Mary Magdalene who wanted to listen and learn from Jesus about how to go about changing the world. Yet, in the Bible, these women were there to serve, in one way or the other, the needs of the apostles or Jesus.

I was a woman in my thirties, with four boys under ten and pregnant once again, striving to live that perfect image and finding my real life coming apart at the seams, with a husband who was breaking under the pressures of economic and emotional collapse going from job dissatisfaction and unemployment to finally a total career change. These women of the Bible weren't speaking to the reality of our lives in the 60s.

On one particular evening, after a busy, demanding day with the children, I went outdoors and stood in the middle of the side yard where I could clearly see the night sky. It was a crisp fall night with no streetlights to obscure what was the most awesome starry night I'd ever seen. And the silence! The silence extended for such a long time that I hesitated to move a muscle. I felt like something was about to happen. During those moments, my soul was filled with what I can only describe as amazing grace; a presence of peace, joy and love, and a sense that all is well. There was a certainty that all creation was vibrant and alive, and that I was just a small part of this amazing experience. Was this the Divine Feminine? Walking reluctantly away from that spot on that night, I was, once again, convinced that there was a divine source or spark of life and that no matter what happened, this source was always there. This loving force transcended feminine and masculine. It was pure love.

I began to look upon the church, upon Mary, and upon Jesus as messengers of this Pure Love. Yet **the place I found it most was within myself through contemplation, meditation, music and nature.** I began to trust that this source was within me too. When this awareness grew stronger, I became even more aware of how institutional religions treated and defined women. Their role was more as a helpmate by providing service and sacrifice to those in positions of authority in society, church and home. Service that springs from love is what we're all called to do. It's a free choice emerging from commitment and a calling from within each person. But often, where women were concerned, their gifts and talents in that service were diminished and dismissed, unless it served those positions of authority. I began to see that their voice wasn't validated and sought after in a way that took them seriously and not in a condescending way. In fact, those voices and ideas were threatening to some of the rigid positions within religions. They were the voices of experience.

My preconceived ideas about my place in the Church were doubly challenged when my husband left me and my children, and I was faced with the reality that I was on my own, to sink or swim. My intuition and decision-making were called on big time, especially as those who represented the Church weren't addressing these real-life situations unfolding in the 70s and 80s.

I attended a few women's group meetings called *Miriam's Circle* at the church. I was willing to be open to the possibility that there might be change within the Church. The focus of *Miriam's Circle* was on supporting the talents and gifts of women in the Church in leadership positions. One focus was on women becoming priests and that was an area where I didn't feel I wanted to get involved and put my energy. It was clear to me that women in the Catholic priesthood was a long way off, and that maybe the Church would never make that kind of leap. My interest in the group was in being supportive of those who were seeking to use their talents in areas other than the traditional women's groups in the Catholic Church which marginalized and separated them. It didn't take long for me to see that these women were treated in a condescending way, almost like children. Rather than staying in that environment and becoming angrier about the way things were in the Catholic Church, I decided to let go of my efforts to become involved there. In many ways, the women appeared to be enabling and complicit in the problem by allowing it to continue. Someone counseled me about becoming too involved with the politics of the Catholic Church and they turned out to be right. Fools rush in where angels fear to tread.

Perhaps these women are on a higher level than angels and have been called to be engaged in this way. I don't know the answer to that. **I only saw people who had gifts and talents in teaching, in service to others and in striving to live out the gospel message of Jesus in a deep and genuine way, but who weren't considered worthy to walk side-by-side with men in decision-making positions.** I observed all this and went to meetings for about six months and knew in my heart I had to walk away and move on with my life.

I wrote this to express the heartache I was feeling. I grew up with and held the belief that we all had gifts to share with the world and needed the freedom to grow and find our purpose:

They spoke of courage.
One by one they gave witness to their presence in the church
They spoke with integrity and wisdom
It was clear they were inwardly free
At peace with themselves and their God

In their heart-of-hearts they know
It is not male or female
It is not conservative or liberal

It is respect and recognition of each person in their own right.
It's listening without defensiveness to the thoughts and ideas of others.
Striving to understand the other's position.

They know that if none of these things are present then we are living a lie.
We're speaking many words with no substance.

Our question is this:
Do we want our sons and daughters to perpetuate that lie?
Or do we want to show them the way of trust and respect.

Is it right to ask women to suppress their God-given call to Leadership?
Or can we walk into the future side by side? Confident that God is with us.

The Institutional Church will survive
But will it survive through the exclusion and heartbreak of those
who rightfully deserve increased leadership roles?
Or will it survive through the adoption of attitudes and values which lead to
Cooperation, Caring, Loving and Forgiveness?

I explored wider ideas of spirituality and heard about the *Omega Institute*. I felt pulled to go there and forced myself to attend some of their day workshops. It was in a beautiful area and I felt I was spiritually home. Some aspects of *Omega* were far beyond what I'd experienced in the Catholic Church. I chose workshops I was comfortable with and that would benefit my spiritual growth at this time of my life. I couldn't afford the cost of their weekend events so I signed up for day workshops. I began to feel myself opening up to a promise of more growth and healing. Yet, at times of trouble or trauma, it seems my GPS is still set to automatically retrieve *Hail Mary, Full of Grace* as a source of comfort and support. She still holds power in my life.

I learned that perfectionism can poison your life. *Want to be happy? Stop trying to be perfect.*[75] It can bring you to procrastinate your life away, out of fear of making a mistake or of not meeting the expectations of others.

---

[75] Brené Brown

Trying to be perfect keeps us from really finding joy in our lives. Whether it comes from the way we've been raised as a child or from our expectations of ourselves as adults, perfectionism holds us back from spontaneity and being more emotionally responsive to others. We're stuck in an unhealthy cycle of looking for approval outside ourselves instead of finding validation within.

The Divine Feminine was there throughout my life. Words of wisdom that entered my consciousness right at the time when I needed it. It was there in the women in my family who broke free of cultural expectations and found their purpose through writing. The Divine Feminine or Goddess movement weren't something I embraced as the total answer. I see it as a concept and force that deserves respect in all of us and from all of us.

The photo of me above is when I visited the place of my ancestors for the first time. When I stepped onto Ireland's turf, I truly felt grounded with a peaceful feeling of coming home. It was where my soul felt integrated with the divine energy I'd been experiencing throughout my life. It connected me to the spirit of my ancestors in such a profound belonging. Recently I found an old photo of my maternal grandmother who I felt very close to. It was faded and I decided to see if I could work on restoring it. I was amazed when her pin, the *Fleur de Lis*, appeared in the photo where it hadn't been clear before. Through the years I'd chosen the *Fleur de Lis* as jewelry pieces and loved them. On researching the meaning behind the symbol, I found that it represented Mary, Mary Magdalene, and the Holy Trinity. Finding this connection with my grandmother was a grace filled moment for me.

When I've been searching and seeking during those times of my life where I felt uncertain and doubtful of myself and the meaning of my life, I've found this poem by Max Ehrman to be a powerful centering contemplation. It's about being One in the Spirit of Love. *You are a Child of the Universe.*

Desiderata

GO PLACIDLY amid the noise and the haste, and remember what peace there may be in silence. As far as possible, without surrender, be on good terms with all persons.

Speak your truth quietly and clearly; and listen to others, even to the dull and the ignorant; they too have their story.

Avoid loud and aggressive persons; they are vexatious to the spirit. If you compare yourself with others, you may become vain or bitter, for always there will be greater and lesser persons than yourself.

Enjoy your achievements as well as your plans. Keep interested in your own career, however humble; it is a real possession in the changing fortunes of time.

Exercise caution in your business affairs, for the world is full of trickery. But let this not blind you to what virtue there is; many persons strive for high ideals, and everywhere life is full of heroism.

Be yourself. Especially do not feign affection. Neither be cynical about love; for in the face of all aridity and disenchantment, it is as perennial as the grass.

Take kindly the counsel of the years, gracefully surrendering the things of youth.

Nurture strength of spirit to shield you in sudden misfortune. But do not distress yourself with dark imaginings. Many fears are born of fatigue and loneliness.

Beyond a wholesome discipline, be gentle with yourself. You are a child of the universe no less than the trees and the stars; you have a right to be here.

And whether or not it is clear to you, no doubt the universe is unfolding as it should. Therefore, be at peace with God, whatever you conceive Him (Her) to be.

And whatever your labors and aspirations, in the noisy confusion of life, keep peace in your soul. With all its sham, drudgery and broken dreams, it is still a beautiful world.

Be cheerful. Strive to be happy.

Elizabeth Russell

From the Roots of my Ancestors

One of my earliest memories is of sitting in the grass with my nana, helping her weed the flowers. She would sing to them, and tell me stories of the fairies and pixies that lived among them.

Nana was Native American. From what nation, she never said. She was two years old when her parents left the reservation somewhere near Kingston, Ontario, and relocated to Grindstone Island in the St Lawrence River.

There are a lot of discrepancies about my nana's birthplace, date of birth, and ethnicity. She was baptized at two years old in the little Methodist church on the island, and that served as her birth certificate, and all mention of the reservation in Canada was wiped out of the family records.

Even so, Nana learned to sing to the plants and live close to the earth. She passed this knowledge on to those who were willing to learn. My mother learned from her, but in my generation, I was the one who resonated with earth energies, and was eager to learn as much as I could from her during our once-a-year visits to the north country.

By the time I was born, Nana had left the island and now lived in a small cottage on the mainland. It was a cozy white house, with flower beds all around it, filled with brilliant flowers in all the colors of the rainbow. In the back yard were some fruit trees, and a white picket fence. We spent most of our time working in the flowerbeds on the side of the house. This is where the magic happened.

I have always been 'sensitive'. Nana was one of the few people who never scoffed or teased me about what everyone else, including my parents, called my *imaginary* friends. As long as I can remember, I have seen angels and spirits. They have always guided me. Although she never said, I always felt that the reason she understood was because she could see these things, too.

Little by little, Nana would coax the fairies and pixies to come out and speak with her. She often spoke a language that wasn't English, and although I never learned to speak it, something inside me understood and accepted what I was hearing. I never saw the fairies as clearly as she did, but I could see little flashes of light and sparkles. I still do, and am grateful for their company, even the little tricks they will sometimes play on me.

Listening to the conversations sounded mundane on the surface, but underneath there was a purpose. Questions about the weather would gather information about upcoming storms that might impact crops, comments on the flow of the St Lawrence River would reveal where there might be better fishing, and – best of all for me – they would tell her where the best berries could be found for picking!

My nana was a quiet woman, not given to chatter. In the afternoons we would sit with cups of green tea and nibble on Nilla Wafers, listening to the breeze come through the window, bringing with it the scent of the flowers we'd been working on earlier. She taught me how to listen to the breeze, to hear its voice and understand what it was saying.

Nana taught me how to connect to the earth, and to not only feel the energy, but to hear the voices of the trees and plants. It wasn't something we spoke about to other people. Instead, it was a special bond we shared that opened my eyes to so many wonders.

Even today, I sing to the plants in my garden as I tend them. I will stand and listen to the wind, feeling its swirling, electric energy. I talk to the birds, the trees, and the fairies and pixies that live around me.

I cherish the knowledge that my nana passed down to me. It helps me feel connected to the Earth, which brings me balance, and helps me heal from the chaos of the world. Her teachings have helped me build a sanctuary, where I often feel her presence as I work in the garden. Sometimes I think I hear her humming along with me.

The last fifteen years have brought about a re-awakening of the gifts I shared with my nana. She passed in 1987, and when I started seeing and hearing all of these things again, I missed her even more because I had no one I could talk to about this.

Through a divorce, and health issues resulting in three near-death experiences, I knew I had to make some serious changes. Learning to take care of myself, as well as I cared for others, was a challenge, but as my gifts re-opened, I found that I wasn't alone.

It started with seeing and hearing angels again, which hadn't happened since I was a teenager. This brought me more peace than I had felt in a long time. I began to explore these relationships, to learn as much as I could about who and what angels are, and how and why I interact with them.

What I discovered about myself on this journey was completely unexpected, but made so much sense to me. And opened up new opportunities for growth and learning.

One particular discovery came during a meditation to visit my *Akashic Records*.[76] It was my first real experience seeing and understanding the energy of the Divine Feminine.

It was a guided meditation, where I connected with my guardian angel, who then took me to the Akashic Library where I could access my personal records. I didn't have a particular question, and it wasn't the first time I had done this meditation, but what I saw on this visit answered a few profound, un-asked questions.

The first thing I was shown was a big cave with a large stone table in the center. There were a few tunnels leading out of the cave, and torches lighting the walls. All around the table were women of various ages. They tended to people sitting at the edges of the cave, and once in a while someone would be led into the cave, and taken to lie down on the table. At this point, a group of women would gather around and lay hands on this person. They would sing, and chant, and I saw one very old woman with long hair and stooped shoulders using a turtle rattle.

After a little bit, the person who had been brought in would either get up from the table, thank the women and leave, or they would dissolve into the table, whereby a prayer would be said for them. This happened over and over, and while it spanned only a few moments in my sight, I knew I was watching generations of women helping and healing others.

Some could be healed. These were the ones who walked out. Some could not, and these were the ones who passed on, shown as disappearing into the table.

In my heart I heard *These are your ancestors. This is where you come from. This is what you are.* This is where I truly began to understand the part I have as a healer, and ties I have to my ancestors, who drew on the balance of the Divine Feminine and Divine Masculine for their healing.

I also learned that **it was not about being able to save every person, but about the love and compassion you put into what you do.** It's about being seeing every living thing through the lens of love and understanding that we are all connected. **What effects one of us, affects all of us. This is why we need to re-awaken the Divine Feminine – so it can help bring balance.**

After this profound experience, I took my first Usui Reiki class. Right from the start, it felt so natural. During my attunement, the Archangel Gabriel came to me,

---

[76] A record of all human events, thoughts, words and emotions, from the past, present and future; believed to be encoded in the ether.

singing and laughing, holding out his hands saying *Dance with me!* I remember laughing with him, and felt such joy.

When I gave my first Reiki session during the class, I began by calling in *all angels who are willing and able to work with me.* I was nearly knocked to my knees by the number of them that showed up. I was not prepared for the response I got, and the powerful energy they brought with them. Archangel Michael appeared at the foot of the table saying *It's about time!* And with him came legions, ranks upon ranks of angels. I was in awe, and not a little overwhelmed.

Though I was the only person in the room to see and hear what was happening, I saw my Reiki teacher take a few steps back because she felt the energy so strongly. The person I was working on remarked afterwards that he had had a profound vision during the time I worked on him.

Thinking back on all of this, I am still in awe that I am connected in this way to such pure Divine Light. The pure love, compassion, and joy of working with the angels never ceases to amaze and astound me. I am humbled and honored.

Eventually, I felt called to take a class on Kundalini Reiki. It was taught as a distance class, but the instructor had such beautiful energy, and the entire experience was just as profound as my Usui Reiki classes.

During each of my attunements, I experienced visions of places and things I've never seen before. Each had something to teach me, and the connections I made are still with me. Each attunement brought me closer to truly understanding what *we are one* truly means. The experiences brought with them a feeling of nurturing love, like a mother's love, both gentle and supportive.

Not long after that eye-opening meditation with the Akashic records, I had a vision. I get visions sometimes, though not often, and they always surprise me. I have had visions of the past, as well as of what I believe to be the future, and some of alternate realities. They always have the same quality to them of a slight fogginess with mild vertigo, but complete awareness of what is happening at the moment it occurs.

One of these future visions happened the day after 'Frankenstorm' (Hurricane Sandy) hit the east coast United States in October of 2012. This was the largest hurricane to hit the Atlantic coast in 2012, and the only one to reach this far from the coast since Hurricane Agnes in the 1950s. The storm had been large and fierce enough that even three hundred miles inland we felt the effects. Trees were knocked down, blocking traffic and opening up gaping maws in the lawns where they had stood for over a hundred years. Streams and rivers flooded, causing people to seek shelter at the local schools and churches because they couldn't stay in their houses. Power was either out or barely there.

The next day we still had streets blocked off and power was still sketchy. The local grocery store is only one and a half miles from my house, so I decided to spend that dreary afternoon sitting in the café there, charging my laptop and phone.

On the walk home, the air was so beautifully crisp and clean. It felt as if so much negativity and anger had been swept away, cleared out completely with the storm. I remember breathing deeply as I was walking, feeling so alive and present in that moment.

It was just around the corner from my house when I saw a completely different view in front of me. Instead of my peaceful, if storm-trodden, street in front of me, I was standing on the steps of the Lincoln Memorial in Washington, DC. It was a grey day, one that promised rain, with cool temperatures and the hint of fall in the air.

I was not alone. There were many other women with me. And some men who identify strongly with feminine energy. We were all in long, dark grey robes with hoods pulled up and partially hiding our faces. A giant circle was forming. There were enough of us that we were easily able to encircle the entire building.

Our hands stretched out gently toward each other, about waist high, but not touching. The energy was barely visible. Palpable, you could feel gently sparking electricity being generated and passed from person to person.

We were gathering this power, and when it built to sufficient strength, we sent it, in waves, into the earth and toward the monument where it became visible as a wall of energy that concentrated into a beam of light which shot up into the sky. When it reached the stratosphere, it spread out to cover the entire Earth in a protective field.

I came out of this vision to find myself sobbing tears of joy and release. It was a clarion call, one that I could not ignore. While there was no date attached to this vision, the message was clearly about the Divine Feminine Re-awakening. It was time for us to step up. **Women will be the ones responsible for protecting and bringing the needed change to the earth.** The energetic balance would be restored between the Divine Masculine and the Divine Feminine.

This happened seven years ago, and I am still waiting for the call to join the circle. I have been told that there is still a chance this event will not need to happen, but if it does, I will be there. I will add my healing along with the others into the earth. Instead of working with one person at a time, it will be a collective effort, embracing the entire planet.

As we embody the nurturing and sometimes fierce energy of the Divine Feminine, we find balance within ourselves. As we find our own inner strength and balance, we affect the world. Every time we influence those around us, that energy continues to expand and impact others.

This is what I saw in my nana, as she tended her garden. It is the same compassion and care that I saw in the ancestral caves. The gathering at the Lincoln Memorial reminds us that we are not alone, and **when we focus our energy together, we can do incredible things.** We have always been able to, we simply need to remember, and then… act.

Doreen Devoy-Hulgan

Walking Forward after Devastating Loss

I am the red-headed, second daughter of an Irish-American Catholic father, and a Norwegian-American Lutheran turned Episcopalian mother. My father, being the man, and being the Catholic, prevailed upon my mother to raise us in the Church. I recall that she, not he, was the one who gave us his religion. Although she declined to convert (and thus had her marriage relegated to the vestibule of the church, not at the altar), she honored her word. It was she that took us to Mass every Sunday when he was out to sea, she who placed the weekly envelope in the collection as the basket came around, she who signed us up for and transported us to our catechism classes and quizzed us on our prayers, and she who cleaned the house and prepared snacks for my dad's high school religion students. She was the one who hosted the parties when we received our sacraments, and she who made sure we abstained from meat on Fridays during Lent. She lit the advent candles and made sure the Baby Jesus made it into the crèche to surprise us as though just-born on Christmas morning. As a child I remember asking her why she hadn't converted and she said because she just wasn't interested. This is probably why we never prayed the Rosary together. Although the Rosary is dedicated to the Virgin Mary – the Catholic epitome of the Divine Feminine – and is a fervent request for her intervention, it is rote, and I think of it as desperate in a sense, and frankly boring. My mother did all the work for none of the glory. None of us are religious as adults. Yet it is no matter; she came by her dedication and attention to detail honestly, and it served us well, despite not preserving souls for the Church, we had an excellent education in western civilization.

Her mother, my GG, was the red-headed second daughter of Norwegian immigrants who passed on their no-nonsense brand of Lutheranism to their eleven children. As much as the Catholics tried to instill in us that we (the Catholics) were God's chosen people, and that non-believers were to be relegated to some level of hell after death, I was never afraid for my mother or my GG. They knew what was up. How did I know that they knew more about life and God and the Universe than the Church would have me believe? I looked at their bookshelves.

As much time and space as the Church took up my youth, books took up more. Each of my parents and my grandmother had unique libraries. My father's collection was expansive and academic. Requiring two rooms to house it in floor-to-ceiling shelving, no matter where we moved, all those books accompanied us. There was even an *Oxford Dictionary* with its own lighted magnifying glass and a custom stand. He loved the classics, poetry and Shakespeare, Arthur Conan Doyle, Mark Twain, George Will, HL Mencken, Hemingway, treatises and essays, biographies (especially of boxers and baseball players and bullfighters), history, classic novels and satire – American, British, French and Irish authors mostly. Despite his career as a naval officer, he was an English literature professor and novelist at heart. I read as much of that collection as I could growing up, and made it through less than half. It is one of my regrets. It taught me to reflect, to comprehend, to reason through an argument, to appreciate a perspective. Through his values, his example, and his library, I learned that women are expected to be intelligent, intellectual, educated and literate. I also learned to appreciate the labor involved in the craft of writing, and the value of story in the human experience. His influence informed the Divine Feminine for me, and this is how it should be. We are not only the product of our maternal lines.

My grandmother's library contrasted sharply with his. Residing in a single half-high bookcase in her dining room, it contained none of his titles, and vice-versa. Her library was precise and practical, just like she was. It clearly reflected her life as the daughter of immigrants who grew up during two world wars. I remember two of her books in particular. There, next to the hard-bound *Reader's Digests* and my grandfather's rarely used psalter, squeezed between the worn Norwegian-English dictionary and the oft-consulted Scrabble wordbook, was a reference on dream interpretation. Next to that, one of Edgar Cayce's books, both of which spoke to me of a world beyond Lutheranism and academia, a world of mystery and magic, intuition and imagination, the world (although I did not know it at the time) of the Feminine Divine. What strikes me is that we never discussed these books, although I probably read them at some point, and she surely did. Otherwise they would not have been afforded space in her house, in her mind, in her life.

My mother's library was a hybrid of the two. Her tastes were eclectic. A nurse and anthropologist by education, she especially appreciated the Tudor period in Europe. Shamans and Kachinas, native peoples and their customs, migration, diseases and epidemics, religions, languages and cooking; her passions were all the things that make humans human. She loved *Asterix* and mysteries, cats and Beatrix Potter. There was *Winnie the Pooh* and *Peanuts*, and tomes of Asian art prints and photographs, *Grey's Anatomy*, *Taber's Cyclopedic Medical Dictionary*, her nursing textbooks circa 1950, and magazines: *National Geographic* and *Smithsonian*. She was an artist in her own right, and many of her shelves housed knitting and needlework pattern books. She was an amazing seamstress with a keen appreciation of color and interior design. And she also loved current novels – all kinds, but mostly historical, and mostly borrowed in huge stacks from the library. In addition to making sure our souls were saved, she also made sure we had library cards in every place we lived, with plenty of opportunity to use them. My father derided her for enjoying popular novels. But I get it. Novels tell the story of the human condition. And as a stay-at-home navy wife, she was often alone with her books. She and I discovered *The Holy Blood and the Holy Grail, Angels and Demons* and *The DaVinci Code*, in parallel fashion, from whence we explored the Magdalene gospels, historical Jesus, and the feminine in the Church. She identified with the feminine, the mystical, the ancestors. Despite this, we didn't really talk about our experience of the divine, except Mom was fond of calling God a woman, which actually made much more sense to me. So while we weren't burning sage (or our bras), or whispering *Hail Marys* together, my grandmother and my parents were showing me the thread of the Divine Feminine in their intelligence, their work ethics, their values, and their libraries. As a child, I had this going for me in the discovery of the Divine Feminine: **open-minded and educated citizens-of-the-world elders, who took me to all the cathedrals, temples and museums we read about in their libraries, and who didn't tell me what to believe.** They did their thing and left the rest up to me.

Fast-forward three decades of bad luck, poor choices, trauma and despair in my life. My first marriage had failed spectacularly and I had three small children and no job. I was living with my second husband who had significant health challenges, (although he adored me and worshiped the ground I walked on). I was drinking daily, often to excess. The Divine Feminine was getting her ass kicked. My mother suffered a debilitating stroke, yet lived. My siblings and I took turns caring for her round the clock. Our relationships disintegrated under the stress. Three months later, my grandmother also had a massive stroke and died within three days. My second husband and I were with her when she passed. Mom lived another fifteen months. Two weeks after her passing, my father revealed his cancer diagnosis. He lived another eighteen months. I was not with either of my parents when they died, and sometimes I regret this.

Nine months after my father's life ended, my (second) husband and only daughter died in a catastrophic car accident.

To summarize: in three-and-a-half years I lost my only living grandparent (whom I adored and who reciprocated), my mother, my father, my husband, and my daughter. My siblings were angry and punitive. All my family, all the people who were my safety net, were gone, with the exception of my two sons. Whenever I think about it, I am flooded with disbelief. As I stood in the front hall on the night of the accident while the highway patrolman was talking about something or other, I had an epiphany. **Despite everything, I was not ready to die. I was going to figure it out, because it wasn't time to lie down.**

Long story short, I persevered. I returned to something I knew: books. I read eight to ten hours a day. I kept showing up, trusting that Life would show me the way.

A year later, I began seeing a psychologist that specialized in trauma therapy. I was especially interested in EMDR,[77] sensorimotor psychotherapy and somatic experiencing. She also had other tools in her bag; some I came to realize were reserved for special occasions.

One day, after having attended sessions twice a week for several months, I entered the office as usual and sat down. After greeting me, my counselor asked me a curious question: *Have you noticed the lights on the wall behind you during our last couple of sessions?* I had not, and my mind immediately went to finding a logical explanation for any such phenomena, even as I turned around to look. There on the wall hovered several small white lights, softened triangles with rainbow caps. I turned to the window to see what prism was hanging in front of it, what raindrop or blemish on the glass had caused such an effect, calculating the time of day, the angle of the sun, the weather. But there was nothing. I looked at her. I asked her when she had first noticed them, and if they were present in any of her other patients' sessions. They had been there more than once, and they had not appeared in any of her sessions with other clients. She asked me if I wanted to see what they were. I nodded and closed my eyes. I began to understand. On my left were my parents and my GG. On my right, my late husband, and in front of him, my precious daughter. My grandmother communicated, without speaking, that they were sorry that they had to leave, and in such short order, so close together. They lamented everything I had been through, all the loss, pain, suffering. She explained that they could help me now, from where they were, much more than they could have ever helped me here on Earth. They told me that all the lack, insecurity and suffering stopped with me. They were going to help me. All I had to do was ask. **I knew I was loved and that no matter what, I was not alone.** I opened my eyes. It was surreal. I don't know exactly what happened that day, but it was life-changing.

To help keep them present with me, I gathered their photos and items that reminded me of them in in an *ofrenda*[78] of sorts, arranging them on my grandmother's dresser which was now mine: framed photos of us, a yellow jade rose that my dad had brought my grandmother from Japan, a *matryoshka* he had brought me from Kiev; a small *Madonna* he had brought from Rome, blessed by the Pope, two angel figurines given to us after the accident, a collectible bear from a friend's mother, the red, heart-shaped candle from grief camp, a framed petit point of Angel Gabriel my mother had stitched, a white feather. I greet them whenever I pass by this little altar.

---

[77] Eye Movement Desensitisation and Reprocessing, a powerful therapy designed to help people recover from traumatic events in their lives.

[78] Spanish for 'offering', a ritual display during Día de Muertos.

Although I had become used to seeing the customary signs of the dead visiting us (hummingbirds, dragonflies, cardinals, pennies), it took some practice to remember to call on them, my ancestor posse. Prior to having them affirm that they were available to me always, I would catch my breath and feel anxious and pressured when I saw signs. I had to quickly acknowledge them and push down the surprise and do it quickly, before they disappeared. But soon I was in the habit of greeting them and asking them what they had for me to learn. I'd breathe deeply, smile, thank them for coming, and ask them to stop by again soon. I had a special sign from my daughter in combinations of the number 1 (she was 11 when she died). At first, I would notice 11:11 or 1:11 and I would greet her. Then I learned that in numerology, this combination of numbers is believed to mean that deceased loved ones are near! I loved that. They were indeed my angels. Then I learned that another interpretation of the repetition of the number 1 is that opportunity, manifestation and connection are all available to me in that moment, and whenever I believe them to be. So whenever I saw those numbers, and sometimes it was four times a day, I would focus intently on a vision I had for myself for that minute, or whatever portion of it happened to be left when I noticed the time.

About three years after the accident, I had come to the logical, and for me spiritual, conclusion that it was time for me to become a nurse. Mom had been an RN, and it was something I had been flirting with for more than thirty years. This meant leaving our farm in Minnesota and returning to Arizona. It was a big move, especially since I hadn't even applied to the program, much less been accepted. I had no job, no place to live lined up, no extra money to pay for school. The decision was made though, and it was time to get comfortable being uncomfortable. Growth is like that.

Fast forward a few weeks and things had started to fall into place. We had a place to live, the boys were in school, I had a job. The application was made and an interview was scheduled for the following Tuesday, the third anniversary of the accident. I wasn't sure how I would be that day. Grief is so unpredictable. But I was set to drive to California for the weekend and was taking it day by day. Thursday evening, I got a call from my advisor. There was a screening exam I needed to take before the interview. This was news to me and cause for distress since I was leaving the next morning, not to return until Monday evening. She suggested I leave a few hours early and stop by the testing center on the way out of town. There was math on this test. And it was four hours long. I agreed to her plan because what was the alternative? I could re-test if needed, but I did not want to have to tell the admissions committee that I had not taken it. The next day would have been my mother's eighty-second birthday. It was an auspicious day. I called on her to help me. I drove to the testing center and within ninety minutes I was done. I had aced both parts. Thanks, Mom! Just like her to give *me* a present on *her* birthday!

Tuesday came. Three years. A lifetime ago and a minute before, all at once. I felt the grief train rumbling in the distance. I had an interview. At 10.45am. I arrived early, practicing box breathing in the waiting area while the grief train got louder. Inhale for a count of five. Hold for five. Exhale for five. Hold for five. It was my turn. I answered their questions without revealing the significance of the day. Inhale for five. Hold for five. I looked at the clock on the wall. It was 11:11. I exhaled. Hold for five. I smiled and inhaled a long, slow deep breath. They were there! I had forgotten to ask, but with that nudge I knew it would all be alright. I added the acceptance letter to the *ofrenda* on October 31st – *el día de los Muertos* – the day of the dead. It was their letter, too. When I completed my nursing degree two and a half years later, my sister pinned me with my mother's pin. It was the end of a book, and the beginning of another.

So you see, the Divine Feminine is what lead us both here, me to write, and you to read, wending her way through my story into yours.

I invite you to **consider how the gifts of knowledge and presence have been given to you by your own ancestors, in life and in death.**

How have your teachers, counselors, healers and pastors helped you recognize and cultivate their presence? What traditions do you honor that include them and their wisdom?

About the Authors

Patricia Iris Kerins, DHP *Scotland and Ireland*
Patricia is an author, sound and voice channel, modern day shamanic coach and spiritual teacher. She is a psychotherapist, hypnotherapist, EFT and Reiki master with thirty years of experience in the world of personal transformation. Combining her knowledge of the mind with her ability to channel the teachings of Mary Magdalene through soul coaching, Patricia helps women heal their wounds and step into their true divine feminine power in a profoundly balanced way.

Patricia is based in County Wexford, Ireland, and works with clients all over the world. She is a spiritual 'Agony Aunt' for national magazine *My Weekly,* and a contributor to *Soul & Spirit Magazine, UK*. Patricia is the author of three books and a forty-nine card divination deck. www.patriciairiskerins.com.

Lynne Meyer *United States*
I'm a native Chicagoan transplanted to Texas. A writer, editor, and artist by preference, I've had a series of diverse jobs, including phone operator, secretary, insurance processor, jewelry repairer, event planning assistant, executive secretary, researcher, literature reviewer, elementary school teacher, and currently technical editor and writer. In a perfect world, I would choose to work outside in the shade with a nice wooded view. The things that light me up are natural settings, children, getting paint all over the place, live theater, and music. Intense, life-long interests are other cultures, spirituality, company over for dinner, and wandering the world for the heck of it. What I've learned so far is that do-overs are not just possible but necessary, spiritual people swear a lot, and the past is a story, not a life sentence to serve out.

Andrea Pollard *New Zealand*
Andrea lives in the multi-cultural wonderland of Auckland, New Zealand. She has had a varied career in health and education but a calling has changed all that. She has walked away from her conventional life and undertaken writing courses, built a travel blog and is now crafting her first novel. Besides writing, her other great passions are walking pilgrimage and transhumance paths, and Italy. Italy's fascinating culture, history, and landscape have seen her return over and over to explore every keyhole

and religious niche from Rome to the mountainous hinterland. She mostly travels solo so that she can hear the stories whispered and weave them into her writing just as her goddesses and heroines demand. www.howfarishappy.wordpress.com

 Maggie Pinsent *South America and England*
World-traveller and speaker of several languages, mother to Dylan, I touched down in the UK in 1994. I made a conscious decision to work at the University of Oxford, so we moved there. I met and married Beloved, Peter. Apart from making a living in administration, I was the Bedel of Divinity – a largely ceremonial position – at the University, which was fantastic fun and I met some extraordinary people. I retired from administration in 2008, and as Bedel in 2016. Peter and I have moved to the north of Northumberland, where we are surrounded by farmland and wild animals, with the beach at Bamburgh Castle for a playing ground. I'm learning to write and can be found in my workshop, hand-building with clay, creating mosaics, and wet felting. I'm a new art and junk journaller.

 Rema Kumar *India*
I was born and brought up in Kerala and Chennai in the south of India and I'm now a textile designer based in Delhi. I work with rural and village-based weavers and master craftsmen the length and breadth of India, fusing traditional and contemporary designs, using natural cottons, silks and wools, and age-old weaving techniques. I create unique, one-of-a-kind creations and my greatest passion is the sari and keeping Indian women's passion for the traditional six yards of fabric alive. My collection also includes stoles, wraps, and home furnishings.

I'm fiercely proud of my country, steeped as it is in thousands of years of art, culture, tradition and history, and I love to lose myself in its thousands of old forts, palaces and museums. www.facebook.com/Kumar.Rema

C. Ara Campbell *Canada*
Ara is a visionary writer, author, and founder of The Goddess Circle. She is a soul guide, cosmic channel, facilitator of The Inner Priestess Awakening Online Journey and Relationship Empowerment & Sacred Love Online Journey, and author of The Astro Forecast. Ara is a modern day mystic dedicated to the rising feminine, living embodied truth, connecting others with their gifts and healing using the natural world. She has been writing and channeling guidance from the unseen since she was young, and intuitively soul coaching using spiritual and natural energies. She can often be found seeking wisdom and solace in the wilds of Mother Earth, capturing the magic of nature with her camera or snuggling her dog Sonny. www.thegoddesscircle.net

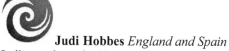

Judi Hobbes *England and Spain*

Judi was born in New Jersey, USA. She is a psychotherapist and supervisor of therapists, working with people for over forty years to facilitate self-acceptance and personal and professional development. Judi is a mother of two and grandmother of three, and is spending her almost-retired years fighting climate change, the current occupant of the White House and enjoying creative expression in art, writing and dancing. www.elantraining.org

Marian Hamel-Smith *Trinidad & Tobago, France*

Marian has been a bilingual secretary, an au pair in France and Spain, an English teacher by default, an organic dairy farmer's wife, an organic gardener, a manager of a B&B and two guest houses, and is now a Mind Body Eating Coach, certified by the Institute for the Psychology of Eating (Colorado). She is the Mother of five children. Her quest in life for Truth from an early age sent her passionately into her religion, but this changed upon the death of her second son. A native of Trinidad & Tobago in the West Indies, Marian has lived in Brittany, France, for over 36 years.

Stella St Clare *United States*

Stella lives in northeast Pennsylvania, at the foot of the Allegheny mountains. She is a psychotherapist by profession and a practicing Wiccan by spiritual persuasion. Stella loves to create potions and lotions and magical elixirs which she stocks in her overflowing pantry, awaiting the day she retires and opens her own little shop of enchantments. She shares an old farmhouse with her husband, two cats, and several lovely, well-mannered ghosts.

Sarah McCrum *England and Australia*

Sarah's work explores how each of us can be fully human and fully alive in an age of exponential expansion in technology. She trained for twenty-two years with two Chinese Masters and she's been an energy coach for twenty years, helping entrepreneurs and gamechangers master their personal energy. She is the author of *Love Money, Money Loves You*, which provides the inspiration for retreats and online programs called The Consciousness of Money. She's also a member of faculty for The Shift Network and a member of the Evolutionary Leaders Circle. www.SarahMcCrum.com

Detta Darnell *England, Ireland and Greece*

Detta is an artist, author, certified life purpose coach and Kaizen Muse Creativity Coach. She embraces the call of the Divine by connecting people to their soul callings and heart whispers, and uses the transformational power of expressive intuitive art forms to help others let go of the need for perfection, procrastination and self-sabotage. She is a Guidess and facilitator of *The Unfinished Woman Retreat* held yearly on her adopted Greek island of Kefalonia. Detta is passionate about helping women of all ages from around the world to reconnect to their creativity, intuition & meaning making. She offers healing art journeys in groups, workshops, gatherings, and one to one. She's also a deep listener and makes a great cup of tea.

www.dettadarnell.com

Sue Fitzmaurice *New Zealand and Nomad*

I'm from Wellington, New Zealand, the coolest little capital in the world. (So says Lonely Planet.) My children grew up and *I* left home at the beginning of 2016 and I've been travelling ever since. I'm a registered nurse, with undergraduate degrees in philosophy and political science, and international relations and international law. I have a Masters in business, and have spent most of my working life in business, running other people's organisations and my own. After leaving the corporate whirl in 2010, I wrote a novel *Angels in the Architecture,* and began a new career as social networker, coach and writer, morphing into full-time writer, editor and publisher. I've since published several non-fiction books of my own, and several from other authors, via *Rebel Magic Books*. In March 2020, I'll host a pilgrimage & retreat tour to sacred sites through France and Spain, mirroring parts of my books *The Accidental Mary Pilgrimage* and *The Deliberate Mary Pilgrimage*. www.rebelmagicbooks.com & www.facebook.com/SueFitzmauriceAuthor

Stacey Phillips, *England*

I was born and brought up Jewish in North London. Most of my working life has been in property development, the family business. I'm mother to two boys, and partner to David who runs our doggy daycare. Our house is a busy one – boys and dogs! I came to spirituality later in my life, particularly after the deaths of my parents. Over the last ten years I've discovered my gifts as a channel and psychic, at the same time that I've suffered a series of autoimmune illnesses. I find expression and growth through art and via my social media at www.facebook.com/FreshMinds1

Swati Nigam *India and United States*

I was born and brought up in India, and moved to the United States soon after I got married. I'm a wife, and mother to two humans, five cats, one fish, and many other critters who come to my doorstep to be fed. I have done my Bachelors in Life Sciences, and I have two masters – MBA and MIS. I gave up the corporate world after my first child was born, and my life changed radically after that. I've trained in several healing modalities: I'm a Reiki Master, Kundalini Reiki Master, Gold Reiki Master, Ethereal Crystals Master, Angel Therapy Practitioner, Past Life Regression Therapist, Theta Healing Practitioner, EFT practitioner, and an Intuitive Life Coach. I have written two e-books: *Learn to See Auras* and *12 Steps to Happiness*. I love animals, plants, all of nature, angels, fairies, watercolor painting, and all things magical. I am always trying to find the magical divine in the mundane.
www.ThePurpleFlower.com

Deb Steele *United Kingdom*

Deb spent many years working as a therapist, supervisor, trainer and facilitator, mostly with women. Her experiences taught her that the healer and the seeker are both one, that giving and receiving are in truth the same, and that our divinity lies in our humanity, not in some realm beyond. Her journey during more recent years has taken her deeper into the inner realms of soul work and she is now moving on to offering Soul Work Companionship one to one and in groups, online and in person. Deb is also ordained as a *OneSpirit* InterFaith Minister.

Martrice Endres *United States*

Martrice Endres is a writer, blogger, yoga teacher, reiki healer, and meditation coach who is passionate about sharing her wellness journey with everyone. She teaches in both group and private settings, sharing her story of self-healing and empowerment. Calling herself a late bloomer, she encourages her students to recognize their own power at every stage of life. www.facebook.com/emmieessentialwellness

Dianne Graham *New Zealand and Australia*

Dianne is an Usui Reiki Master and energy healer with the ancient wisdom of her Maori culture in her DNA. She offers meditation and self-healing techniques that create lasting change and is known for her inherent understanding of our inner child and how that impacts on our limiting beliefs later in life.

She is a gifted communicator, facilitator and teacher who is always sharing her knowing with others. Her passion is to connect people to their true soul essence through conscious conversations. Her powerful range of energy sprays are used by many other healers to complement their work.
www.facebook.com/DianneGrahamShapeShifter

 Alison Smith *United Kingdom*

I am a Human Potential Facilitator, and a 21st Century Priestess-Poet. My skills and qualifications include counselling, coaching, circle work, reiki healing, teaching, philosophy and creative writing. I help women to connect back to their authentic self and soul essence, and access deep inner wisdom to create new stories of freedom, connection and empowerment.

I am the founder of *The Wellspring*, and *Radical Rising Sisterhood*, two online communities for creative women on a mission to change the world.

I love the Northumberland Coast where I grew up and have an affinity with islands. My sacred animal is the cat, and my soul home is Crete. www.thegardenway.co.uk

 Tia Christiansen *United States*

Tia is a certified Energy Empowerment Coach, Reiki Master, and founder of the *Dream Sculpting Institute*. She has been a Lead at two Fortune 500 companies, and was a music festival and custom event producer with twenty years experience across the United States, central Europe, and Japan.

Tia helps successful career women and entrepreneurs reclaim their divine feminine power and lead with heart. Her *Authentically You* leadership program focuses on finding fulfillment in all areas of life, including optimum health, mental clarity, unlimited wealth, and energetic alignment. www.dreamsculptinginstitute.com

 Maddison Bee *Australia and England*

Maddison is twenty-five and lives on the south coast of England. She has an undergraduate degree in Eastern Philosophy and Social Studies. She spent twelve years studying the art of Kyokushin Karate and is now exploring other disciplines such as yoga, *T'ai chi*. She uses the physical discipline taught in her combative training to deepen her spiritual practices through meditation and movement. She is currently building her platform as an independent author. She hopes that her testimony will inspire women to find their strength again and through honouring their inner voice, reclaim their personal power.

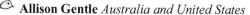 **Allison Gentle** *Australia and United States*

Allison is an Australian teacher, student and writer, and the mother of two adult children. In pursuit of her purpose, she upped sticks from the Blue Mountains in 2017, took a year-long road trip across the USA, and is now doing a PhD in Literacy Teaching and Learning in New York.

Melanie C. Toppin *The Netherlands and Germany*

Melanie C. Toppin is a certified child & youth coach, and writer of fantasy and spiritual education books. She is co-author of *Chocolate & Diamonds for a Woman's Soul: Stories of Resilience, Grace & Faith* and *Better Woman Better World.*

She is the founder of Toppin Solutions, online coaching for kids and young adults. Her flagship program is *Embrace Your Inner Queen*, designed to help young girls grow up confident and passionate about their purpose in life. When she's not writing, she's either spending time with her cuddly cat Kyra, studying to becoming an educator, immersed in the worlds of other writers, or dancing and singing through the house. www.toppinsolutions.com

Mary Louise Malloy *United States*

Mary Lou has arrived at a place where looking back on the good and the bad along the way brings her a sense of peace and contentment. She received her Bachelor of Arts degree at the age of fifth-six and continues to be a life-long learner. Her children and grandchildren have given her many cherished experiences as they follow their life journeys. Life has blessed her with much along the way and she hopes to have many years ahead for sketching and watercolor painting, creative writing and traveling when she's able to. She is the author of *Me in the Middle,* a memoir of lessons learned along the way. www.meinthemiddlewrites.com

 Elizabeth Russell *United States*

I'm a recovering public school Spanish teacher originally from Binghamton, New York. I have lived in both Spain and Taiwan and have strong family ties to the St Lawrence River. At the age of fifty, I returned to school to pursue herbalism. After graduating with my Holistic Health Practice, Natural Products Manufacturing, and Herbal Retail Management certificates, I launched Lizbeth's Botanicals (herbal products & body care) and Linden Tree Intuitive (wellness mentoring, herbal workshops, and Reiki). I have previously published a *Mindful Mandala* coloring book, and am currently working on a second coloring book and a book on flower essences. My passion is helping people on their journey to self-love and self-care using herbs, flower essences, mindfulness, and more. www.lindentreeintuitive.com

Doreen Devoy-Hulgan *United States*

After the break-up of her first marriage and then losing her grandmother, mother and father in quick succession, Doreen lost her second husband and daughter in a catastrophic car accident at the age of forty-six. Coming to terms with the stark reality that no one was coming to save her, Doreen began a journey of self-discovery and post-traumatic growth. Her process during the first three years of her recovery, led to certifications as a Human Potential Coach, Reiki Master, and registered nurse. She is also a Spanish language professor. Although writing has always been part of her life, the work featured here is her first non-academic publication. Look for her memoir *One Small Thing: Walking Forward after Devastating Loss* in the near future. Doreen spends her time between Minnesota and Arizona.
www.facebook.com/OneSmallThingNow

A Tribute to the Authors

As a business consultant in 2005, I received a phone call one day from an Englishwoman living in the back and beyond of the South Island of New Zealand, asking for help with marketing the luxury lodge she managed. She said she couldn't afford to pay me but she could give me an amazing luxury weekend including spa treatments and energy relaxations. I was in! Sarah McCrum has been one of my closest friends and confidantes, and frequent collaborator and coach, ever since. Sarah, you are always up for pretty much anything I suggest, as we have been for each other through our growing and changing careers for nearly fifteen years. In many ways you are responsible for much that is me, or at least for assisting it to emerge. Thank you for everything you do and have done for me and for my family. You are one of my life's greatest blessings.

Stacey Phillips and I had been Facebook friends a year or so, when in 2011, a bunch of similar friends – none of whom had met in person – got together for a crazy mad long weekend in Boston, USA. We came from all over the globe, Stacey and I travelling the furthest, she from London. Two years later, I had taken my daughter out of school for the year to travel the world, and we stayed a couple of days in London with Stacey and her family. And then after my children grew up and I left home in 2016, Stacey's home and family became one of my own several adopted homes and families – in fact, my main one, to be fair. We've been an inspiration and support to each other – and one of each other's best critics – through a multitude of 'stuff'. Stacey, you are a soul sister if ever there was one, and I love you to bits.

I first met Detta Darnell at a workshop run by Julia Cameron in Bristol in late 2017. We were breaking into groups and I literally saw her across a crowded room, pointed at her, and said You! I'm with you! Detta, you were the first to rise to the occasion for this book – isn't that just so you – and the first to complete your story, despite the massive journey it took you on. You are a shining light and nobody makes me laugh as much as you do. I love you so much. Thank you for your beautiful art – I cannot imagine any other cover for us now.

Swati Nigam and I had been part of the same Facebook group of inspirational page owners and I got to know her when she gave me an angel reading in 2014 and identified the unusual (to say the least) guardian angel I'd first been told was with me thirty years earlier. Swati, you have taken me on a journey into parts of my own Self that I didn't know were there, and you've been the most loving and kindest of friends. You're also a complete nut, and I love you.

Margaret Pinsent, Marian Hamel-Smith and Doreen Devoy Hulgan, it has been a privilege to walk a few steps with you on the worst journey a mother can take. You are the bravest of souls and I'm in awe of you. You have all shown me great kindness, warmth and hospitality, and your courage in sharing your stories as beautifully as you have is inspirational. Those stories break all our hearts but offer hope to many who may also have suffered such unspeakable grief. Thank you. I met Doreen in 2016, having been Facebook friends a while, when we met up to attend a Saturday workshop with Esther Hicks in Sacramento. The deaths of her husband and daughter were still very recent but she told me and two other friends the story of that night over lunch with the most extraordinary power that we were transfixed as much with Doreen as with her story. The two of us spent the next day wandering Haight-Ashbury in San Francisco – it was a special weekend. I met Margaret at a women's retreat I co-hosted with Detta Darnell in Greece in 2018. Her son's death was also still very recent and she allowed all her grief and vulnerability to flow however it wished in the cradle of other women's love. It was transformative – only a few months later, I saw a newly empowered Margaret when she hosted me for a few days in beautiful Oxford. I met Marian on my return from France to England at the end of 2018. I was cleaning out the myriad of saved 'favourites in my Google Chrome settings when I came across her personal Facebook page among them. I had no recollection of how or why it was there, but I messaged her and before I knew it she was hosting me in Brittany, taking me to visit Mont St Michel and other beautiful parts of the north-west of France.

I met Patricia Kerins in Scotland in 2016, at her home in the countryside between Stirling and Loch Lomond. We had been Facebook friends for a while, connected as we were with various Scottish circles, Patricia much more than me of course. I think I'd been in her house not five minutes when, having expressed some fog about what I was doing with some part of my life at the time, she bade me close my eyes and guided me into a deep and enquiring meditation. Scots are known for being no-nonsense. I later attended a weekend workshop with her in Edinburgh, which was my first opening to the magic of Mary Magdalene. Patricia has an ability to provide the right words – the absolutely right words – in the right moment, and to channel a powerful healing energy with them. She is a deeply empowering soul with whom it's my absolute privilege to be acquainted. Thank you, Patricia, for contributing our Foreword, and for your support of me and this book.

I met Dianne Graham, my countrywoman, at Sarah McCrum's home on the Sunshine Coast in Queensland in 2013, the year I took Ruby out of school. Dianne lights up rooms she walks into. She is the singularly most radiant person I've ever met. We have a deep, and as yet mostly unexplored, connection that binds our New Zealandness and our Celtic heritages. Dianne will be co-hosting The Accidental Mary Pilgrimage tour and retreat with me in March 2020.

In May and June 2016, I accidentally found myself in a tiny village in the Himalayas, attending a month-long arts festival as guest writer and blogger. Rema Kumar, and her husband Puneet, were both participants and we shared a house in the village. I wrote a blog about Rema:

Rema Kumar has one of the warmest, most authentic smiles you'll see anywhere. You know when you meet her that here is a beautiful person, and her personality is such a match to her work: full of colour and style and elegance.

Rema designs fabrics and clothes, most particularly saris. They're stunning. She's like the Gucci of India.

Rema is a living, breathing example of being authentically happy. I adore her, and Puneet, and am grateful for their many kindnesses and hospitality. Their joy in their art is a treasure.

I don't know how I became Facebook friends with Lynne Meyer but we've basically never not been Facebook friends. We met briefly in 2011 when I visited Texas – it was so not long enough, and it was way too long ago, and we are well due for a do-over. Lynne is one of those naturally smart, witty people whose way with words you just wish you shared. She is big of intellect and equally big of spirit. Since we have managed to excoriate on social media all the same loathsome people in the world for as long as we have, we are clearly soul sisters. Keep doing you, Lynne, you're effing brilliant.

In early 2018, I pitched up at Judi Hobbes' gothic mansion house flat in Manchester to dog sit her darling Willow and Sam for ten days. As is generally the case with house and dog sitting, you get to know people's dogs better than you get to know them, except Judi asked me back early this year and I accepted with pleasure. My suggestion that she consider a piece for this book came at a time when she was making space in her life for artistic pursuits, including writing. We've not spent half the time together I'd like to, but I've no doubt that will unfold as it will.

I've not personally met Allison Gentle, Elizabeth Russell, Maddie Bee, Melanie Toppin, Andrea Pollard, Mary Lou Malloy, Alison Smith, Deb Steele, Ara Campbell, Stella St Clare, Martrice Endres, or Tia Christiansen, although their contributions and stories are no less for that, and I *feel* like I've met some of you. Certainly I've chatted with several of you live online.

Allison has been a client of mine and it's been a privilege to walk with her through massive changes in her life, upping sticks from Australia to attend a PhD programme in the United States – she has a brilliant mind and a fabulous way with words.

I've been Facebook friends with Liz Russell for some time – again I don't know how, but she is a consistent and welcome, warm and glowing presence in my news feed.

Maddie pitched up at the suggestion of a mutual friend. She is the youngest of the women here and it's been a delight to have her contribution.

Melanie Toppin joined one of my online courses some years ago and we've just been in and around each other on Facebook ever since. I didn't know she had this story to tell until she told it. I love that.

Andrea Pollard got in touch with me via my writers group (which she had joined at the suggestion of a mutual close friend) when I mentioned this project. As a fellow Kiwi, I was thrilled that she joined; her story is unique and inspiring, and her telling of it is rich and compelling – I'm excited about her forthcoming novel!

Mary Lou approached me earlier this year to help edit and publish her memoir *Me in the Middle*, so I knew she had a story to add and she has been generous in her contribution. Her joy at new wisdom and her active and inquiring mind are an inspiration.

Deb Steele, Stella St Clare and Martrice Endres are all members of the Facebook group I host for my first pilgrimage retreat and tour to France and Spain in March 2020, and so that was a logical place for me to inquire of anyone's story. They got in touch and their stories are diverse and beautiful and full of healing.

I literally sent Alison Smith an invitation to submit accidentally – she accepted just the same. (There are no accidents.) Again, her story is unique and brings themes both similar and different to the others here.

Tia Christiansen arrived at the suggestion of Sarah McCrum and it's been a pleasure to get to know her through her story and the back and forth emails that have marked the writing and editing of each woman's story. Tia's corporate journey, and subsequent semi-bewilderment with it, are not dissimilar to my own, and I have much respect for anyone able to reflect on the vast comforts and appeals of that whirl.

Last but not least, I have been a follower and admirer of *The Goddess Circle* on Facebook and Instagram for a while and felt sure whoever was behind it must have a beautiful story to tell – thank you Ara Campbell. You have one of the gentlest and softest of souls here – the sort with fire at its core.

I feel sure I will meet you all in good time. I look forward to it.

It has been an extraordinary privilege and pleasure to read all your words. Thank you for allowing me to nudge you, question you and edit you. It's a brave thing to put your story in someone else's hands. You have enriched my world in a multitude of ways.

Sue

Our Books

LOVE MONEY
MONEY LOVES
YOU

Money talks.
Are you listening?

Sarah McCrum

PATRICIA IRIS

VIVA VOCE
- The Living Voice -

Lift your Vibration, accelerate Inner Healing with
powerful Voice-Work
guided by the Archangelic Realms

Beach Stones
Poems from a Wild Greek Island

Detta Darnell

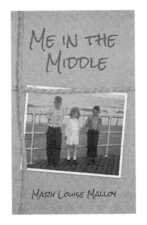

ME IN THE
MIDDLE

MARY LOUISE MALLOY

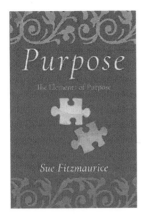

Purpose
The Elements of Purpose

Sue Fitzmaurice

Purpose 2
Making Sure Your Purpose Finds You

Sue Fitzmaurice

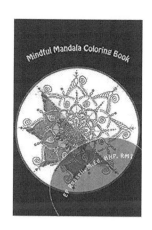

Recommended Reading

Authors
Louise Hay
Brené Brown
Toni Morrison
Alice Hoffman
Alice Munro
Edna O'Brien
Maya Angelou
Jean Shinoda Bolen
Clarissa Pinkola Estés
Caroline Myss
Mary Beard
Sue Monk Kidd
Naomi Wolf

Non-fiction
Crones Don't Whine – Concentrated Wisdom for Juicy Women, Jean Shinoda Bolen
Goddesses in Everywoman, Jean Shinoda Bolen
Mary and Early Christian Women, Ally Kateusz
The Tao of Physics, Fritjof Capra
Women Who Run with the Wolves, Clarissa Pinkola Estés
Celebrating the Southern Seasons ~ Rituals for Aotearoa, Juliet Batten
The Beauty Myth, Naomi Wolf
Becoming, Michelle Obama
Wild, Cheryl Strayed
Shameless, Nadia Bolz-Weber
Sacred Contracts, Caroline Myss
If Women Rose Rooted, Sharon Blackie
The Gospel of The Beloved Companion ~ The Complete Gospel of Mary Magdalene, translation & commentary by Jehanne de Quillan
Women & Power, Mary Beard
Sisters and Prophets, Mary L. Sleevi
Ethiopia with a Mule, Dervla Murphy
Black like Me, John Howard Griffin
I Shock Myself, Beatrice Wood
As Gypsies Wander, Juliette de Bairacli-Levy
Sinning Across Spain: Walking the Old and New Camino, Ailsa Piper

Travelling with Pomegranates, Sue Monk Kidd & Ann Kidd Taylor
Initiation: A Woman's Spiritual Adventure in the Heart of the Andes, Elizabeth B. Jenkins
The Heroine's Journey. Women's Quest for Wholeness, Maureen Murdoch
Untie the Strong Woman, Clarissa Pinkola Estés
The Wild Girl (the Fifth Gospel), Michèle Roberts
Drum & Candle, David St Clair
The Suppression of Women's Rites also published as *When God was a Woman,* Merlin Stone
The Altar of My Soul. The Living Traditions of Santería, Marta Moreno Vega
Autobiography of a Yogi, Paramahansa Yogananda
I, Phoolan Devi, Phoolan Devi
Awakening to the Spirit World – the Shamanic Path of Direct Revelation, Sandra Ingerman
You Can Heal Your Life, Louise Hay
Our Bodies, Ourselves, Boston Women's Health Collective
The Second Sex, Simone de Beauvoir
Sex, Death, Enlightenment, Mark Matousek
The Return of the Mother, Andrew Harvey
Caravan of No Despair, Mirabai Starr
Ever Widening Circles, Joanna Macy
Flight into Freedom, Eileen Caddy
Crossing to Avalon, Jean Shinoda Bolen
The Sophia Code, Kaia Ra
Chasm of Fire, Irina Tweedie
At the Root of This Longing, Carol Lee Flinders
Anna, Grandmother of Jesus, Claire Heartsong
Cave in the Snow, Vickie MacKenzie
The Silver Wheel, Elen Tompkins
Success is the Quality of Your Journey, Jennifer Jones
Lessons of the Heart, Patricia Livingston, with Henri Nouwen
Our Lady of the Lost and Found, Diane Schoemperlen
Simple Abundance, Sarah Ban Breathnach
Something More, Sarah Ban Breathnach
The Chalice and the Blade, Riane Eisler
Legends of the Madonna in Art, Anna Jameson
Alone of all her sex, Marina Warner
Longing for Darkness, China Galland
The Hebrew Goddess, Raphael Patai
Drawing Down the Moon, Margot Adler
In a Chariot Drawn by Lions – The Search for the Female in Deity, Asphodel P Long.
The book of Mary, Nicola Slee
Language of the Goddess, Marija Gimbutas
Maiden, Mother, Crone, Claire Hamilton
Incidents in the Life of a Slave Girl Written by Herself, Harriet A. Jacobs
Wild Power: Discover the magic of your menstrual cycle and awaken the feminine path to power, Alexandra Pope & Sjanie Hugo Wurlitzer

The Lost Sisterhood – The Return of Mary Magdalene, the Mother Mary, and Other Holy Women, Julia Ingram
Belonging, bell hooks
When the Drummers were Women – A Spiritual History of Rhythm, Layne Redmond
Summoning the Fates – A Generational Woman's Guide to Destiny and Sacred Transformation, Zsuzsanna Budapest
Soul Retrieval – Mending the Fragmented Self, Sandra Ingerman

Celtic
Echoes of the Goddess. A quest for the Sacred Feminine in the British Landscape, Simon Brighton & Terry Welbourn
The Ancient Celts, Barry Cunliffe
Early Irish Myths and Sagas, Jeffrey Ganz
Celtic Goddess. Great Queen or Demon Witch? Claire French
The Gods of the Celts, Miranda Green
The Ancient British Goddess. Goddess Myths, Legends, Sacred Sites and Present Revelation, Kathy Jones
The Woman's Companion to Mythology, Carolyne Larrington
Goddess – Myths of the Feminine Divine, David Leeming & Jake Page
The Goddess, Power, Sexuality and the Feminine Divine, Husein Shahruhk

Native American
The Wind is My Mother. The Life and Teachings of a Native American Shaman, Bear Heart, with Molly Larkin
Buffalo Woman Comes Singing. The Spirit Song of a Rainbow Medicine Woman, Brooke Medicine Eagle
Lakota Woman, Mary Crow Dog, with Richard Erdoes
The 13 Original Clan Mothers, Jamie Sams
The Afterlife of Billy Fingers, Annie Kagan

Fiction
The Bone People, Kerri Hulme
My Brilliant Friend, Elena Ferrante (*Neopolitan* series)
Eat Pray Love, Elizabeth Gilbert
Woman of God, James Patterson
The Ministry of Utmost Happiness, Arundhati Roy
Mists of Avalon, Marion Zimmer (series)
The Color Purple, Alice Walker
The Lost Sisterhood, Anne Fortier
Circe, Madeline Miller
The Firebrand, Marion Zimmer Bradley
Practical Magic, Alice Hoffman
Snow Crash, Neal Stephenson
The Dragonriders of Pern, Anne McCaffrey (series)

REBEL
MAGIC

www.rebelmagicbooks.com

Printed in Poland
by Amazon Fulfillment
Poland Sp. z o.o., Wrocław